STRESS BURNOUT

An Annotated Bibliography

T. F. Riggar

Southern Illinois University Press

Carbondale and Edwardsville

Copyright © 1985 by the Board of Trustees, Southern
Illinois University
All rights reserved
Printed in the United States of America
Edited by Dan Seiters
Designed by Kathleen Giencke
Production supervised by Kathleen Giencke
88 87 86 85 4 3 2 1

Library of Congress Cataloging in Publication Data

Riggar, T. F.
    Stress burnout.

    Bibliography: p.
    Includes index.
    1. Burnout (Psychology)—Abstracts.   I. Title.
BF481.R53 1985   158.7   84-5447
ISBN 0-8093—1186-0

Contents

To S. W. R. without whom nothing is possible

Preface

Professional helpers face a variety of on-the-job
stressors as well as those associated with working
with persons in need of help. The process has been
fully articulated and addressed in the growing body
of research literature termed professional burnout.
But as most of us must ask, just how important is
stress burnout to the line practitioner or counsel-
or? I was recently asked to address a state-level
counselors annual association's meeting on this very
topic. The counselors present, as have those in
over ten states, were very interested in "burnout."
They, as have many others, reported very strong
fears concerning the danger they perceived. Many
reported a basic bottom-line fear that it would soon
affect their job or the adequacy of their efforts.
In addition, these counselors express dissatisfaction with the effects inflation has had upon their
salaries, with the loss of prestige "helping" has in
the eyes of society, and with the future of helping
the changing client. The most important thing,
however, was the counselors' lack of knowledge about
the phenomena of burnout. There does exist a need
for a useful, specific compilation of the burnout
literature. I now have the pleasure of introducing
one such product in T.F. Riggar's <u>Stress Burnout</u>.
 The helping fields have once again solidified their
futures. In my discipline, rehabilitation counseling, alliances with other allied health fields
(i.e., occupational, physical, and recreational
therapies) have produced concrete

acceptance of the rehabilitationist as an active member of the total rehabilitation approach. We have seen as rehabilitationists the first recognition of our professional training and endeavors by the insertion of the word qualified in front of "rehabilitation worker" for the 1984 rehabilitation legislation. In fact, rehabilitation counseling is a strong, growing concern. Further, with the often maniacal concerns for survival, many counselors are beginning to look toward the resolution of more pressing occupational concerns. The text you are about to review marks a major resource for those practitioners and researchers beginning to professionally address job stress and satisfaction as occupational concerns.

Stress Burnout will evidence that professional burnout is a concern for each and every facet in human services. The stresses that come from intimate involvement with clients and their bids for day-to-day survival can become quite substantial. Coupling these stresses with those of working in the human-service setting create normally high levels of professional burnout. For example, the job turnover rate of 25% among rehabilitation counselors in state agencies offers eloquent evidence of the ultimate cost of these combined forces. Stress Burnout offers counselors a precise and condensed annotated body of easily useable resources addressing the symptoms, causes, and strategies for overcoming professional burnout. Most importantly, the text presents its efforts in a cross-referenced model that allows for building a more in-depth understanding of burnout before it crushes the counselor. As the text literally presents most of the existing literature, counselor-practitioners and researchers will be able to identify those citations and resources that best match their needs.

Perhaps the most significant mark of a profession is its ability and willingness to investigate major issues that affect it as a discipline. Rehabilitation counseling has identified worker satisfaction and burnout as a priority concern that we are facing in delivering quality case services.

Professor Riggar's efforts provide us with the first
major up-to-date vehicle to address those concerns.
While most of the manuscripts appearing in research
literature are descriptive, empirical research
concerning burnout is being conducted. Stress
Burnout will make future efforts much more manageable, while stimulating even more refined thought.
Indeed, as we begin to understand the scope of
satisfaction and burnout in rehabilitation, we can
begin to build strategies to address them. The link
between satisfied and energized workers with commitment and quality work products has been recently
touted by the quality control groups in industry.
Now it is our turn to learn from them.
  My personal appreciation of Dr. Riggar's work stems
from a professional capacity. As a researcher
currently involved in addressing the issue of
burnout in the allied health professions, I find
Stress Burnout to be an invaluable tool. I look
forward to its dissemination and fervently hope it
finds its way onto many rehabilitationists
bookshelves and desks.

David K. Hollingsworth
School of Allied Health Professions
Louisiana State University Medical Center
December 26, 1983

Acknowledgments

No book, particularly one of this nature, can be the work of a single individual. In this sense the contribution of Dr. Jerome R. Lorenz, Director of Rehabilitation Institute, Southern Illinois University, who allowed the time and provided faculty support is significant. Dr. Samuel Goldman, Dean of the College of Human Resources, for his understanding of the time and effort involved in research, as well as the administration and management of the Word Processing Unit, on which this text is typed, is significant. Ms. Linda Patrick who operates the Word Processing Unit within the College of Human Resources, was able to put up with poor direction, missed deadlines, bad communication, and computer illiteracy on my part and still produce this quality project.

In addition to professionals within the author's immediate environment, considerable credit must go to Jim Simmons, Associate Editor of Southern Illinois University Press, whose patience, understanding and forebearance when working with faculty is nothing short of amazing. Providing parameters, appropriate suggestions, worthy comments, and in general making the process flow smoothly allowed this book to reach its conclusion.

Perhaps the most important work done was that of Graduate Assistants within the Rehabilitation Institute. Over a period of three years many students contributed to this work, researching and digging out articles and books, annotating and outlining the best ones and finally suffering

through the seven proofreading stages that were
necessary to condense the 1,000+ pages to the best
of what exists today.   Special acknowledgement
should go to Constance Garry and Elizabeth Brown for
proofreading the final galleys.   Thanks goes to
those students who pulled it all together: Joseph
Dowd, Peggy Dunn, Regina Daniels, Ruth-Marie Cham-
bers, Raquel Alencar, Beth Pascucci, Sam Lacy, Mary
Bruckner, Scott Bullen, Karen Stepp, Concetta
Wheaton and Karen Kirschke.

Finally, but certainly not lastly, very special
thanks goes to those secretaries who slaved over
revision after revision of 1,000+ pages.   Kathy
Miller, Judy Weithorn, Denise D. LaBerdia and
Darnecea Moultrie, the human word processors, truly
allowed this project to come to fulfillment.

Introduction

Billions of dollars are lost each year to the
American economy because of workers who can no
longer function adequately in, or cope successfully
with, their jobs. More than just the monetary loss
to the country is the loss suffered by the people in
the process. In recent years the signs and symptoms
of these problems, i.e., turnover, absenteeism,
lowered productivity, psychological problems, etc.,
have become increasingly predominant in our society.
Although the problems we face are complex and
varied, a considerable portion of the concerns
related to work and worker productivity has been
found to be caused by what is colloquially known as
stress and burnout.
  This colloquially understood syndrome is particularly prominent in those professions that deal
primarily with people. The intense involvement with
people over long periods of time in emotionally
demanding roles leads directly to the stress burnout
syndrome. Such intimate occupational involvement is
especially evident in the human-service professions.
The quality of work life for helping professionals
has apparently reached a state where the people who
intend to help are not only hurting their clients
and patients but harming themselves.
  It is to find solution to this pervasive problem
that this book has been developed. Caring individuals, themselves often caught in the duress of the
syndrome, may use this text to gain greater awareness of causes, sources, and potential coping
strategies. Although not a how-to book the contents

examine in considerable detail all of the most
relevant literature available today. In this sense
the compendium at the back of the book will allow
human service professionals the opportunity for
greater awareness of the stress burnout syndrome.
Perhaps the first point to be considered concerns
what the term itself means.
  As generally used the term <u>stress burnout</u> is
sufficient for many purposes. However, as a scientific identifier the word lacks specificity and
definition. In fact, so varied is the range of
burnout that many specifiers have been used in the
professional literature to attempt to isolate and
examine specific parts, or the syndrome as a whole.
Examples of these terms include:

neurological meltdown	professional stagnation
tedium	occupational stress
occupational fatigue	melancholy
job stress	overwork/overload
job strain	

  Due to the lack of exactness that exists despite
all efforts by investigators, a broad, overall
delineator is used herein to define the wide-ranging
and involved syndrome. This condition, which we
call stress burnout, can be defined as all of those
past and current references to problems on the job
that result in a negative interface between per-
son-environment= organizational fit.
  A syndrome exists because of the characteristic
pattern of signs and symptoms that usually occur
together. It should be clear, however, that the
only thing stress burnout defines is the pervasive
complexity of all of the works cited that attempt to
delineate and identify the problem. To attempt to
define the condition itself is difficult. The
literature abounds with definitions, all of which
are different yet share certain
striking commonalities.
...when professional role envisioned during counsel-
or training conflicts with real work demands on time
and energy.

...victims of stress overload.

...to deplete oneself, to exhaust one's physical and mental resources.

...to wear oneself out by excessively striving to reach some unrealistic expectation imposed by oneself or values of society.

...a process in which the professional's attitudes and behavior change in negative ways in response to job strain.

...to fail or wear out or become exhausted by making excessive demands on energy, strength, or resources.

...a syndrome characterized by loss of productivity, energy, and interest in their jobs by staff members.

...a pervasive mood of anxiety giving way to depression and despair.

...the therapists' failure to muster the reserves necessary to remain effective on the job.

...the emotional exhaustion resulting from the stress of interpersonal contact.

...when staff lose all feeling and concern for clients and treat them in detached and even dehumanizing ways.

...emotional exhaustion and attitude shifts.

...loss of caring characterized by an emotional exhaustion in which the professional no longer has any positive feelings, sympathy, or respect for clients or patients.

...a progressive loss of idealism, energy and purpose experienced by people in the helping professions as a result of the conditions of their work.

...always having incomplete tasks competing for your attention in the present.

...a debilitating condition involving the development of negative emotional, physical, and psychological reactions to occupational stress.

...a condition produced by working too hard for too long in a high-pressure environment.

...prolonged involvement either with a few extremely troubling cases, or with too many cases.

Purpose

It is not our purpose here to finally resolve the stress burnout syndrome. Due to the abundance of existing literature we have attempted to examine the best 1000+ publications and to glean from them the most pertinent information. By abstracting or annotating the most complete and comprehensive books and articles we have enabled the reader to appreciate the scope of the syndrome and the depth of this undertaking.
Throughout, the best materials available have been sought, examined, and condensed. Computer searches, hand searches, and other bibliographical and references sources were used to obtain the most relevant materials. Once obtained each article or book was scrutinized to determine whether its contribution was sufficient for inclusion in this text. Those finally selected were carefully outlined to present the most salient points while still doing justice to the original material and its author(s).

Use

This text may be used in a number of ways. Those not familiar with the syndrome may simply leaf randomly through the pages, selecting to read interesting annotations that catch the eye. Individuals seeking something specific about the syndrome are able to directly examine the issue through the use of the detailed contents at the back of the book.
The table of contents provides the three major categories into which material is collated. These are:

Signs/Symptoms
Causes/Sources
Coping strategies

We feel that this text facilitates examination of this syndrome by the reader in a number of ways. The first is to stimulate interest in stress burnout. Such interest, and continued research, will allow the more speedy remediation of problems

in the future. The second particular about the text
is that it enables the reader to eliminate long-term
and onerous research (which in itself could cause
the syndrome to occur). The articles and books have
been annotated in such a way that those interested
in a cursory or in a global examination need not
examine the original material. The thoroughness
with which the original manuscripts have been
outlined often eliminates the necessity for further
research. Lastly, the contents represent the most
comprehensive compilation of information related to
the syndrome to date. Despite the multitude of
articles and books available, each has its own focus
and is not generally intended to be
all-encompassing. We have taken everything available and organized it so that anyone wishing to
review the literature on any aspect of the syndrome
may find relevant references.

 For each of these three major categories a number
of subdivisions are provided. In this way the
reader may directly locate the source of certain
material. Each of the subdivisions lists citations
of authors and year. Once a citation is found it is
only necessary to find the reference through the
alphabetical listing of authors last names. A
casual examination readily reveals the method by
which all materials are categorized.

Annotated Bibliography

Adams, J. D. Improving stress management.
  Social Change Ideas & Applications, 1978, 8(4),
  1-4; 9-10.
The importance of managing stress is emphasized by
the several billions of dollars lost each year due
to the decrease in productivity and increased
sickness rates. The main premise herein for improving stress management is that each individual, not
the physician, is responsible for his or her own
well-being.
There are four types of stress or stressors. Type
I refers to recent events on the job. These changes
include: major changes in policies or instructions,
more hours of work, a sudden increase in the pace of
work, and procedural changes.
Stress Type II involves recent events away from
work. These changes include restriction of social
life, marriage, death of family member, and serious
illness.
Stress Type III involves job conditions such as too
much work, too little time, conflicts, and ambiguity.
Stress Type IV involves conditions away from work
such as pollution, noise, concern over economy, and
anxiety about children's activities.
One study found a positive correlation between
chronic health conditions and the frequency with
which managers were experiencing the above stress
types. A stress-management program should emphasize
an approach that is holistic and integrative. One
such program includes discussion, reading materials,

and a 20-minute slide presentation on the sources and responses to stress. In addition a variety of suggestions for effective stress management is given. A diagram is provided illustrating: 1) the sources of stress, 2) individual variables that either diffuse or intensify stress (personality, situational factors, quality of support), 3) available coping strategies (self-management, organization improvement, use of support systems), 4) psychophysiological manifestations of stress, 5) outcomes (work effectiveness, health, growth, and satisfaction).

Five self-management practices are:
1. Vigorous regular exercise.
2. Nutrition.
    a. Good eating habits.
    b. Vitamins and mineral supplements.
3. Letting-go techniques.
    a. Centering and focusing.
    b. Relaxation/meditation/prayer.
    c. Finishing unfinished business.
4. Self-awareness.
    a. Needs, desires, idiosyncracies.
    b. Congruence/assertiveness.
5. Personal planning.
    a. Time management.
    b. Positive life choices.

Adams, J. D. Guidelines for stress management and life style changes.   The Personnel Administrator, June 1979, 24, 35-38, 44.

Some of the primary factors that create stress are very difficult to change. These include an individual's personality, inherited characteristics, interpersonal support inherent in the environment, and the nature of the organization where the person works.

Within each area there are things that can be done to manage stress effectively. There are several guidelines that help in making changes in order to achieve a less stressful and more healthy life style. By following these guidelines, a gradual

process of life style change can take place that
will not be as overwhelming.
 Self-management techniques include:
1. Good nutritional habits.
  a. Balanced diet, regular meals.
  b. Maintenance of weight control.
  c. Moderate use of alcohol & tobacco.
  d. No smoking.
2. Good exercise habits.
  a. Regular exercise to improve
   cardiovascular fitness.
  b. Regular recreational exercise for
   tension reduction and diversion.
3. Self-awareness.
  a. Understanding of personal needs.
  b. Assertive behavior and role
   negotiation.
4. Letting-go techniques.
  a. Regular relaxation techniques, e.g.,
   meditation, prayer.
  b. Seeking closure on tasks and
   interpersonal situations--finishing
   unfinished business.
5. Personal planning.
  a. Effective time management day to day.
  b. Life and career planning for long term.
Creation and use of supportive relationships are
important and should include being aware of the
effect friends, family, and acquaintances have on
us. If the relationship is stressful and cannot be
improved, deal with it, then set it aside.
The approach to organizational improvement that
will affect stress levels on the job most effectively include: two-way flow of information; identification and change of stress provoking norms; role
clarification; clear, concise objectives; and
performance standards for all employees. These
changes in an organization involve many people and
must be created in an organization before significant stress reduction is possible.
Many stress-management programs fail because they
promote a "one best way" technique. Individuals
must deal with stress in a manner in which they are

comfortable.   Problems of stress should be dealt with one at a time.   Individuals should not attempt to change their life-styles all at once; they often may become discouraged and revert back to the old way of dealing with situations.   Making life-style changes that will help us withstand the stressors we encounter takes time.   It is difficult for people to make personal changes rapidly.   When making life-style changes it is better if we make them one step at a time.   Our chances for success are greater if we do not attempt to change all at once.   We should also think in terms of what we want our life style to be five years from now.

Adler, J., & Gosnell, M.   Stress: How it can hurt. Newsweek, April 21, 1980, pp. 106, 108.
Air traffic controllers present a textbook picture of psychological stress but in a study of this occupation it was found that by some measures the controllers are actually healthier than the rest of the population.   The study of stress offers no simple answers and experts are increasingly questioning long-accepted assumptions about illness and stress because they are simply not proven.   This article discusses how stress interacts with other factors to affect health.
Stress has much more subtle effects on the body's endocrine, nervous, and immunological systems and research is now focusing on how stress may create conditions in which the disease takes hold instead of stress "causing" a disease.   Current animal research on how the body deals with stress is discussed in relation to uclers.   Some of the findings are that early experience and social environment seem to affect susceptibility to diseases, and suppression of the immune system may be the causitive factors relating to stress and disease.
In research on the relationship of stress to hypertension, scientists found that baroreceptors, which function as blood-pressure monitors, built into the walls of the arteries detect increased pressure and signal the heart to slow and tend to

numb the brain's response to unpleasant stimuli. The body may seek this natural anesthesia by raising the blood pressure. Hypertension may then be a side effect of stress, rather than a direct result of it.

In a three-year study of 416 air-traffic controllers it was found that the incidence of hypertension was two to three times the expected level for men of that age group; but they did not have more total illness. The factor that seemed to have the most influence was the attitude the men had to their work. Controllers who were dissatisfied showed a significantly increased risk. The intensity of the stress appears to be less important than the way it is handled. Examples are offered to corroborate this statement.

In handling stress, some of the effects have been factors in stress-related illness. An increased incidence of disease has been associated with poor individual coping mechanisms, the lack of support systems, and lonliness.

Aiken, W. J., Smits, S. J., & Lollar, D. J. Leadership behavior and job satisfaction in state rehabilitation agencies. Personnel Psychology, 1972, 25, 65-73.

State rehabilitation agencies have spent little time, energy, or money to increase the effectiveness of supervisory personnel. The focus has been on rehabilitation counselors on the basis that counselors are the direct link between the rehabilitation agency and the handicapped client.

The study reviewed used the same rationale: that the supervisor is the direct link between the state rehabilitation agency and the personnel providing services to clients. There is very little research dealing with supervisory behavior in state agencies. Industry has been engaged in studying the behavior of supervisory and mangerial staff for many years. It is difficult to apply industrial results to state agencies due to the fact that rehabilitation and industry differ in two essential ways:

1. Rehabilitation, as defined in this study, is a governmental activity rather than free enterprise.
2. Industry more clearly defines production and quality.

Supervisors have traditionally been promoted from the counseling staff. The rapid expansion of rehabilitation in the past decade resulted in the promotion of counselors to supervisory positions, new counselors hired who were not fully trained in counseling, and an expansion of rehabilitation services to individuals who had not received services previously, i.e., public offenders, drug addicts, chronically unemployed, alcoholics, welfare recipients, and the severely disabled. Due to these drastic changes in the service-delivery system, the supervisory skills of a supervisor are of vital importance to undertrained and inexperienced counselors. The supervisor must be skilled in the educational-consultative activity in which he helps the untrained counselor develop skills and attitudes to provide services to clients. This study represents an attempt to isolate those leadership behaviors and job satisfaction that counselors see as functioning within state agencies.

A random sample of 342 counselors was drawn from personnel lists in 31 participating state rehabilitation agencies. Of the 342 counselors sampled, 230 returned complete and usable materials, while 28 returned had one or more incomplete items. The statistical analyses are based on the 230 complete sets of survey materials.

Several scales of the Leader Behavior Description Questionnaire, form XII, were selected. Form XII represents the fourth revision of the questionnaire, which developed out of a theory of role differentiation and group achievement and subsequent research on the hypothesized subscales. The three subscales selected for use in this study were:

1. Initiation of Structure--clearly defines own role, and allows followers to know what is expected of them.

2. Tolerance of Freedom--allows followers scope for initiative, decision, and action.
3. Production Emphasis--applies pressure for productive output.

Alexander, R. J. "Burnout out" versus "punching out." Journal of Human Stress, March 1980, 6(1), 37-41.

Air traffic control is a unique occupation that requires high physical and mental standards often-times accompanied by clear signs of burnout. Symptoms include insomnia, anxiety, depression, nightmares, fear of midair collision, and increased alienation from work.

Those controllers experiencing such symptoms run high risks of early retirement due to medical reasons. Under the Federal Employers Compensation Act those controllers who retire due to job related medical disabilities are eligible for compensation for loss of earning capacity. This early retirement usually results in a rapid improvement of symptoms, within months. They also become eligible for a new career provided for under the Federal Aviation Administrations Second Career Program, as well as collecting medical disability under the FECA through the Department of Labor.

Present procedures used in determining controller disability appear to be simple and vulnerable to the charge of fraud. Much work is needed in the area of psychiatric disability determination to inspire confidence that the public, disabled controllers, FAA management, and the evaluating physician will be well served.

Allen, D. W. Hidden stresses in success. Psychiatry, May 1979, 42, 171-176.

"Conventional measures of success include the attainment of wealth, position, esteem favor, or eminence, but these things, without an accompanying enforcement of self-esteem, cause stress, emotional discomfort or strain." Self-esteem is pleasure in success; pretensions are the inner set of what a

person expects of himself. Success divided by
pretensions equals self-esteem. Accordingly, as
success increases and pretensions decrease,
self-esteem increases. Many therapies and religions
focus on reducing pretensions. By reducing the size
of the goal, self-esteem can be increased and
measure of stress-free success can be rendered.
  Behind stress lies unconscious dilemmas that are
built into the character or cognitive structure in
inner, unattainable sets or in internalized double
binds, in conflicting expectations or demands on the
self. Stress can be caused by the fear of competing
or the fear of shame or guilt as a result of competing. These feelings can be remedied by viewing
victory as an extension of achievements rather than
as an act of "killing off" another person. To
understand causes of stress related to success, one
needs to know the inner, personal meaning of the
success, the nature and source of the ambition, and
what factors focus libidinal and aggressive forces
in that ambition. Stress can result if personal
success is vicarious success for another person;
stress can result if the challenge of the road is
all, and the end is nothing.
  Plateaus need to be set and reached in order to
experience success. Stress results from not knowing
what pace to set or what plateaus can be reached.
Moving from plateau to plateau also involves stress
resulting from change to status, living environment,
and friends. Stress is involved as progress in the
hierarchy is made; the requirements change perhaps
from conformity to independence and innovativeness.
Public focus also elicits stress from constantly
being examined in the media; exhibitionistic needs
may be satisfied, but a feeling of shallowness may
also exist. Success at the lower levels is much
more tactile and defined; as one progresses up the
ladder, personal definitions of success become
unclear. "Regardless of the degree, there must be
success in both work and love or there is an incurable strain."

Antonovsky, A. Breakdown: A needed fourth step in

the conceptual armamentarium of modern medicine. Social Science and Medicine, 1972, 6, 537-544.

The concept of breakdown is suggested as a fourth step in the concerns of modern medicine. Modern medicine concerns itself with controlling the outer environment and immunization when dealing with sickness or illness. Another factor is that there may be multiple causes for a disease, going beyond germs, toward the awareness of deprivational and stress diseases. The definition of breakdown is conceived by the author as various degrees and combinations of factors. It is defined as any state or condition that:

1. Is directly painful to the individual (from not at all to severely).
2. Limits him functionally (from not at all to severely).
3. Is characterized by being (not acute to acute or life threatening).
4. Is recognized by the medical institution of the society in which the individual lives as requiring under its direction (nothing to active therapy).

From the etiological standpoint, the author sees multiple causation as responsible for breakdown. Tension is noted as gratifying and rewarding in two ways: pleasurable as in a sexual experience, and second as the value of the experience itself, which could be useful to the individual in the future. The imbalance is then not pathogenic. Antonovsky states, "It is, rather, the prolonged failure to restore equilibrium which leads to breakdown. When resistance resources are inadequate to meet the demand, to resolve the problem which has been posed, the organism breaks down."

The resistance resources mentioned include adaptability, (to a role that suits the individual best), profound ties, (to immediate others), and the ties between an individual and his total community, (identifying with the community). Finally it is felt that a new health profession is needed, that is, something to augment resistance sources prior to breakdown. The author sees a need for new

directions in research, epidemiologic and social,
studying the factors that can lead to breakdown or
even death. Thus the medical efforts mobilize to
focus on a specific disease and specific therapy for
that disease, while it is suggested (in the case of
breakdown), that therapy be built upon resistance
and coping resources.

Armstrong, T. B. Job content and context factors
   related to satisfaction for different occupational
   levels. Journal of Applied Psychology, 1971, 55,
   57-65.
   This study is based on the relationships between
satisfaction for the two kinds of job factors and
overall job satisfaction. In addition, importance
ratings for these same job factors were examined to
shed light on the problem.
   This research was based on content-context job
factor dichotomy. The main hypothesis stated that
the favorable feelings toward such content factors
as achievement contribute to overall general job
satisfaction but do not generally contribute to job
dissatisfaction per se. A review of the literature
indicated that the research on Hertzberg's theory
revealed that the job-satisfaction study used both a
high- and low-level occupation and examined the two
kinds of job factors on both satisfaction and
importance dimension.
   In this study, the rationale of Darley and Hagenah
relative to occupational level was used to test the
main hypothesis of Hertzberg's theory.
Two hypotheses were formulated for this study:
   1.   For the high-level occupational group, the
        job-content factors make a relatively
        greater contribution to overall job
        satisfaction than do the job context
        factors.
   2.   For the low-level occupational group, the
        job-context factors make a relatively
        greater contribution to overall job
        satisfaction than do job-content factors.
   A questionnaire was developed by conducting a pilot
study. The sample consisted of engineers and

assemblers because both occupations are classified
in the technology field with engineers as professionals and assemblers at the semiskilled level.
The first hypothesis was accepted and the second
hypothesis was rejected. These results challenge
the common stereotype held for semiskilled workers,
that is, that they merely trade their time at work
and seek security and economic features in order to
cope with life's basic needs. Confirmation of the
first hypothesis on the other hand supports previous
research using high level groups.

It is further concluded that job satisfaction
remains a vital concept, in that it has an important
effect upon success and satisfaction in nonjob areas
of life.

Atkins, B. J., Meyer, A. B., & Smith, N. K.
Personal care attendants: Attitudes and factors
contributing to job satisfaction. Journal of
Rehabilitation, July/August/ September, 1982,
48(3), 20-24.
To learn more about the role of personal care
attendants, a study of 56 attendants in Dane County,
Wisconsin, was made. The authors of the study were
interested in the high turnover rate of PCAs (personal care attendants) and what could be done to
make the job more appealing. In addition, PCAs were
surveyed regarding their attitudes relative to job
duties and personal values. The goal of the study
was to attain a better understanding of attendant
care and to improve employer-employee relationships.

The 56 attendants who participated in the study
were administered three scales. To "examine the
effect of attendant on the attendant-employer
relationship and to determine if any particular
attitudes toward the disabled correlated with PCA
job satisfaction/length of employment" the ATDP
(Attitudes Towards Disabled Persons) scale was used.
Personality traits were measured with the Gordon
Personal Profile (GPP) and the Gordon Personal
Inventory (GPI). For demographic information and
specific job-related questions the Current Attendant

Profile (CAP) and the Former Attendant Profile (FAP) were used.

The results of the study are as follows: Forty-three (43%) percent of attendants are less than 27 years old. Seventy-nine (79%) percent of the attendants are single and seventy-five (75%) percent have no dependents. Most attendants (88%) work for employers whose ethnic heritage is the same as theirs. For half of the attendants surveyed the main source of income is as a PCA. Almost half (45%) of the PCAs had no prior contact with the disabled. Factors PCAs liked best were: "being able to help others (38%) and doing something worthwhile (36%)." Job aspects that were liked least: "low salary (27%), lack of fringe benefits (18%), and odd hours (14%)." Two major reasons given for attendants quitting were: "change in school schedule (23%) and the employer died or needed more care (20%)."

Suggestions made by PCAs to improve the job included: fringe benefits, support groups, attendant training, and employer training. The characteristics PCAs look for in employers were: treating employees with kindness, fairness, respect, knowing their care needs, ability to give praise and criticism, and acting as independently as possible.

Austin, J. J., & Jackson, E. Occupational mental health and the human services: A review. Health and Social Work, 1977, 2 (1), 92-116.
The many social workers who hold responsible management positions in the mental health field are in a position to influence the development of innovative mental health programs. However, most of these innovations reflect a preoccupation with specific client problems and fail to address the issues of occupational mental health within the larger context of job satisfaction and occupational and union mental health services.

Some authors have begun to question the value of the work ethic in this country, claiming that work dominates the lives of most Americans. Herzberg has indicated that the basic reason for working is economic necessity. He also found that safe, pleasant working environments, job security, and fringe benefits all contribute to keeping a person happy with a job. Ginzberg has pointed out the following possible sources of worker tension in the work place: (1) isolation, (2) tight supervision, (3) work groups that include increasing groups of minorities or women, (4) a reduction in management's loyalty to older workers, (5) displacement of higher echelon workers who have extensive employment contacts, (6) anonymity in rapidly growing organizations, (7) excessive demands on young executives for mobility, with increased strains on marriages, (8) technological advances, (9) increased leisure time for workers who cannot afford to pay for leisure activities, and (10) preferences for hiring younger workers over older ones.

To reduce demands on workers it is recommended that employers (1) provide opportunities for workers to update their education while still working, (2) reduce employer arbitrariness in making, interpreting, and enforcing rules, (3) increase workers' opportunities for self-expression, and (4) give increase support to workers who are experiencing personal crises.

The importance of maintaining easily accessible mental health services is revealed by Leeman, who found that 60% of all workers treated in an onsite center were unable to name one other source to which they could have gone for help.

Bach, G. The George Bach self-recognition inventory for burned-out therapists. Voices, 1979, 15(2), 73-76.

Fifty-seven items are included, which provide a self-assessment of one's current level of "Burned-Outness." This excellent list relates to the physical and mental well-being of the therapist and reflects the therapist's affective abilities with clients.

Whether you consider yourself mildly or more severely burnedout will depend on how painfully you experience your level of burnout or how tolerant you

are in handling the occupational hazards of your profession.
The following is a list of characteristics of burnout:
1. Exhaustion and easy tiring.
2. Disenchanted with work.
3. Feeling isolated, socially, psychologically, and physically.
4. A growing apathy toward patients.
5. Inescapable boredom.
6. Problems outside of the work environment.
7. A growing unprofessionalism in all areas of work.
8. Cynical.
9. An unhealthy increase in risk-taking behavior.
10. Outside concerns take precedent over clients and work in general.

Bailey, J. T., & Walker, D. D. Rx for stress: One hospital's approach. Supervisory Management, August 1982, 27(8), 32-37.
Burnout has been found to be a contributing factor in high rates of absenteeism, frequent complaints of illness, cynicism, lowered work performance, low morale, and turnover. A number of organizations have realized the detrimental effects of employee stress on organizational goals. An attempt to combat burnout has been made by the Stanford University Hospital since its nursing staff provides good candidates for burnout in an atmosphere of pressure and emotions. The following are the results of this case study.
A stress audit of 129 intensive-care-unit nurses was conducted through a free-response questionnaire to determine the nature of their stress. Based upon these results, 15 training modules were developed as well as a number of workshops for dealing with specific stressors. One third of the nurses found the number-one stressor to be interpersonal relationships (conflicts with staff, physicians, administrators, and residents). To combat this,

workshops on conflict resolution and training modules on group process, communication, assertiveness, and conflict resolution were implemented. The second most common stressor was identified as direct patient care activities (death of patients, unnecessary prolongation of life). This was handled through workshops on death and bioethics, training modules on crisis intervention, problem solving and ethics. The third most common stressor was management of the unit (inadequate staffing). Action taken on this problem was to close units temporarily, intensify recruitment efforts, increase the number of RNs, involve nurses in decision making relative to scheduling and other job-related procedures and policies. Fourth was physical work environment. This was dealt with by remodeling the physical plant. Fifth was knowledge and skills. Specific training modules were developed in needed areas to handle this. The sixth area was administrative rewards. This was dealt with by negotiating new contracts covering such items as salaries and fringe benefits.

As a result of this study, it became clear that one of the most urgent needs of nurses was a full-time nurse consultant. A running program for nurses was started, providing training materials on prescribed medication as well as aerobic dancing and other exercises, saunas and hot baths, relaxation exercises, autogenic training, biofeedback, guided-imagery exercises, problem solving, and seminars on time management and assertiveness training. Opportunities for singing, playing, or listening to music were also provided.

The following guidelines were developed to help deal with burnout: "recognize that everyone is vulnerable to stress and burnout and acquire an understanding of the signs and symptoms of stress." Conduct surveys to determine the stressors of your employees and take appropriate action. Get the personnel interested in physical fitness, weight control, stopping alcohol abuse, and stopping smoking. Clarify job descriptions and evaluation criteria and offer help with career development.

Allow employees to participate in decisions relative to staffing, scheduling, and other policies affecting their jobs."

Ball, W. R.   Emotional stamina--the practioner's dilemma.   Counselor Education and Supervision, 1977, 16(3), 230-269.
Counselors often give a lot and get little in return, and deal with emotional stamina in a close and personally demanding relationship. Beginning counselors often are not prepared to face the disparity between theory and reality or between the emotional-psychological demands and the net result of counseling effort which results in them leaving the profession soon after training. Training programs should point out that the practitioner can expect to feel an emotional-psychological energy drain. Direct feedback from the client can replenish this energy but is a rare occurence.
The counseling relationship is incomplete in that it occurs outside the mainstream of public life, with social and intimate relationships limited. The counselor often is faced with minimal return from the client. Full relationships outside the counseling setting help to restore some of the lost energy. In addition, counselors often need time to relax and be away from other people after a full day of counseling.

Bardo, P.   The pain of teacher burnout: A case history.   Phi Delta Kappan, December 1979, pp. 252-254.
Teacher burnout is a phenomenon all too familiar to many adults working in the modern public school. Symptoms include high absenteeism, lack of commitment, abnormal desire for vacations, low self-esteem, and an inability to take school seriously. The National Education Association currently attributes much of the problem of burnout to teachers' pervasive sense of having lost control of their classrooms. Students appear to be simply refusing to do the work that leads to learning. Conscientious teachers often struggle to make lessons more

interesting in hopes of motivating the student.
However, the more a teacher tries, the less that
seems to be accomplished. Many teachers appear to
suffer from guilt, feelings of frustration, and
disappointment. Eventually these feelings lead to
burnout, and for many, leaving the profession is the
only solution. The NEA estimates that at least 30%
of American teachers would like to be doing something else.

Barnes, M. R., & Crutchfield, C. A. Job
   satisfaction- dissatisfaction. Physical Therapy,
   1977, 57(1), 5-41.
   Job factors that result in feelings of satisfaction or dissatisfaction were studied in a sample of
25 physical therapists engaged in private practice
and 25 physical therapists employed as chiefs of
departments in Pittsburg, Washington, and Baltimore.
The intention of this study was to determine the
meaningfulness of work for a sample of physical
therapists and to compare the behaviors of organizational physical therapists with those in private
practice.
   Three factors of job satisfaction that were statistically significant for both organizational therapists and private practitioners were achievement,
salary, and responsibility. Only one factor,
policies and administration of the organization, was
significant in job dissatisfaction for both groups.
   Achievement was the most readily identified source
of motivation for all the therapists studied. For
private practitioners the source of achievement was
directly related to the patients, while organizational therapists' satisfaction and achievement
were derived from seeing the results of their
administrative efforts to develop and maintain an
efficient, effective service-business.
   The work itself was viewed by both groups of
therapists as having positive as well as negative
attributes similar to those of achievement. Responsibility was found to be a significant motivator for
both groups and inadequate income was not found to
be significantly dissatisfying to either group.

Working conditions were found to be statistically significant for private practitioners because of too much work, but were not significant for organizational therapists.

Organizational policies and administration were highly significant in measuring job dissatisfaction for each group. Organizational therapists were dissatisfied largely because of disagreement over goals. The factor for private practitioners was caused by difficulty in interpreting government policies and regulations and the ambiguity of goals between agencies and therapists with respect to the patient.

Herzberg's two-factor theory of job satisfaction-dissatisfaction was used as the model for this study. If this theory is correct in relation to physical therapists, then administrators and educators who teach physical therapy management theory should become thoroughly aware of the factors that provide satisfaction and dissatisfaction for physical therapists.

Baron, A., & Cohen, R. B. Helping telephone counselors cope with burnout: A consciousness-raising workshop. Personnel & Guidance Journal, 1982, 60(8), 508-510.

Telephone counselors experience high levels of burnout because of the stress inherent in the occupation. The inability of the counselor to see "facial and other physical cues, the inability to track a client through the crisis process because of the one-shot nature of telephone counseling, and the inability actually to observe behavioral changes over time in the callers can all lead to a heightened sense of frustration and disillusionment."

To formulate a workshop crisis for counselors and address the issue of burnout, three areas were studied. These included: symptoms of burnout; sources of burnout (professional and organizational); and formation of contracts to cope with stress and disillusionment. The workshop consisted of six half-hour sessions which covered: "personal symptoms of burnout, personal contributions to burnout, and professional contributions to burnout, organizational contributions to burnout, highlighting positive work aspects, and exploring personal and organizational ways of coping with burnout." The sessions include questionnaires and discussions that allowed individuals to express their opinions and suggestions.

It is important to recognize that people experience burnout to varying degrees and have certain needs to be met as a result of this phenomenon. The objective of the workshop is to assist counselors in identifying their needs and finding suitable solutions to resolve their disillusionment or frustration.

Barrow, J. C., & Prosen, S. S. A model of stress and counseling interventions. Personnel and Guidance Journal, Sept. 1981, 60(1), 5-10.

Stress occurs when any demand is made upon the body that originates from a stimulus or situations. Stress is usually a result of a change in the body's homeostasis. The body responds to stress via three stages: alarm, resistance/adaption, and exhaustion. The alarm stage is controlled by endocrine hormomes, which ready the body for "fight or flight." Resistance/adaptation brings "the individual's dominant defenses into play." The final stage, exhaustion, results when the ability to cope is extinguished.

Emotional stress, which is prevalent among many clients, usually occurs in the adaptation stage and is psychologically disruptive. If the stress is prolonged or of great frequency, it can cause negative reactions such as: degenerative diseases; depletion of body energy and resistance levels; disruption of thought processes or acquisition of behaviors in opposition to maintainance of good health.

A model was developed to explain the interactions of stress and self-regulation. The model incorporates environmental and individual variables that are important in the regulation of stress. The

model is composed of six stages: envirnomental
demands, mental processing (internal and external
cues), mental activation, organ reaction, internal
feedback, and action to change environment. When
analyzing the effect of stress on mental processing,
it is important to consider that "the network of
beliefs, expectations, values, and other mental sets
is more pervasive than transient thoughts and is
really at the heart of important differences in life
style." Much of the stress produced in individuals
today causes basic physiological responses but
cannot be relieved by physical actions.

   In an effort to reduce stress, interventions should
be made. These actions should be made at the
stress-producing stage and implemented either
cognitively or behaviorally. Counselors can assist
the client in identifying the suitable intervention
for reducing the stress. Some intervention methods
include "training in such areas as assertiveness,
leadership, and helping skills." Other methods are
development of time management and involvement in
self-management groups. Another intervention,
"stress inoculation," was developed to help clients
understand and identify maladaptive behaviors and
emotions. The use of values clarification is
important in identifying and establishing goals in
order to reduce stress.   This type of intervention
also allows "a person to gain perspective on the
kinds of demands appropriate to make of oneself."

   Interventions useful in the stage of mental activation encompass those that stimulate the central
nervous system. Relaxation response, biofeedback,
transcendental meditation, and sensory awareness
training are all methods that have positive effects
in the reduction of stress. Clients learn how to
reduce blood pressure, and tension levels through
the practice of certain "coping" behaviors such as
deep breathing, autongenic training, and relaxation
exercises. After an individual learns to recognize
the "internal cues of stress," he is able to relieve
these sources of stress through the use of relaxation response exercises.

The conclusion drawn from use of the interventions is that it allows counselors to determine successful methods to be used in individual causes of stress management.

Batlis, N. C. Job involvement and locus of control as moderators of role perception/individual outcome relationships. Psychological Reports, Feb. 1980, 46(1), 111-119.

A considerable amount of research has been devoted to documenting the impact of role perceptions on the attitudes and behavior of organizational members. The theory of role dynamics includes two constructs that have received special attention in the literature, role conflict and role ambiguity. Role conflict is best understood as "a simultaneous occurrence of two or more sets of pressures such that compliance with one would make compliance with the other more diffiuclt." Role ambiguity refers to a situation in which clear, consistent information regarding role requirements is perceived by the individual as unavailable. Role conflict and ambiguity have been generally correlated with job dissatisfaction, anxiety and tension, and propensity to leave the organization.

Results have not always been consistent. Variables frequently have been different for role conflict and role ambiguity and have varied from sample to sample. These conflicts have led investigators to the moderating effects of variables such as a need for clarity, need for achievement, need for autonomy, ability, and higher order need strength. While personality variables would be thought to affect the relationship between role stress and individual reactions, the available data permits few worthwhile generalizations.

This study was designed to examine the moderating influences of two personality variables previously demonstrated as significantly affecting the relationships between perception of the organizational environment and individual outcomes. The first variable, locus of control, was selected because of significant measure correlations with perceptions of

effort-performance expectancies within an academic
setting. The other variable selected was job
involvement, defined as "the degree to which the job
situation is central to the person and his identity."
Job involvement has been found to be an effective
moderator of relationships between perceptions of
organizational climate and overall job satisfaction.
It was found that variations in the work experience
are likely to have strong affective consequences for
people for whom work is an essential component of
their identity, those with high job involvement.
Nonjob-involved persons should manifest less extreme
reactions to environmental conditions such as role
stress.

Beech, H. R., Burns, L. E., & Sheffield, B. F. A
    behavioral approach to the management of stress: A
    practical guide to techniques. New York: John
    Wiley & Sons, 1982.
I.   Occupational Stress and Stress Problems.
    A.   Types of occupational stressors.
        1.   Problems of work load.
            a.   Work overload.
            b.   Work underload.
        2.   Problems of occupational frustration.
            a.   Role ambiguity.
            b.   Role conflict.
            c.   High degrees of specialization.
            d.   Poor career development
                  guidance.
            e.   Poor communication.
            f.   Problems of bureacuracy.
        3.   Occupational change.
            a.   Scientific developments.
            b.   Promotion.
            c.   Relocation.
            d.   Organizational restructuring.
            e.   Redundancy.
            f.   Retirement.
        4.   Other sources of occupational
              stressors.
    B.   The effects of stressors on the

individual.
1. Physiological.
2. Behavioral.
3. Cognitive.
II. The Behavioral Approach.
A. Society and mass media.
B. The approach of psychotherapy.
C. The approach of behavioral psychology.
D. Self-help methods.
III. Identification of Stressors: Behavioral
Analysis.
A. Components of behavior.
1. Behavioral excesses.
2. Behavioral deficits.
3. Behavioral assets.
a. Motivational analysis.
b. Developmental analysis.
1) biological factors.
2) sociolgical facotrs.
3) behavioral factors.
c. Analysis of social
relationships.
d. Analysis of the
social-cultural-physical
environment.
B. Behavioral analysis of anxiety and fear.
C. Self-report measures.
D. Behavioral observation.
E. Role playing tests.
F. Interpersonal performance test.
IV. Relaxation Techniques in the Control of
Tension.
A. Historical aspects of progressive
relaxation training.
B. Benefits of deep relaxation.
C. Points to bear in mind about relaxation
training.
D. Progressive muscle relaxation exercise.
E. Basic training program.
1. Relaxation of the arms.
2. Relaxation of the facial muscles.
3. Relaxation of the neck muscles.
4. Relaxation of the shoulders, chest,

    E.   Uses of biofeedback.
    F.   Biofeedback and general relaxation.
    G.   Biofeedback and stress-related disorders.
    H.   Biofeedback and headaches.
          1.   Biofeedback training sessions.
          2.   Migraine headaches.
    I.   Biofeedback and hypertension.
    J.   Areas of application.
    K.   Advantages of biofeedback.
IX. Vulnerability, Coping Skills and Personal
    Stresses.
    A.   Elements of stress reaction.
          1.   Basic temperamental variable.
          2.   Coping skills.
          3.   Actual stresses.
          4.   Type A personality.
    B.   Stress-problem identification.
    C.   Referral for specialist attention.
    D.   Selection procedures.
    E.   Monitoring functions.
    F.   Redundancy counseling.

Beehr, T. A. Perceived situational moderators of the
    relationship between subjective role ambiguity and
    role strain. Journal of Applied Psychology, 1976,
    61(1), 35-40.
While most previous research deals only with
investigating the relationship between role stress
and role strain, this study was based on the hypothesis that three situational characteristics-group
cohesiveness, supervisor support, and autonomy-can
be moderators of the relationship between role
strain and role stress. In addition, the variety of
roles and organizations was greater than in previous
studies so that the results would be more representative of phenomenon that are widely dispersed in
the world of work. This study was a search for
situational moderators of the relationship between
one organizational stress (role ambiguity) and four
psychological strains (job dissatisfaction, life
dissatisfaction, low self-esteem, and depressed
mood).

Specific hypotheses were that role ambiguity is more strongly related to role strains a) among people in noncohesive groups, b) among people with nonsupportive supervisors, and c) among people in nonautonomous roles than among people in autonomous roles.

A sample of 651 workers employed in a printing company, a small research and development company, two automotive supply companies, and four service departments of a hospital were interviewed in 90-minute structured sessions in the respondents' homes. Although the measures of all variables were subjective, it can be argued that the perceptions of the subject are important in stress research because strain may be largely an individual's reaction to his subjective environment.

Role ambiguity was found to be significantly related to the four strains for the sample as a whole. Job dissatisfaction is the strain most strongly correlated with role ambiguity. Life dissatisfaction has the weakest relationship to ambiguity in the work role. Group cohesiveness was found to moderate the relationship between role ambiguity and low self-esteem. The implications of this study are that even if there is a stress, people in roles with certain situational charac- teristics, especially automony, do not suffer from it. It is not clear, though, whether supervisor support was an adequate force to alleviate feelings of stress individuals; peer support, on the other hand, may be an effective means of support alleviat- ing stress.

Job dissatisfaction was found to be more strongly related to role ambiguity in cohesive than in noncohesive groups. In contrast, for persons in cohesive groups the relationship between role ambiguity and low self-esteem is weaker than it is for those in noncohesive groups. It is suggested that peer support in a cohesive group alleviates internalized blame for situations caused by role ambiguity. Autonomy was found to be the strongest and most inconsistent moderator of the relationship between role ambiguity and role strain. Stress can be decreased in organizations by increasing autonomy of the member roles.

Beehr, T. A. Work-role stress and attitudes toward co-workers. Group and Organizational Studies, 1981, 6(2), 201-210.

Factors that influence satisfaction with an employment position may result in: overall job dissatisfaction, low self-esteem, depressed mood, and fatigue. The source of these factors are: role ambiguity, role overload, and underutilization of skills.

One hypothesis used to explain this phenomenon is role theory. This theory assumes that the social system is a source of role definition and that it can be blamed for stress that is created and felt. Individuals having difficulty with their role may exhibit this through their actions. A primary method used is withdrawl. Withdrawl is manifested through absenteeism and reduction in communication, both of which "protect the individual from stress [but] are dysfunctional for the organization."

To study the impact of role theory, work-role stress, and attitudes toward coworkers, a survey was conducted among 468 employees in 5 midwestern organizations. Factors studied were: the relationship of role ambiguity, role overload, and underutilization of skills to role strains such as low self-esteem and dissatisfaction. The second set of factors considered the impact of role stresses on relationships with coworkers.

Specific items were measured such as role stresses, including role ambiguity and underutilization of skills. Measurement of role strain included overall job dissatisfaction, life dissatisfaction, low self-esteem, depressed mood, and fatigue. Results of the correlations were positive in most categories. "The correlations between the role stresses and job dissatisfaction appeared to be the strongest, and the correlations between the role stresses and life dissatisfaction were the weakest." Similarly, "role ambiguity was most strongly correlated with dissatisfaction with role clarity,

second most strongly correlated with dissatisfaction
with coworkers, and least strongly correlated with
dissatisfaction with the nonsocial facets of the
work role-pay and comfort."
Conclusions drawn from the study indicate that role
stress is a primary influence on attitudes, social
interaction, and role expectations. Role stress
also influences behavior in employee turnover and
absenteeism.

Beehr, T. A., & Gupta, N. A note on the structure
  of employee withdrawal. Organizational Behavior
  and Human Performance, 1978, 21, 73-79.
  Employee withdrawal from an organization can take
many behavioral forms: absenteeism, lateness,
turnover and psychological manifestations. These
different forms of withdrawal may be positive or
negative, with absenteeism being the lesser and
turnover the more serious. The purpose of this
study is to determine the direction and the relative
strength of the relationships among the forms of
withdrawal.
  Data was collected from 651 employees from 5
midwestern organizations by obtaining personnel
records, professional interviews, and supervisor's
rating of their subordinates.
  The results show that a positive relationship
exists among the various types of withdrawal, with
low to moderate strength. While all forms of
withdrawal reveal themselves together, their relative severity may be varied, depending on their
correlates.

Bennett, W. Stress could lengthen your life.
  Vogue, October 1979, 330, 388.
  Having a sense of control over stressful conditions may be a severe element protecting people
from harmful reactions. Yet, many people in highly
stressed occupations do report experiencing considerable satisfaction from their work.
  It is becoming more and more evident that how you
react to the situation, not the situation itself, is
what counts. Stress may become a burden or a

challenge, but what really counts is the way one
copes and the extent to which one can cope. Some
people just seem to lack an inner monitoring device
for regulating the work-rest-recreation balance.
They seem to have such a compulsive need to work
that they deny the existence of fatigue and push
themselves beyond reason.

Individual differences in the response to stress
are determined by a variety of influences and
constitutional factors. Men and women handle stress
in different ways and even react dissimilarly at the
biological level. But women experience stress
similar to that of males in the conflicts they both
encounter: by their roles and self-image, and by
struggling against job discrimination and lowered
self-esteem that begins early in adolescence. Women
differ from men in the way they handle stress by
talking about their negative experiences: they are
more satisfied with the kinds of support they
receive when they are troubled than are males.
Women also have a milder biochemical response, they
produce less adrenaline than do males, which is the
most significant change to the reaction of stress.
Physiologically females react less markedly to
stress, but psychologically they suffer more than
males do.

Biologically women are better equipped than men to
deal with stress. They seem to be protected by
their moderate adrenaline production. Yet they are
still handicapped by cultural liabilities in dealing
with stress. But they do have an advantage: their
willingness to share their problems and their
ability to develop social networks that are supportive in difficult situations.

Berlin, I. N. Resistance to change in mental health
    professionals. American Journal of
    Orthopsychiatry, January, 1969, 39(1), 109-115.
    Mental health professionals resist change because
such change may reduce their status, financial
return, sense of personal satisfaction, and feeling
of competency. Constant challenge to ideas or
efforts may require one to reaffirm one's

efficiency, knowledge, or capacity to resolve
problems better than anyone else. These feelings
may stand in the way of collaboration. Professional
personal satisfaction depends on one's learning a
certain body of knowledge and becoming proficient
and comfortable in its use. The therapeutic position is one of safety, noninvolvement, and power.
  Status in the mental health profession is often
exemplified by the psychoanalyst who treats individual clients for high hourly fees. The changing
needs for mental health services challenges this
status. Uncertainty and the questioning of tradition among professionals is anxiety-provoking and
threatening; new forumlations in theory and practice
are feared. Resistance may be due to fear of
discovery that one is not as competent or effective
as one had hoped.
  Altered status also may be at the base of resistance to change. A variety of professional and
nonprofessional community representatives now want
input into mental-health programming, thus threatening the expert status of the therapists themselves.
Consultation and coordination are becoming more
important aspects of the mental health professionals, thus lessening the uniqueness of the job and
the direct client contact. By reducing autonomy,
the public health model threatens professionals
trained in individual work. Pilot models of collaboration are needed to supply proof that consultation
can provide rewards in new ways even though power
and former ways of gaining job satisfaction are no
longer intact.

Bermak, G. E., Do psychiatrists have special
  emotional problems? American Journal of
  Psychoanalysis, 1977, 141-146.
  Psychiatry has been described as having an identity crisis: a combination of the previously developed sense of self and a newly developed professional self that provides a solid professional stance.
  A questionnaire was sent out to 75 San Francisco
Bay area psychiatrists which dealt with the emotional problems involved in their practice.

Psychiatrists have emotional difficulties that are special to them and their work: 60% agreed that psychiatrists' emotional problems originated in their work, while 40% agreed that the emotional problems originated in the personality of the psychiatrist. Special problems that exist -- particularly isolation, physical aloneness in the practice of psychiatry, the inability to communicate with others about patients due to confidentiality which creates a high degree of isolation, and personality problems that interfere with their ability to achieve intimacy outside the office -- are all special difficulties faced by psychiatrists with emotional problems. It is also important to note that the control of emotions, awareness of deep emotional issues in oneself, ambiguity in the field itself, the emotional drain of constantly being empathic, and long delays in achieving results in the treatment of patients, are all burdens and sources of strain to the emotional psychiatrist.

These special emotional problems should be approached by psychiatrists in two ways. First, psychiatrists should maintain high levels of training, including continuing education with peer supervision. Second, personal therapy should be encouraged positively for all in the field.

Berstein, A. J. Burnout in human services. Human Development News, February-March, 1982, p. 4.

Burnout is a phenomena that exists not only because of the emotionally draining, frequently frustrating, and rarely satisfying work but because the human-service worker has lost the ability to be flexible and adaptable to changes in the system. The burnout of human-service workers is made analogous to both flames and rust. Some long-term employees become locked "into habit patterns that become encrusted and rigid." Other workers have not burned out as much as they lack motivation or fuel for the flames to cause combustion.

Burnout is the result "of a particular lifestyle, a particular pattern of behaving that leads to feelings of dysphoria." Individuals who are depressed do not have any fun or experience pleasant events. They tend to reduce social contacts when under stress or under a heavy workload. Socialization, in the form of nonwork conversation and lunch dates, is reduced to the point that work begins to have a negative impact by causing the worker to become more demanding of himself and others. Feelings of helplessness are reduced by changing the worker's perception and having him make a commitment to implementing a new behavior.

Finally there is the effect of interpersonal factors on burnout. A person suffering burnout seeks support from others and usually receives sympathy for the frustration he is experiencing. After a prolonged period of time of complaining, the burned-out individual no longer continues to receive sympathy and understanding from others. In the extreme, this causes the person to become bitter and have feelings of alienation. Communication is an important factor in the treatment of burnout. The communication patterns of the burned-out individual give a good indication of the depth of depression.

Frequently, it is difficult to remedy the effects of burnout because of the inability of persons to objectively examine it as a "job dissatisfaction syndrome." It is believed that conceptualization of burnout may be a part of the problem as much as it is a solution.

Bies, F., & Molle, B. What to do when you've had it up to here. Glamour, 1980, March, p. 32A.

Career counselors and industrial psychologists view "career burnout" as a syndrome that affects most working people at one time or another and one that is termed a distinct malady of the working world. Stress, boredom, and job dissatisfaction all contribute to career burnout.

Some psychologists believe career burnout can only be resolved by changing one's career, or modifying one's current job in some way. Burnout generally occurs when people begin to question their own personal values, or feel that what they are doing just isn't important anymore. But one thing that is

important is that alcoholism, risk of heart attack,
and disease can all be aftereffects of the burnout
process.

Burnout is the most severe stage of stress, and
each year thousands of people in the medical profession are victims of the syndrome. Their energy is
depleted, their clincal work begins to seem dis-
tressing and dull, and their midafternoon clients do
not usually receive the same degree of attention as
those received in the morning. After a full day of
dealing with depressed clients, they usually go home
depressed themselves. As a result of this, many
decide to leave their professions because it is too
draining. In many cases, the nature of a profession
or industry, the pressures, hectic schedules and
time demands, can push a highly talented and qualified person toward burning out.

Suffering a career burnout does not necessarily
mean you must change careers. A reappraisal of
one's goals and expectations can remedy the feelings
of being burned out. Some ways of gaining perspective include: forced vacations, short-term sabbaticals, and seeking out individuals who can offer
support. Taking a mental health day off from work
when needed is very helpful, as well as involving
oneself in a variety of work skills, instead of
intense concentration in one area, and exercising
regularly. If this all fails then a career change
is probably the solution, but only after the goals
and expectations are thought out carefully. Analyzing motives, desires, and financial situations are
of great importance, as well as possible alternate
routes.

The major preparation in considering a career
change due to burnout is to gather as much information as possible about a number of other interesting
companies. But keep in mind "the grass always seems
better on the other side of the fence, but it's just
as hard to mow."

Blake, R. R., & Mouton, J. S. Grid approaches to
    managing stress. Springfield, IL: Charles C.
    Thomas, 1980.

A framework for understanding how diverse attitudes and behaviors interrelate and how they predis-
pose one person to one illness and another to a
different illness is provided by this book.

Using the grid system that has been successfully
applied in many areas of managerial and social
sciences, the authors present a comprehensive and
coherent system for analyzing the role stress plays
in illness and for applying this knowledge to
prevention and treatment. They verify that specific
forms of stress cause specific physiological responses. They show why and how this specificity
hypothesis is more accurate than the idea that
stress undifferentially lowers resistance to bring
about an unpredictable breakdown at the organism's
weakest point.

A review of the interrelationship of mental states
and physical systems, current conception on the
mental programming of death, somatic responses to
experiential trauma, the placebo effect,
biofeedback, exercise, and diet are discussed.

The grid is then introduced using two axes; it
graphically depicts an individual's concern for
things or outcomes on the one hand and his concern
for people on the other. Each axis is divided into
nine segments so that coordinates can be used to
define the person's grid orientation: his attitude
toward the world around him.

The grid offers direct access to the field of
stress and stress management in a single, coherent
presentation. This includes (1) a framework for
thinking about and analyzing differences in human
adjustments, (2) concrete case examples that illustrate the use of the grid in specific episodes of
behavior, (3) an analysis of how grid maladjustments
become evident in stress-related illness and diseases, (4) a diagnostic strategy useful in making
grid evaluations, and (5) a critique of new and
significant approaches to treatment and prevention
via changes in the behavioral aspects associated
with illness.

Individual chapters detail the five basic grid
orientations or styles and reveal the various

combinations of concern for things and people. Each
orientation is analyzed with respect to motivation,
conflict, extremes of passivity and negativity
within that orientation, focal stress, and implications for the individual's mental and physical
health.
  The information and theories presented to this
point are then applied to concepts and practices of
prevention and treatment. The former is discussed
with respect to the role of will and intentionality
in bringing about change, short-term prevention
through risks associated with specific grid styles,
prevention through a positive attitude toward good
everyday health practices, and long-term prevention
through appropriate childrearing practices. Treatment receives equally thorough analysis in discussions of techniques such as relaxation,
biofeedback, assertiveness training, desensitization, and flooding. The final chapter
encapsulates the thesis of the book by placing
health and illness in a social perspective.

Bloch, A. M. Combat neurosis in inner-city schools.
  American Journal of Psychiatry, 1978, 145(10),
  1189-1192.
  The causal relationship between continued environmental stress and strain and symptoms of psychological and psycho-physiological manifestations of
traumatic war neurosis or combat neurosis has been
clearly established. "Classroom teachers in inner-city schools are seeking treatment for symptoms
of continual psychological stress and physical
assaults that result in temporary and sometimes
total decompensation." For political reasons the
quantitative and qualitative extent of these stresses is unknown.
  Fear is a common defense mechanism causing changes
in respiration, blood pressure, and catecholamine
secretions. Sustained arousal can culminate in
disease such as hypertension or peptic ulcer.
Teacher symptoms are similar to those of combat
neurosis; emotional tension, cognitive impairment,
and conversion symptoms.

Two hundred fifty-three teachers from Los Angeles inner-city schools who were victims of psychological stress and physical stress and physical trauma were studied. Combat-neurosis studies were used as guidelines in assessing the evaluation results. Because the teachers' contracts provided medical coverage, a well-documented medical record was available to trace symptoms developed during the teaching career. Important life stress events and medical symptoms could usually be correlated.

Almost all the clients had some psychophysiological manifestations of long-term stress including fatigue, blurred vision, dizziness, and irritability. Of the 28% who had sustained actual physical assault, those who had been attacked without provocation or did not know the assailant experienced the greatest difficulties. Almost 80% of the teachers who succumbed to sustained stress were categorized as passive, rigid, and moderately obsessional. They were unable to strike back when assaulted. Threats of attack were often more psychologically disabling than the event itself.

Because 68% of the teachers were discouraged by other faculty from talking about the incident, they were denied an opportunity to gain support and for reality testing. Most requests for transfers were denied. Principles often were indifferent or fault-finding with the subtle message given that one should not report the incident.

In applying guidelines used in studying war survivors, it was found that the teachers were suffering similar symptoms. Severity of the event, chronicity of the stimulus, unexpectedness of the event, lack of counter-balance to unpleasant stimuli, and impaired morale were found to be important factors of stress.

To minimize the impact of violence, psychological training of the teachers must be implemented. Rehearsing and familiarizing teachers with potential violence can be useful. Improving morale can be affected by providing teachers an opportunity to share experiences with others. The teachers must feel the unconditional support of the administration. Teacher rotation to less stressful schools is recommended every two to three years.

Boronson, W. The workaholic in you. Money Magazine, June 1976, p. 32-35.
Many Americans work constantly, some because they really enjoy it and others because it is a compulsion beyond their control. The work addicts or workaholics may end up in deadend careers, with poor health, or with an early death. Knowing the warning signals of becoming a workaholic may be helpful in warding off these results.
Constant workers may be work lovers (work hard and long by choice and can stop without withdrawal symptoms) or workaholics (work constantly perhaps to prop their self-esteem or status, having a difficult time in nonwork situations). Although workaholics inevitably keep getting promoted because of their diligence, a lack of imagination keeps them from getting to the top rungs. Continual work violates one of the bases for developing original solutions, i.e., moving away from the problem to develop perspective.
Often people work long and hard because they fear losing their job, cannot do their job as well as they think they should, or because they want to escape emotional problems. Change in work pace should be done gradually; suddenly switching from hard work to idleness may bring the onset of a variety of physical and psychological illnesses. Many companies are now requiring employees to take vacations each year rather than accruing time over several years. The author emphasizes developing outside interests to develop a change of pace.

Boy, A. V., & Pine, G. J. Avoiding counselor burnout through role renewal. Personnel & Guidance Journal, 1980, 60(11), 161-163.
Counselors are bombarded by conflicting role demands that lead to burnout. Counselors become personally and professionally discouraged because the professional role envisioned during counselor

training conflicts with real work demands on their time and energy.

There are nine suggestions to help counselors clarify their goals and roles:

1. Spend the major portion of the working day counseling clients.
2. Know clients authentic needs. Do not get caught up in activities of a funding agency or that are currently popular.
3. Carefully select the organization for which you want to work.
4. Associate with committed, concerned colleagues.
5. Develop a sense of organizational involvement. Use theinfluence to help the client.
6. Be reasonably committed to a theory of counseling.
7. Engage in self-assessment.
8. Periodically examine the counseling role. Resist time-consuming, noncounseling activities.
9. Retain an attitude of hope.

Bricklin, M. Take it easy, doc. Prevention, June 1981, 33(5), 24-30.

This deals with physician burnout from the extensively quoted statistics on work time allowed in other types of jobs. For instance, a pilot may only be airborne for 30 hours a week. A truck driver may only work a ten-hour stretch on the road. Laws regulate the working time limits in most industries in which the health of others is directly in jeopardy from operator exhaustion. However, doctors, especially interns and residents, are expected to work a normal 14-hour day, plus be on call every other night. Even established doctors who are finished with medical school and residencies generally work a 54-hour week. Research from the U.S. Department of Labor shows clear statistics that work injuries increase rapidly above a 40-hour work schedule. A survey of doctors shows that one out of four doctors work 70-80+ hours a week.

Studies conducted at the University of Southern California show that as the amount of time spent on the job increases the attitude of the doctors becomes more mechanical. Furthermore, one out of four medical students seeks psychiatric counseling; 36% of doctors use tranquilizers or other chemicals to excess, and 17% have been hospitalized for psychiatric reasons.

The author suggests that doctors become more flexible, imaginative, and sympathetic. Doctors in other countries are willing to strike if their work load is too extreme. The statistics in the United States suggest that there will soon be many more licensed physicians than is needed and the practice hours could be reduced.

Brief, A. P., & Aldag, R. J. Correlates of role indices. Journal of Applied Psychology, 1976, 61, 468-472.

Role conflict and role ambiguity have been found to be negatively related to indices of satisfaction and performance and positively related to anxiety, tension, propensity to leave the organization, and termination of employment.

Research has shown that individuals high in HONS (higher order need strength) exhibit a stronger relationship between job characteristics and job satisfaction than do those lower in HONS. Individuals high in HONS would respond more negatively to role conflict and role ambiguity than would those in lower HONS.

As a result, job characteristics such as skill variety, task identity, task significance, autonomy, and feedback from the job itself have consistently been found to be related to various affective states of the worker. In addition, individual differences such as introversion, flexibility, need for cognition clarity, achievement, and independence have been found to moderate various role perception-personal outcome relationships.

Briley, M. Burnout: Stress and the human energy crisis. Dynamic Years, July/August 1980, p.

36-39.

People who burnout are victims of stress overload. They become negative, easily frustrated, and find it increasingly difficult to deal with others and themselves. They feel emotionally and physically exhausted. They may suffer from insomnia, lingering colds, gastric distress, and headaches.

Persons between 40 and 55 years old are most prone to burnout. Individuals in our society who are among the most dedicated are those most prone to burnout.

Not only human service workers but also artists, writers, and business persons burn out. Unnecessary pressure, long hours, monotony, poorly defined responsibility and goals, conflicts among employees, and favoritism all foster distress.

Distress accounts for more lost time and lost productivity than all other causes put together. Estimates of American business losses are as high as $500 billion a year in productivity from tardiness, absenteeism, high turnover, low output, and escape habits such as drinking.

Burnout can be prevented or cured by following these eight steps:
1. Watch for symptoms.
2. Share your reactions, feelings, and concerns with your coworkers and get a sense of support from them.
3. Take time out at work each day for less stressful tasks.
4. Assign priorities to each task and do the most important first.
5. Allow for vigorous exercise each day and for a relaxed lunch away from the office.
6. Allow a "decompression period" each day between the time you leave work and arrive home.
7. Replenish yourself. Find new interests.
8. Rest and relax. Structured relaxation techniques such as meditation are a great help.

Brocher, T. Understanding variables in occupational

stress. Occupational Health and Safety, March
1979, 48(2), 26-29, 30-31.

Research indicates that under the pressures of
stress, physiological reactions with secondary
psychological consequences, as well as psychological, psychosocial, and sociocultural stressors,
which can cause psychosomatic as well as physiological changes and stress adaptation syndromes, can
occur in various occupational positions. In this
study, connections between organizational structure
and the rate of stress symptoms are examined. The
study demonstrates that the consequences of bureaucratic processes in organizations are directly
responsible for stress reactions among various
professional groups.

The data presented was based on 20 years of experience with workers who attended the former Menninger
Seminar for Industrial Mental Health. More than
20,000 workers over a period of 20 years from
various occupations were represented in the data
collected. All of these various individuals participated in intense five-day seminars, three-day
workshops, and/or individual and organizational
consultations. Investigations in stress conditions
were based on three areas to obtain sufficiently
reliable data: (1) a general health survey; (2) a
personal history survey that would include early
childhood and psychosocial development data; (3) an
organizational survey relating methods of performance evaluation, patterns of supervision, degrees
of job satisfaction, perception of work conditions,
and potential for career development. The primary
task was to identify which stress factors are
directly work related, which are the result of
organizational pressures and/or specific subgroup
dynamics, and which are carried over from person-
al-conflict situations in the family or during
crucial development periods of the life cycle.

The data collected indicated and confirmed that
promotion, reward, status, and demotion usually
occurred between the ages of 35 and 45. Insecurity,
inadequacy, and the fear of failure increased during
these years when many individuals are confronted

with disturbing psychosocial problems that contribute to psychological stress symptoms. Specific tasks, occupational positions, and the organizational environment produce different degrees of stress. In organizations, the main stress factors that may produce a definite variable of physiological disorders are based on dependency needs versus dependency fears. Both factors are related to self-esteem and the need for acceptance. The need for adequate training and consultation was indicated as being beneficial in stress reduction for all supervisory staff.

Brown, T. Coping with stress--some practical approaches. School Guidance Worker, May 1977, 32(5), 39-42.
Unmanageable stress is becoming an increasingly serious problem in modern living, and relaxation techniques are published in the popular press with increasing frequency. These two factors dictate that counselors and psychologist will be in greater demand to help others cope successfully with the debilitating effects of stress.
There are a number of relaxation techniques that are of practical value in dealing with stress:
1.   Progressive relaxation involves a systematic tensing and relaxing of the various muscle groups, leading to overall physical relaxation.
2.   Autogenic technique involves formulae or exercises that emphasize feeling of heaviness and warmth in the limbs require passive concentration on heartbeat and breathing, cultivation of warmth in the solar plexus area and coolness of the forehead.
3.   Anxiety Management Training is a packaged program that was found useful for clients suffering tension from single specific causes, multiple tensions, or those suffering from "free floating" anxiety.
4.   Savasana is a yoga relaxation technique that involves visualization of an

imaginary trip inside the body with
appropriate suggestions for relaxation.
5. Benson's relaxation response is a very
simple technique based on four components:
a quiet environment, a mental device or
stimulus, a passive attitude, and a
comfortable position.
Stress, a complex phenomenon having multiple
causes, responds to a variety of treatment
modalities and strategies. Two other approaches
include biofeedback and hypnosis. The former
requires expensive equipment and latter expensive
training.

Bryan, W. L. Preventing burnout in the public
interest community. The Grantsmanship Center
News, March/April, 1981, 9(2), 14-27; 66-75.
High risks, uncertain rewards, overwhelming workloads, and little evidence of results in the public
interest or social change work force are resulting
in increasing rates of burnout victims. Individuals
in these work forces must incorporate a more
holistic perspective of themselves and their colleagues or burnout will continue to increase and
severely limit long-term effectiveness of their
organizations.
Burnout describes a situation in which one recog-
nizes the imbalance in life that is caused by the
intensity of commitment to the job and the resultant
feeling that one must escape from that work situation. Some of the reasons public-interest workers
are susceptible to burnout are:
1. Intense external pressures on public
interest organizations.
2. Lack of clear direction in the work
environment.
3. Lack of organizational and personal
processes for saying "no."
4. Uncertainty of rewards.
5. Lack of security.
6. Illusiveness of success.
7. Intensity of the work place.
8. Ralph Nadar syndrome.

9.   Lack of appropriate work habits.
Some people are more susceptible to burnout than
others--often manifested by public interest workers'
efforts to work on all kinds of issues and ignore
their health.
Suggestions for preventing burnout emphasize that a
sense of balance is essential to a person's life.
Suggestions are divided into three categories:
1.   Things a public interest organization can
     do to prevent burnout.
     a.   Organizational planning.
     b.   Evaluation: organizational effective-
          ness and individual staff.
     c.   Reward systems.
     d.   Atmosphere of centeredness: appro-
          priate balance in daily living
2.   Things the individual worker might do to
     prevent burnout.
     a.   Develop personal support groups.
     b.   Planning: how and when personal
          needs are to bemet.
     c.   Stress management techniques.
     d.   Preventive health techniques.
     e.   Having fun.
     f.   Spirtually.
3.   Development of a public interest profes-
     sion.
The commitment that led most individuals into
public interest work is not left at the office, it
lives within the individuals. Public interest
workers must recognize themselves as whole people
and maintain balance in their lives to prevent
burnout. They need to "recognize that work is not
everything: life is."

Campbell, S. J., & Frail, L. J. Inpatient
    psychiatric social workers: Their job
    satisfaction and dissatisfactions. Smith College
    Studies in Social Work, 1975, 46(1), 42-43.
    Research was conducted to explore the sources of
job satisfaction and dissatisfaction of inpatient
psychiatric social workers in 9 teaching hospitals
in the Boston area. The data was collected through

questionnaires and interviews of 26 young social workers, who averaged 2 years postgraduate employment and 1 year employment at their present job.

The results indicated the social workers were satisfied with the amount of responsibility they had for clinical tasks and/or shared responsibility for a wide range of clinical functions. Family work was the central feature of their work. Dissatisfaction resulted from the amount and quality of social work supervision, intense conflicting staff relationships, blocked mobility of hierarchy, and lack of group unity. The conclusion is that these findings suggest possible reasons for the high turnover rate among workers on inpatient wards.

Campbell, W. Looking at the when and why of staff turnover. Health and Social Services Journal, 1977, 87(9), 1272-1273.

This study reports the reasons for staff turnover during a four-year period in a psychiatric unit operating along therapeutic community lines.

The criteria monitored were the number of staff who leave every year, their grade, the length of stay and reasons for leaving, and the time of year in which people chose to leave.

A terminal interview or questionnaire was not used; but an informal chat was held with respondents prior to their departure. The author was not willing to claim a great deal of validity for this reason.

Reasons for leaving are proposed for consideration under the following headings:
1. Promotion.
2. Retirement.
3. Further training.
4. Ill health (physical and mental).
5. Unsuitable--dismissed or resigned because of unsatisfactory performance.
6. Dissatisfaction--"unhappy" in their jobs for various reasons.
7. Others--this covers marriage, pregnancy, emigration, temporary workers.

Caplan, R. D., Cobb, S., & French, J. R. P., Jr.

Relationships of cessation of smoking with job
stress, personality, and social support. Journal
of Applied Psychology, 1975, 60(2), 211-219.
This study was conducted to examine degree of job
stress, personality types, and level of social
support. The method used was a questionnaire to
which 200 male administrators, engineers, and
scientists responded.
The major findings of this study indicate that the
ability to quit smoking was related to amount of
perceived job stress. Persons who had been unable
to quit smoking, compared to those who had quit,
appeared to have more job stress in terms of quantitative workload, deadlines, and responsibility.
The significance of personality type as it relates
to cessation of smoking as indicated in the study is
revealed that persons with Type A personality: that
is competitive, hard driving, and involved in work,
were least likely to quit smoking than persons with
Type B personality, which is the opposite of Type A
personality.
Social support moderates the effect of stress on
ability to quit smoking in that decreases in the
work load and responsibility were associated with
increases in the quit rate only for persons with low
social support. The study stressed that when social
support is high, the level of job stress may be less
of a motivating factor in the cessation of smoking
than other motivations.
It is suggested in this article that what is needed
to further clarify smoking behaviors is longitudinal
studies to see whether reductions in work load,
responsibility for persons, and other stresses may
aid quitting.

Caplan, R. D., & Jones, K. D. Effects of workload,
role ambiguity, and Type A personality on anxiety,
depression, and heart rate. Journal of Applied
Psychology, 1975, 60, 713-719.
The Type A personality is described as hard
driving, persistent, and involved with work. This
type of personality was studied as a conditioner of
the effects of quantitative work load and role

ambiguity on anxiety, depression, resentment, and heart rate among 73 male users of a university computer system.
Stress, personality, and psychological strain were assessed by questionnaire and heart rate was measured.
In studying stress, the differentiation was made between the objective and subjective forms. Objective stress was measured independently of a person's environmental perceptions, whereas subjective stress relies on self-report.
Stress has the greatest effect on strain in the hard driving, involved Type A person. The higher the status of people's occupations, the more involved they were in their work. These highly involved people obtained greater emotional rewards from their successes, but they also paid a greater psychological price when they faced the prospects of failure in their work role.
Type A personality workers would be of great value to organizations devoted to productivity and achievement. However, the research also suggests that these same individuals may contribute to their organizations at some cost to their own mental and physical health.

Carpenter, H. H. Formal organizational structural factors and perceived job satisfaction of classroom teachers. Administrative Science Quarterly, 1971, 16, 460-465.
Organizational factors such as line and staff arrangements, prescribed communication channels, and span of supervisory control may influence the degree of teacher adaptation in educational systems, the degree of role conflict experienced, as well as the teaching process itself. In this study, the relationship between formal structural types of school organizations and the perceived job satisfaction of classroom teachers was tested.
Six school systems of approximately 5000 students were identified and classified as tall, medium, or flat (independent variable). Teachers' salaries, fringe benefits, and other economic factors were

similar. The hypothesis tested was: In tall,
medium, and flat organizational structures, there
will be no significant differences between teachers'
perceived needs satisfaction as measured by a Maslow
type instrument. Significant differences were found
between discrepancy scores of teacher groups in the
three structural types. It was suggested that basic
job security needs and self-actualization related
needs were not affected by factors of formal organizational structure. However, a decrease in some
teacher socialization process and perceived job
prestige as the steepness of the organizational
ratio increased was indicated. In addition, it was
also indicated that as the structural type became
taller, the teachers' feeling of prestige in the
community, perceived opportunity to participate in
setting school goals, and perceived professional
authority associated with the teaching position
appeared to decrease. No consistent trends were
indicated, but differences were found between the
majority of needs. The results support conjecture
that flat organizational structures tended to have
employees with higher levels of job satisfaction
than did taller organizational structures.

Casas, J. M., Furlong, M. J., & Castrillo, S.
    Stress and coping among university counselors: A
    minority perspective. Journal of Counseling
    Psychology, 1980, 27(4), 364-373.
    Within the last 10 years, researchers have direct-
ed increasing attention toward ethnic minority
clients in the area of mental health. However,
there has been a virtual absence of research with
regard to the ethnic minority provider of services.
Little has been written regarding the stress that
these professionals experience in their work environment.
    Maslach contends that helping professionals in
general must work harder and more intimately with
people because of institutional care and treatment
for personal problems. As a result, more internal
pressures result, leading to an emotional overload.

This obviously works against the professional,
having negative consequences.

Situational stressors can contribute to burnout.
Burnout may be characterized as "(a) physical and
emotional exhaustion; (b) loss of self-confidence
and a balanced perspective . . . (c) inability to
maintain the caring and the commitment that was
initially brought to the job; and (d) loss of
concern for the people with whom one is working even
to the point of blaming them for their own vic-
timization." All of the characteristics, however,
are relative to the general symptomotology of
burnout. Research regarding stress and burnout
experienced by enthic minority counselors specifically is warranted.

A study was completed on ethnic minority counselors
employed in colleges and universities that were
primarily Anglo. For purposes of this study, ethnic
minority included "Asian, Black, Hispanic, or Native
American groups." These professionals were asked to
repsond to a questionnaire regarding stress, counselor roles, self-help agencies for dealing with
stress, people who could assist them in times of
stress, and preferred characteristics of the individual providing help for stress. Results indicated
that most of these counselors felt that they have an
adequate self-help network. Some, however, felt
that their self-help network was not sufficient to
assist them in dealing with stress on the job.
Those connected with inadequate self-help agencies
indicated that they experienced more stress on the
job than those with adequate self-help networks. In
short, counselors with inadequate support agencies
reported primary sources of stress as conflicts with
employers and supervisors, absence of support for
their role as a "minority counselor," no opportunity
for job advancement, and a lack of contact with
minority professional peers. On the other hand,
counselors with adequate support networks identified
their sources of stress as lack of sensitivity of
nonminority supervisors, personal expectations
placed on them by the university and minority
community, etc. There was a large amount of

consistency between both groups in the area of
perferred sources of help. There was some difference, however, with regard to preferred characteristics of the individual who is to provide services.

Chance, P. That drained-out, used-up feeling.
  Psychology Today, January 1981, 88-92.
  Burnout is to deplete oneself, to exhaust one's
physical and mental resources. To in effect wear
oneself out by excessively striving to reach some
unrealistic expectation imposed by oneself or values
of society. Burnout is especially likely for those
in the helping profession: social workers, psychiatrists, psychologists, teachers, nurses, doctors,
and welfare workers. The burnout victim is disillu-
sioned, irritable, exhausted, and depressed. The
clients of burnout victims also suffer. They
receive shoddy care from people who have become
cynical and hostile and who are often contemptuous
of people they were once eager to help. The cost of
burnout in bureaucratic inefficiency and wasted
dollars is staggering. The burnout victim becomes
the clockwatcher, the chronic absentee, the work
dodger. Various authors agree that the immediate
cause is a mismatch between effort and results.
Because good intentions are met with low pay,
impossible workloads, miles of red tape, inadequate
training, low prestige, and ungrateful clients, the
ideal of helping people becomes very difficult.
Experts claim that it is up to the individual worker
to do what he or she can. The individual should
become aware of the problem, separate work from the
rest of life, develop outside interests, get additional training, and abandon unrealistic expectations. It is also good to redefine the job
whenever possible, or to change jobs when necessary,
in order to reduce the work load or improve work
conditions. Too little stress and we rust out; too
much stress and we burn out. Stress is the problem
and stress management is the solution; hence,
relaxation exercise, attitude and awareness, and
diet are important in coping with stress. The
psychotherapeutic stance states that the "real cure"

is closeness. Others make the distinction between
burnout and tedium. The symptoms of the two conditions are identical but only burnout comes from
working with people. Burnout is also thought to
occur in stages that are identified as: enthusiasm,
stagnation, frustration, and apathy. The advocates
of the "stage" view of burnout recommend Glasser's
Reality Therapy as an effective intervention. More
important than identifying the phenomenon is taking
crucial steps to apply solutions. Some find that
society is somehow at fault, and they point to
mobility, change, urbanization, affluence, bureau-
cracy, or mechanization as the culprits. As the
price of burnout becomes more apparent, there will
be pressure to do something about it. To do that,
we will inevitably have to do something about the
social problems against which burnout victims do
battle.

Cherniss, C. Professional burnout in human service
   organizations. New York: Praeger, 1980.
   Findings from an intensive, longitudinal study of
28 new public professionals describes how individuals' adaptation to stress gives rise to a unique
phenomena called burnout. Burnout refers to a
process in which the professionals' attitudes and
behavior change in negative ways in response to job
strain. In addition to these negative changes in
thought and behavior related to the job, there are
physical and behavioral signs. These include
chronic fatigue; frequent colds, the flu, headaches,
gastro-intestinal disturbances, sleeplessness,
excessive use of drugs, decline in self-esteem, and
marital and family conflict. Burnout adversely
affects the professional's performance in a variety
of ways. These include the loss of enthusiasm,
idealism; higher rates of absenteeism and turnover;
and in some cases, burnout may lead to physical
abuse of clients.
   The longitudinal study was approached from a social
ecological perspective, i.e., the interaction
between the individual and the social environment.
The research indicates that the major sources of

stress are: the problem of competence, i.e., most new public professionals did not feel completely prepared for their roles; the clients were not always motivated, cooperative, or grateful; bureaucratic interference, i.e. politics and paperwork; boredom, from routine work; lack of variety and challenge; and unsatisfactory relations with peers. The research suggests changes in attitudes toward work that occur in the process of adjusting to the syndrome.

Cherniss, C., & Egnatios, E. Is there job satisfaction in community mental health? Community Mental Health Journal, 1978, 14(4), 309-318.

After a discussion on the importance of job satisfaction, this study presents data concerning current levels and sources of job satisfaction in community mental health centers.

In their pilot study four major reported sources of frustration and work alienation for the staff were: (1) a feeling of inadequacy in performing many activities, especially those for which the staff had received poor training and supervision; (2) lack of direct and immediate feedback concerning results in many work activities; (3) excessive paperwork; (4) role conflicts, poorly defined objectives, sudden changes in personnel and rules, and the constant need to deal with "politics."

The results of the study reported that the average community mental health staff member scored relatively low in satisfaction with work but close to the median in satisfaction with supervision and coworkers. Correlations between the aspects of work and job satisfaction were drawn in the areas of organizational quality ("poor communication" and "inefficiency"), clarity of program goals, ambiguity of role expectations, and adequacy of communication in the agency.

The results also suggest that if the trends emerging from the sample exist in programs in other parts of the country, administrators may find increasing difficulty in recruiting and retraining staff, pressure for staff unionization, internal conflict and dissension and ultimately a deteriorization in the quality of services.

Unfortunately, many of the forces that contribute to burnout are beyond the control of individual professionals in their work organizations. There are cultural and historical factors that must be addressed by society if professional burnout is to be overcome.

Cherniss, C., Egnatios, E. S., & Wacker, S. Job stress and career development in new public professionals. Professional Psychology, November 1976, 7(4), 428-436.

The first year or so of a professional career in a public institution is often seen as a time of challenge and stress. The shared hardship of new professionals often creates a bond among the newer members. "Public professionals" are individuals who provide services requiring a high degree of knowledge and/or formal training and who work in public institutions.

By looking at the experiences of the new professional, the researchers hope to be able to see more clearly how the public situation affects the thinking of all professionals. The inquiry concerning stress on the public professional focused on three questions: (1) what are the sources of job stress for new professionals, (2) what are the effects of job stress on performance and career development in public professionals, and (3) how does the nature of the work setting influence the new professionals attempt to cope with high levels of potential job stress?

As soon as new public professionals begin thinking about the first day of work, job-related stress may begin. Two major aspects of role performance appear to be missing in most professional training programs. Public professionals do not study their own role even though the major area of "role performance" clearly involves working with individuals or groups in a helping relationship. Public professionals are constantly required to manipulate the system in order to function effectively; for the new professional this can have lasting affects. Thus, the helping process and the organizational dynamics of public institutions are two crucial areas of performance for which few professionals are prepared. They become acutely aware of this lack when they begin their careers, and until socialization in these areas catches up with them, stress and anxiety can be severe.

Professionals in training are exposed to the new concepts. However, when they leave school and begin their careers in public institutions, institutional constraints do not allow them to perform their roles in the new ways they are taught. Due to the bureaucratic structure there is incompatibility between tasks that requires quick personal responsiveness and hierarchy structure. Stress related to performance in the job role may increase the likelihood that professionals will blame the recipients of their service for problems that occur and will not examine the potential contribution of their own theories, techniques, and behavior.

Role-related stress in helping professionals also has been identified as a source of dehumanizing behavior toward welfare recipients, mental patients, clients, and other groups or consumers. This occurs in part because professionals who are responsible for providing services are overwhelmed by the problems they are asked to deal with. Job stress is not necessarily bad. Its impact on the new professional's role behavior and career development depends on how it is coped with.

Many of the aspects of the social climate that had been stressful eventually became viewed as advantageous. The lack of clear-cut expectations and structure provided much greater autonomy and freedom for a relatively more experienced, secure, self-confident individual. Thus, the social climate and work setting will not affect everyone the same way.

Christensen, J. Burning and burnout. English Journal, April, 1981, 70(4), 13-16.

This article on burnout cleverly uses the metaphor of fire to make certain points about burnout and the implications for dealing with burnout. Typical signs of burnout are addressed such as sleep problems, depression, apathy, anger, and fatigue. However, the focus is on how to deal with the "fire" that teaching engenders without getting irreparably "burned." Using the resource of Celtic invocations this author suggests some specific remedies. The first Celtic invocation reminds that fire needs constant renewal and therefore people need physical and mental renewal also. The second innovation deals with the need of people for each other in that the Celts obtained fire from one another in a special ceremony. The implication for burnout recovery is that we need to "feed one another's fires" both emotionally and practically whenever possible. The third invocation dealt with spreading out the fire at night to keep it just burning but not flaming. This refers to the effort to keep our mental states alive in the midst of pressures from parents and administrations. This is further reinforced by reminding teachers that the sparks of learning that are generated by the teacher in a classroom are not necessarily a daily occurence, but that they do spring from the teacher's deep joy of learning.

Some specific remedies geared to teaching include in-service training, regional conferences on teacher's real needs, national institutes to let teachers learn together, visiting scholars who can come to teachers if the teachers can't get away, and master teachers being released to travel and help other teachers.

Clark, C. C. Burnout: Assessment and intervention. Journal of Nursing Administration, September, 1980, 10(9), 39-43.

Burnout is a major factor of the nursing administrators' unwillingness to justify their own right to health and well-being. Characteristics contributing to burnout include: extra long hours of dedication, taking work home due to workload, a feeling of

personal responsibility if the work does not go
well, along with anxiety and guilt.

Symptoms of burnout experiences are: fatigue,
exhaustion, head and backaches, depression, and
psychosomatic complaints, as well as other problems,
depending on the individual and the situation.
Suggested procedures to use to minimize the effects
of burnout and decrease its potential in the organization include: the opening up of communication
with oneself, adequate nutritional intake, relaxation by meditation, outlets for stress, and establishing peer and counselor support systems. To
protect the organization, administrators need to
learn to identify potential burnouts, along with
establishing new workable atmospheres to eliminate
its possible occurance. By limiting the number of
hours worked, by taking periodic breaks and establishing work hours, by shifting tasks among personnel to allievate boredom and frustration, and by
sharing duties and responsibilities, burnout can be
controlled.

The pressures experienced by the nursing administrators and their staff can never totally be
removed, only minimized. The proposed preventive
strategies can enhance the potential threat to
personal and professional effectiveness.

Cleland, C. C., & Peck, R. F. Psychological
   determinants of tenure in institutional personnel.
   American Journal of Mental Deficiency, 1959, 63,
   876-888.

What are the characteristics of the attendant who
remains for a long period of time on a ward for
mental defectives? Through a screening battery,
previous studies have tried to determine who would
make good employees The major difficulty with this
approach is deciding who is "good" and who is "bad."
Attendants in mental hospitals and those working in
state schools have been lumped together, casting
serious doubts on the credibility of the results.

The present study used tenure as an indicator of a
"good" employee for two reasons: (1) that the best
attendant was of little service if he left the

institution after a short period; and (2) that some correlation between satisfactory service and tenure was inevitable.

The state school is seemingly a "cultural island." The hierarchy of command is definite, the "behind the walls" isolation from the community is easy to perceive, the self-sufficiency of the physical plant, and the absence of rapid change in the patient population all contribute to this.

Despite an estimate of their importance, attendants are low persons on the ladder, as revealed by the formal organizational chart. The analysis of the attendant's role revealed that the type of personality pattern that received satisfaction for service to patients was what Erich Fromm defined as "authoritarian."

Coburn, D. Job-worker incongruence: Consequences for health. Journal of Health and Social Behavior, June 1975, 16(2), 198-212.

This article examines the consequences for a person's health at work that is perceived as excessively complex or excessively simple. It analyzes the incongruence between the demands of the job and the capacity of the person to cope with them in relationship to general psychological well-being and role incapacity and health status.

The items that were measured are job incongruence: work overload and underload, attitudes towards the job, health status, and role incapacity.

The findings show that work overload is associated with low dislike and high stress; work underload with high dislike and low stress. The data demonstrates that job incongruence is highly related to attitudes towards the job. Support is given to the thesis that work that is below one's perceived capacity is heartily disliked and work that is above one's capabilities is perceived as stressful.

The data support the hypothesis that job congruence is associated with lower well-being. The underloads show a greater percentage "not too happy" than the overloads, while the overloads have a greater

percentage high on psychophysiological
symptomatology.

The relationship between perceived incongruence and
self-assessed health showed that the extreme overloads and underloads do perceive themselves as in
relatively poorer health than the rest of the
population, but the difference between groups is
very small. In general, only the extreme underload
and overload showed much variation from the general
population on either self-assessed health or role
incapacity.

This study has shown that both work overload and
underload have consequences for the worker. Job
demands in excess of capacities do appear to be
related to lower psychological well-being, and in
the case of extreme incongruence, to poorer health.
Low job demands and high capacities tend to be
related to lower overall morale and a moderate
incidence of psychological symptoms.

Some limitations are the degree to which health
status is a direct product of physiological reaction
attributed to the job or to which it is mediated by
workers' psychological reactions to the work situation. The evidence presented suggests psychological
and physiological responses are alternative reactions rather than both being part of a single
response sequence.

Cohen, J. B.   Health care, coping, and the
    counselor. Personnel and Guidance Journal, 1978,
    616-621.

Physical health is intimately linked to mental
health. The medical point of view of restoring and
maintaining health has been linked to the body.
More recently, proponents of holistic medicine have
been arguing that the treatment of disease merely
begins with the recognition of symptoms and must
move from there to the complexities of the individual in his of her various roles. Social
epidemiology, the study of social factors as they
affect distributions of diseases, is prominent among
these new areas of disease research. Theories of

stress and coping play a large role in social epidemiology.

Early theories of stress were concerned with physiological responses; stress was originally defined as environmental conditions requiring adaptive responses. These are called "stressors." However, this view is inadequate because it provides no explanation of differing reactions to the same stressor both between different persons and within the same person, and because it assumes people are mere victims of external events. Thus, a more accurate view would recognize the interaction of physical, sociocultural, and psychological factors.

In a study of pregnant women, the rate of complications in women with high stress was nearly normal (46%), but was almost 91% in women who reported few psychosocial resources to combat stress.

Coping techniques are either instrumental or palliative. Instrumental techniques try to solve problems. Palliative techniques try to minimize the effects of the problem without solving the problem. Palliative techniques include the use of drugs and alcohol, denial, and avoidance. Prolonged exposure to stress can cause breakdown because it requires a great expenditure of energy, thus reducing the person's ability to respond to other internal demands.

Social support tends to alleviate the effects of stress. Social support is defined as approval, esteem, and succor from others. One study found that women exposed to severe events but who lacked social support were 10 times more likely to be depressed than women who had social support.

Counselors can help provide needed social support by providing the client with helpful information, by acting as a confident, or an informed listener, and by defining a client's weaknesses and problem areas.

Cole, S., & Lejeune, R. Illness and the legitimation of failure. American Sociological Review, June 1972, 37, 347-356.

The initial crux of this article appears to be the relevance of what impression people have of themselves. Both medical doctors and social scientists agree as to the importance physiological and social-psychological factors have on the determination of objective and subjective states of health.

This study deals with the hypothesis that a person's inability to perform a specific role pattern leads to that person defining his or her health as poor. Also discussed is the relationship between definition of health and performance roles of wives and mothers among working class black women.

In the study participants were asked to define their own state of health in terms of fair, good, or poor. Once separating the two major focuses of illness, physiological and psychological reasoning, determining the cause and corresponding effect on the person's mental health will become more apparent.

Causal order, difficult to discuss without longitudinal data, was dealt with in a most simplified manner. The report merely showed that the relationship between self-defined failure and health persists even when the issues such as symptoms, number of doctor-patient contacts, and number of reported illnesses are controlled.

Welfare recipients attach their own stigma to their lower status when comparing their own social structure with the dominant force of the upper class society. While the survey indicated that over half of the respondents receiving welfare felt ashamed, a larger sampling felt that they should act and be grateful, which in turn led to the feeling of inferiority and a lowering of status. While persons on the welfare role who consider themselves to be in this position for only a short time do not need to rationalize their own predicament, persons who have given up hope of ever bettering themselves will develop a strong sense of justification.

Health is perceived as physiologically determined, and hence, beyond the control and range of the person. A person not fulfilling his expected social role due to poor health is generally not stigmatized because of this failure. Poor health in this report seems to be the legitimizing factor in justifying a person's poor performance in his or her society. How persons define their own health influences their lives. If you think that you are unhealthy, you will act ill. If you do not strive for more and better, you are acting out a form of deviance.

The bottom line is that people who have high rates of self-defined failure will also represent a high degree of poor health.

Colligan, M. J., & Murphy, L. R. Mass psychogenic illness in organizations: An overview. Journal of Occupational Psychology, 1979, 52(2), 77-90.

There is concern that contagious psychogenic illness occurs frequently and that psychogenic factors play a contributing role in the etiology of the illness. The phenomenon of contagious psychogenic illness is defined as "the collective occurance of a set of physical symptoms and related beliefs among two or more individuals in the absence of an identifiable pathogen."

Common symptoms of this malady are nausea, dizziness, headache, and weakness, which usually disappeared after treatment. Other symptoms occuring frequently in adolescent groups were catatonic posture spasms, muscular twitching, and simulated gonorrheal vaginitis. Symptoms usually appeared after an event such as the smell of a strange odor (gas); use of a new solvent; insect bites; rumored or actual epidemics. An important variable identified was the need to assiciate a physical cause, not psychological, to the illness. A large percentage (93%) of individuals experiencing symptoms were female. This finding suggests that women are more prone to manifest symptoms, suggestive of psychological stress or anxiety, due to their social role of being more sensitive/susceptible to their environment and to emotions.

"Contagious psychogenic illness appears to be a social phenomenon affecting a certain proportion of normal population under conditions of psychological/physical stress." Individuals affected by this phenomenon tended to have a higher rate of absenteeism and hospitalizations than those not affected.

It is suggested that this action may be a coping mechanism rather than an indicator of poor health. Factors that may contribute to contagious psychogenic illness are: environment, boredom, production pressure, physical stressors, labor-management relations, and lack of communications. The manner in which individuals cope with these factors may determine their ability to withstand or reduce the impact of psychogenic illness. Factors such as work-place characteristics may increase overall level of stress. Examples of this are: excessive noise, air contamination, poor lighting, and temperature variation. Work related problems came under the general categories of: excessive pressures from supervisors, conflicting orders from supervisors, and too little authority for the amount of assigned responsibility. Workers feeling loneliness and isolation are able to reduce the impact of stress by use of coping and adaptation mechanisms. It is suggested that information that focuses on sources of stress and ways to cope with it may have an immunizing effect.

Convergence and contagion are defined in relation to their effect on behavior. "Contagion refers to the spread of behavior from group member to member, one person serving as the stimulus for the imitative act of another. Convergence refers to situations in which group members have, independently of one another, developed common response patterns which are expressed simultaneously." Poor employee-supervisor relations have caused a reduction in employee self-esteem. Recognition of a physical agent may cause the externalization of its resultant symptoms. Recognition of possible stressors gives validity of symptoms to others experiencing the same discomforts as well as disinhibiting the expression of symptoms in others. It has been shown that as an epidemic progresses, the severity of symptoms is reduced. Factors influencing behavior are: level of stress and strain, sociometric patterns, and informational supports.

Colligan, M. J., Smith, M. J., & Hurrell, J. J.

Occupational incidence rate of mental health
disorders. Journal of Human Stress, 1977, 3(3),
34-39.

The National Institute of Occupational Safety and
Health conducted an investigation to determine the
relative incidence of mental health disorders,
health problems of a psychogenic nature, and mortality from stress-induced or stress related disorders.

Data was collected from the records of 22 mental
health centers operated by the state of Tennessee.
This involved an examination of the admission
records to determine the incidence rate of diagnosed
mental health disorders for 130 major occupations;
those occupations were employing 1,000 or more
workers in the state. These occupations were then
rank-ordered in terms of the degree of stress and
related health problems they encompass. Selection
criteria was based on occupation, age, and residen-
cy.

The study indicated that health technicians showed
the highest incidence of mental disorders. Of the
top 22 occupations, it is interesting to note that
due to particular stressors present in the hospital
environment that are conducive to the development of
mental disorders, 6 are related to hospi-
tal/health-care operations. The responsibility of
caring for and interacting with people who are ill
can be emotionally demanding, subjecting the health
professional to considerable stress. Women and
health-related workers in particular are more likely
to report mental health disorders than the general
population due to a heightened sensitivity to and
acceptance of emotional disturbance. Women were
also more likely than males to receive treatment
from one of the mental health facilities.

This study was intended to provide a basis for
defining job situations posing health problems due
to their stressful demands. Follow-up research is
needed to examine the relationship between job
stress and mental health, designed to control sex
differences in the reporting and/or actual incidence
of mental health disorders.

Collins, G. R. How to handle burnout. Christian
   Herald, Dec. 1979, 102(3), 17-20.
The term burnout is but one of many that has taken
on new meaning in the English language. It is
described as a feeling of physical and emotional
exhaustion that comes after we have had prolonged
involvement with people and work situations that
demand our time, energy, and strength. Burnout is
not characteristic of any profession in particular,
but is prevalent in many careers.

A recent study was completed at the University of
California in Berkeley in which hundreds of people
were interviewed. All of them were experiencing
difficulty coping with emotional stress resulting
from intimate involvement with troubled individuals.
The study was concluded after discovering several
ways of knowing when burnout is developing. Some
include:
1.   We detach ourselves from other people. We
     become less involved, allowing for
     self-protection and pressure reduction.
2.   We begin to run down physically.
3.   We are influenced psychologically.
     Discouragement, low morale, impatience,
     self-contamination, forgetfulness, a
     hypercritical attitude, inefficiency and a
     "what's the use" attitude can all slip
     into our thinking.

Researchers have discovered a burnout prevention
strategy. First we need time alone. Research has
proved that this is essential to prevent burnout.
Secondly, burnout can be prevented when there are
"shared responsibilities." The belief that no one
else can help is a sure road to burnout. Lastly,
support is needed to prevent burnout. Close contact
with people who can give encouragement and a different perspective is helpful.

Cooper, C. L., Mallinger, M., & Kahn, R. Identifying
   sources of occupational stress among dentists.
   Journal of Occupational Psychology, 1978, 5(3),
   227-234.

Dentistry is potentially a stressful occupation with pressures that have led to stress-related illnesses such as coronary heart disease. These may be due to environmental factors or stressors such as work overload, poor working conditions, unsatisfactory work relationships, inherent characteristics of the individual and his behaviors. This study examines the relationship between causes or sources of stress and of the manifestations of physical ill health.

The data consisted of a 15-item questionnaire aimed to measure individual job pressures at work. It was distributed to 150 dentists who attended the California Dental Association in 1977. Potential stress-related characteristics and a number of personality traits were studied.

The results indicated the pressures from work stem from trying to maintain and build a practice, too little work, administrative difficulties, coping with difficult patients, high anxiety, and age. Those dentists who are at high risk tend to be older, anxiety prone, less emotionally stable, and feel that others perceive them as inflictors of pain. However, much more research is needed to establish links between the working conditions of dentists and physical health associated with coronary risk factors.

Cooper, C. L., & Marshal, J. Occupational sources of stress: A review of the literature relating to coronary heart disease and mental ill health. Journal of Occupational Psychology, 1976, 49, 11-28.

In both the United Staes and the United Kingdom illness results in the loss of large sums of money and much productivity due to loss of man hours. The primary illnesses responsible for the loss are: cardiovascular diseases, mental, psychoneurotic and personality disorders, nervousness, and headache. These disorders are suggested to result from negative environmental stressors such as role conflict or poor working conditions, which may aggrevate present, but hidden, physical characteristics.

Features of stress at work that cause certain behaviors or disorders to become evident are: "the dimension or characteristics of the person, the potential sources of stress in the work environment, . . . [and] outside relationships and events . . . which have an impact in the workplace." The environmental stressors of the worksite are directly related to specific aspects of the job. Another source of pressure results from the manner in which an individual copes with stress at work.

Factors intrinsic to a job are a primary source of stress. Evidence suggests that some intrinsic factors, if repetitive and dehumanizing, may adversely affect physical health. Quantitative and qualitative overloads may cause breakdowns in both individuals and organizations. These overloads may prompt an increase in a negative behavior (increased cigarette smoking) or increase the likelihood of illness. Indicators of stress- drinking, absenteeism, low motivation, low self-esteem-increase when quantitative overload is too great.

Major areas of occupational stress that impact on the individual and personality are: role in the organization, career development, relationships at work, and organizational structure and climate. Confusion about work role, duties, and responsibilites cause stress to be experienced by the worker. Role ambiguity impacts negatively on physical and mental well-being. Worker experience, lower job satisfaction and self-confidence, higher job tension, increased blood pressure and pulse rate, lowered motivation, and depression. The higher the worker is on the organizational ladder the greater the relationship between role ambguity and coronary heart disease. The inference drawn from this is that as we move toward clerical, and managerial, and professional occupations we may be increasing the likelihood of occupational stress due to identity problems and other interpersonal dynamics and less to the physical conditions of work.

Stressors that impact on career development involve promotion, status incongruence, lack of job security, and thwarted ambition. The stress manifests itself ranging from psychological symptoms to marked physical disorders, which often culminate in mental illness. Studies indicate that when an individual moves through the corporate structure at a pace he is satisfied with he experiences less psychiatric illness. Stress results when "role conflict generated from incompatible expectations of a social position may yield psychological disturbances and frustrations."

Conclusions drawn from the research suggest that the type of work, the work environment, and individual personality all interact to create stress. This stress can be positive or negative depending on its type and the individual's ability to cope with stress. Negative effects of stress result in illness and disease.

Cooper, C. L., & Payne, R. (Eds.) <u>Current concerns in occupational stress.</u> New York: John Wiley & Sons, Inc., 1980.

The purpose of this book is to highlight some of the more interesting research developments and coping strategies in the field of occupational stress. The book is divided into three sections. Section one focuses on some of the more vulnerable occupations or jobs at risk and the nature and characteristics of these jobs that create stress and strain. The stressors involved in repetitive work, hazardous occupations, entrepreneurial/managerial functions, and the problems associated with being in jobs at which role boundaries are explored. Many of these are of current concern to employers, trade unions, and governments in terms of the limitations they impose on the quality of work life and productivity.

The second section explores contemporary aspects of work life that create occupational stress. The effects of the movement toward dual-career families, the stressful consequences of job transfer, the impact on the individual and the organization of different methods of evaluation, the psychological and medical impact of retirement and the effect of the values of Western society toward achievement and

Type A behavior are examined. The characteristics
of various jobs that act as sources of stress and
create medical, social, and psychological problems
for individuals at work are identified.
  In the third section, various ways in which one
might cope with stress is examined as well as
techniques for reducing managerial stress and other
aspects of organizational stress among employees.
Finally, exploration of ways in which social support
and participation at work alleviate many of the
occupational stressors is presented. In this
section the attempt is not to provide a totally
comprehensive package of "flavor of the month"
stress reduction programs, but rather to provide the
various approaches that have been used by people in
a work context to reduce the press of work life.
  The chapters of this book are as follows:
      Introduction
      Part I - Jobs and Occupations at Risk of Stress
      1.   Hazardous Occupations and the Heart of
           Malcolm Carruthers
      2.   Repetitive Work
      3.   Stress and the Entrepreneur
      4.   Boundary Roles
      Part II - Contemporary Aspects of Work Life
           that Create Stress
      5.   The Effect of Job Transfer on Employees
           and their Families
      6.   The Impact of Retirement
      7.   Type A Behavior in the Work Setting
      8.   Evaluation Practices as Stressors in
           Occupational Settings
      9.   Stress and the Two-Career Couple
      Part III - Coping with Stress
      10. Organizational Stress and Social Support
      11. Coping with the Stress of Managerial
           Occupations
  Extensive reference lists are provided at the
conclusion of each chapter.

Cooper, T. Stress: How to manage it. _Vogue_, Jan.
  1979, _169_, 149-171.

This was an interview with Dr. Theodore Cooper, Dean of Cornell University Medical College. He states that stress is the pressure of everyday life, that it spurs us on to greater achievement and makes life more interesting.

Dealing with stress on a day-to-day basis is mostly common sense: get enough sleep, eat well, relax enough, and have the support of friends and family. Exercise is an excellent antidote to stress. Being able to put a problem out of your mind when you have done all that you can do towards it also helps. There may come a point when you have done all you can do, and the pressure still becomes unbearable. This is the time to seek professional help.

How do you know when you have reached that point? Dr. Cooper says when you have anxiety that is persistent and sometimes incapacitating. Depression, chronic fatigue, irritability, headaches, indigestion, diarrhea, and palpitations are other warning signals. The way a person copes is revealing. Drinking more, or eating more, or eating less, or finding it hard to get to sleep are factors that often occur. In each case there is a departure from the normal pattern. People try to adapt by changing something else.

Stress mnagement today is based on the premise that you can adapt to stress. A person cannot adapt to stress by withdrawing from the community into isolation. This is a copout by trying to pretend that pressures do not exist. When pressures are not dealt with, they manifest themselves in various ways like those mentioned above.

Cooper, T., & Edson, L. Stress, stress, stress. Across the Board, 1979, 16, 10-19.
Stress can be both good or bad. The good causes individuals to forge ahead against obstacles, the bad causes illness. Yet, few medical professionals accept stress as a medical condition. However, more and more doctors are reporting patients with symptoms that seem to have no organic base; some claim that 50% of patient visits are attributable to stress.

Friedman and Rosenman have found that hard, aggressive personalities (Type A) are more prone to heart attacks than individuals who are more passive and procrastinating. Dunbar supports this; in studying coronary victims, she found their lifestyles filled with deadlines and compulsive striving. Dembroski and Glass also found highly competitive, hostile individuals to be more likely to develop heart disease.

Stress also affects the digestive system. The mucus lining of the stomach has been found to be affected by mood changes, thus linking stress to ulcer development. Diabetes has been shown to be more severe under stress conditions.

The body's immune system also seems to be affected by stress. Headaches and colds are common before speaking engagements and it is now thought that changes in the immune system due to stress make the body less resistant to germs. Moreover, allergy patients experience more severe symptoms during stressful conditions.

Although the body reacts physically to stress, tissue changes are not caused directly by emotions. How the body will react is not known beforehand. Freedman suggests two related but separate responses the body makes -- the automatic nervous system and neuroendocrine system response.

Based on case histories of psychosomatic disorders, lists of common stressors that can affect an individual's health are available; the Holmes Social Readjustment Rating Scale lists 45 traumatic life events according to adjustment required with death of a loved one, divorce, going to prison requiring the most adjustment. Changes in job status-either loss or promotion-can also promote stress conditions.

Individuals faced with stressful working environments can alleviate stress in several ways-allowing time after work to unwind, self-help devices (meditation, biofeedback, primal breathing), and exercise can be effective in reducing stress. When such approaches do not work, drugs can be effective to treat anxiety or depression. Four leading groups

of drugs used are discussed. Knowing oneself and
what conditions cause stress are the bases for
determining what approach can be most helpful.

Cummings, T. G., & Cooper, C. L. A cybernetic
   framework for studying stress. Human Relations,
   1979, 32(5), 395-418.
This theory of stress is derived from the framework and concepts of cybernetics, or systems control. Cybernetics is concerned with the use of
information and feedback to control purposeful
behavior. The basic premise of this theory is to
reduce deviations from a specific goal-state.
   Cybernetic theory provides a comprehensive portray-
al of the person-environment interaction. It
emphasizes time, formation, and feedback. The
temporal dimension provides research into the
dynamic aspects of stress. Time is thought to be
one of the most neglected parameters of the problem.
The focus is on information because it mediates the
person-environment relationship. The idea of
feedback recognized that coping behavior is purposeful, directed by the knowledge of previous effects.
   Living systems must maintain themselves in a state
of homeostasis if they are to survive. They have to
keep a variety of variables in motion: import,
transportation, matter, energy, information, and
export. Forces that counteract this must be dealt
with. Here the living organism is directed to keep
this system functioning. When forces disrupt this
homeostasis beyond the range of stability, then the
organism must cope. Stress is any variable that
disrupts the smooth functioning of the system. This
places a strain on the organism it may or may not be
able to reduce.
   The cybernetic theory is the application of
homeostasis properties of living systems within the
comprehensive framework of studying stress. The
concepts of stress, threat, strain, and adjustment
process serve as useful starting points for defining
and making operational the empirical referents of
these distinct aspects of the personal-environment
fit. Specifically these stresses and threats refer

to external factors that disrupt the person's
prefered steady state; the former affect the person
in the present, the latter affect the person in the
future. Strain is the actual disturbance of the
internal steady state. Adjustment reduces this
state.
The cybernetic theory provides a useful framework
for studying the stress cycle. The theory draws
attention to information that is often otherwise
neglected.

Daley, M. R. Burnout: Smoldering problem in
   protective services. Social Work, September 1979,
   24(5), 375-379.
   Individuals who work in organizations that offer
child protective services suffer from an exception-
ally high rate of burnout. It is not uncommon for
workers to become burnedout within two years. This
high turnover rate is very expensive for the
agencies, both in terms of personnel and monetary
resources. Burnout seriously reduces the number of
workers able to help clients and increases the need
to train additional personnel. The phenomenon of
burnout is defined as "a reaction to job-related
stress that varies in nature with the intensity and
duration of the stress itself."
The symptoms of burnout, i.e., low worker morale,
absenteeism, high rate of turnover, are manifested
through warning signals. A common warning signal is
"a worker who exerts increasing amounts of effort
but seems to be accomplishing less."
The characteristics of employees who exhibit the
states leading to burnout are similar. In the
initial state people exhibit an inordinate amount of
energy to do a good job. They often put in large
amounts of overtime and quickly became exhausted
only to become frustrated by the additional tasks
that demand their attention. Individuals who stay
in the field often become petty bureaucrats. In
some workers, stress becomes so great that they must
leave their situation either by transferring or
quitting.

Job-related stress can be positive. In the early stages it is a challenge to workers, causing them to have increased motivation and productivity. If stress is left unchecked it can result in burnout. The likelihood of this happening can be reduced if the worker is given periodic rewards or rest periods.

Common examples of burnout causes are: "barriers to the attainment of goals, which generate frustration; uncomfortable working conditions; necessity of reconciling incompatible demands; ambiguous role perceptions." Caseworkers often are unable to spend much time with their clients because of the enormous amounts of paperwork. Due to large caseloads workers frequently are unable to see cases through to completion. They encounter stress when they discover a client has not received the needed supportive services. The problem workers find most frustrating is the lack of a tangible index of success for use with clients. Evaluations are based on subjective criteria and workers frequently are uneasy about the validity of their evaluations. Another category of stressors for caseworkers is that of working conditions. A caseworker may find himself in circumstances that are dangerous, unhealthy, or unwanted by the client. Role ambiguity for the worker is reflected in his doubts concerning how to behave as well as the demands expressed by various interest groups. Workers may have difficulty reconciling the duties of the protective service agency with those of the institutions.

Approaches and strategies used to prevent burnout include: sanctioned time-out; supervisory support; peer group support systems; and judicious rotation of job assignments. Workers can reduce the likelihood of emotional burnout by limiting the time spent in direct contact with clients. It is important that supervisors monitor caseworkers and demonstrate empathy for them to help relieve feelings of alienation or uncertainty concerning job performance. Administrators also play a vital role in decreasing the likelihood of burnout among their workers. They can do this by rotating jobs,

developing career ladders in direct service, opening
two-way channels of communication with staff, and
implementing sound training programs for workers.
Development of career ladders offers workers options
to continue working in the field of social work
while allowing them to advance themselves.

Daley, M. R. Preventing worker burnout in child
   welfare. Child Welfare, 1979, 58, 443-450.
   Although theories on the cause of burnout vary,
there are two key dimension of any definition: the
time-related concept of wearing out and the feeling
of estrangement. Because the process of burning out
is gradual, a worker may not recognize it. Some of
the symptoms of burnout are: minimizing involvement
with the client, treating clients as cases, not
persons, and working harder and longer hours but
accomplishing less.
   In the initial stages the body mobilizes defenses
to cope with job stresses. This may enable a person
to maintain effectiveness for a while, but prolonged
exposure results in exhaustion. The worker may then
quit, become a bureaucrat, or breakdown physically
and mentally.
   To prevent burnout, rest periods must be long
enough for the body to replenish its energies and
for the effects of stress to dissipate. Turnover
causes a loss of financial resources invested in
training workers and causes loss of productivity
while training replacements. Of contextual factors
inherent in the job and working conditions, only the
amount of feedback showed significant correlation to
burnout.
   Personal factors include career motivation.
Unfortunately, social workers seek direct interaction with clients, but this constitutes only a
small portion of the job-related activities. Thus,
workers don't get expected rewards from working with
clients. Other personal factors include work
overload and job responsibility. Line workers
burnout more frequently than administrators.
   Organizational factors contributing to burnout are
large caseloads, formalized rules, centralized

authority, large span of supervisory control, a high
percentage of time required for administrative
tasks, and inability to provide adequate services
for clients. Availability of time-outs, peer and
supervisory support, and sharing of cases reduce
likelihood of burnout. Strategies for reducing
burnout include: making time-outs available,
facilitating peer support, providing feedback,
improving training, regulating caseloads, and
developing career ladders in direct service.

DuBrin, A. J., Fowler, J., Hoiberg, L., Mathiott, J.
E., Morrison, F., Paulus, P. C., Prince, E.,
Stein, S., & Youngs, B. B. Teacher burnout: How
to cope when your world goes black. Instructor,
January 1979, 56-62.
Teacher burnout is caused by a number of factors
that seem to be distinct to the teaching situation.
This burnout is culminating in a number of the same
factors that characterize burnout in other occupations: depression, exhaustion, ulcers, migraines,
alcoholism, drug abuse, and turnover.
This article presents a number of diverse and
creative responses to burnout geared both to the age
and experience of the teacher reading it and to the
diverse work assignments within the teaching profession. Some of the basic techniques of avoidance or
cure are participation in further training, teacher
support groups, hobbies, leisure activities, relaxation, and exercise. Other more creative and
specific ideas include study tours to foreign
countries and changing schools. Others work on a
sharedcontract basis with another teacher or participate in a peer- evaluation program that sets
specific growth goals and provides for feedback and
evaluation. Some teachers hire older students to do
paperwork, while others reschedule their days to
accomodate their own needs and those of their
students. The article suggests that if a teacher is
happy away from school, then burnout is the problem
and the solutions are many.

Duemer, W., Walker, N., & Quick, J. Improving work

life through effective performance planning. The
Personnel Administrator, July, 1978, 23-26.
Stress-related consequences such as respiratory
disease, digestive problems, and cardiovascular
problems can be modified or managed through a
program of stress reduction, which focuses on a type
of planning called management by objectives. This
planning involves the employee and the supervisor
cooperating in planning and goal setting. Benefits
of this type of planning include improved communications, improved planning, and reduced uncertainty
and stress of changing job responsibilities.
The study was conducted in a division of a life
insurance company by means of a questionnaire,
examination of absentee records, and interviews.
Role playing in small groups was a part of the
process.
Some of the results include more challenging work
goals, increased clarity and reduced confusion in
the employee's work goals, assistance for supervisors to give feedback about job performance, and
encouragement for employees to participate in
setting their own goals. Another result is that as
clarity of work assignments and goals increases,
confusion is diminished and absenteeism is reduced.
Furthermore, the study found that high and low
levels of competition are detrimental but that
moderate levels of competition have a positive
effect on job performance.

Dunham, J. Staff stress in residential work. Social
Work Today, 1978, 9(45), 18-20.
The major responses of social workers, psychiatric
nurses, and doctors to stress are exhaustion and
increasing rigidity in the performance of their
tasks at work and becoming more remote from their
clients. These responses were identified as burnout
syndrome in research done by Maslach, who also
reported fewer stress symptoms when the workers were
able to consult with their colleagues or were
invited to participate in decision-making and had
developed constructive ways of ventilating their
feelings. This author presents the results of a

exploratory study on which residential social
workers were asked to report on their stress situations and stress responses as well as the recommendations they would make to reduce and prevent
stress. The major stress situations reported were:
reorganization and other changes; role conflict and
role uncertainty; poor working conditions; and
communication difficulties. The behavior of the
children and adolescents who are placed in residential homes and schools is also reported to cause
considerable staff stress. The poor working conditions in schools and homes included in this
research consist mainly of working unsocial hours,
irregular duty time, poor transportation and facilities in rural areas. Communication difficulties
were reported as important stress factors. The
barriers to effective interprofessional communication and cooperation with workers who are based
outside the institution are caused by differences in
qualifications and professional experience.

Recommendations as to the ways to reduce or prevent
work stress include, the importance of thorough
preparation, good support from colleagues, and
effective interprofessional communication and
cooperation. Additional recommendations for improving the working conditions include: better pay,
reasonable time-off which should not be eroded by
moral obligations, more full and active social life
outside the school, long regenerating holidays, an
increase in the feeling that these professionals are
doing vital and unique tasks.

These results agree with other research that has
pointed out some of the characteristics of a healthy
organization. In those studies the healthy physical
and social conditions will be established by giving
the employees the following opportunities:
1. Influence the decisions that affect them.
2. Be engaged in meaningful activities.
3. Feel a sense of belonging to their work
   groups.
4. Satisfy their needs for self-esteem.
In residential homes with these characteristics,
the staff will find opportunities for personal

growth, development of competence, and awareness of self-fulfillment.

Edelwich, J., & Brodsky, A. <u>Burnout: Stages of Disillusionment in the Helping Professions.</u> Human Sciences Press, New York, 1980.

Burnout is referred to as a progressive loss of idealism, energy, and purpose experienced by people in the helping professions as a result of the conditions of their work. Any kind of involvement that people form is vulnerable to doubt, disillusionment, and an eventual exhaustion of energy. The same kinds of physical symptoms of burnout commonly observed in human services personnel can just as easily be found in the high pressure work of business. Business, however, does not carry the high social cost that the human services professions do.

Vocations in the human services are characterized by several sources of frustrations that may eventually lead the most dedicated person to ineffectiveness and apathy. Some of these sources of frustration are: noble aspirations and high initial enthusiasm, lack of criteria for measuring accomplishment, low pay at all levels of education, skill and responsibility, upward mobility through the administrative channel, sexism, inadequate funding and institutional support, inefficient use of resources, and high public visibility coupled with popular misunderstanding and suspicion.

This book explores the stages of disillusionment and the interventions that may assist a person out of burnout. Based on extensive interviews with social workers, psychologists, counselors, teachers, and other professionals, the authors explore the causes of burnout and proposed constructive intervention methods for individuals and institutions.

The process of disillusionment progresses through the following stages:

1. Enthusiasm--the initial period of high hopes, high energy, and unrealistic expectations, when one does not yet know what the job is all about. It is when one

      does not need anything in life but the
      job. Overidentification with clients and
      excessive and inefficient expenditure of
      energy are major hazards of this stage.

2.   Stagnation--one is still doing the job,
      but enough reality has filtered through to
      make one feel that it might be nice to
      have some leisure time, money, etc. The
      emphasis now is on meeting one's own
      personal needs and the issues of money,
      working hours, and career development now
      become important.

3.   Frustration--effectiveness in doing the
      job and the value of the job itself are
      questioned. The limitations of the job
      situation are now viewed not simply as
      detracting from ones personal satisfaction
      and status, but as threatening to defeat
      the purpose of what one is doing. Emo-
      tional, physical, and behavioral problems
      can occur at this stage.

4.   Intervention--whatever is done in response
      to or in anticipation of enthusiasm,
      stagnation, frustration, or apathy. It
      breaks the cycle. Some interventions are
      more effective than others in the long run
      and the trick is to find the ones that
      produce lasting change.

The chapters included in this book are:

1. What is Burn-out?
2. Recognition and Scope of the Problem
3. Idealistic Enthusiasm
4. The Small World of Stagnation
5. Career Dead End
6. Politics and Powerless
7. The Givens of the Systems
8. Frustrations, Reactions, and Consequences
9. The Retreat into Apathy
10. Realistic vs. Unrealistic Interventions
11. Problem-Solving On and Off the Job

Emener, W. G. Professional burnout:
  Rehabilitation's hidden handicap. <u>Journal of</u>

Rehabilitation, January/February 1979, 45(1), 55-58.
There are numerous intrapersonal and environmental conditions that are unique to the field of reha- bilitation and that contribute to burnout of reha- bilitation professionals. The rapid changes in the scope of services, prioritized population groups mandated at the congressional level, reorganization- al human-service structuring at state levels, advancements in rehabilitation knowledge and tech- nology, and fluctuations in social economic, and employment aspects of living, have been overwhelm- ing.

There are a number of symptoms that help identify the condition called burnout. They include: being tired all the time and unable to get enough sleep; easily tired muscles; colds that seem to linger on and on; headaches that seem to crop up during the day; becoming more introverted; bored and easily discouraged; quick to be angry and frustrated; and feeling as if everyone is against you.

It is the idealistic people who enter the field and gradually become overcommitted to their work who can easily become burnout candidates. The top three causes include: responsibility without necessary authority to accomplish tasks; responsibility without necessary resources to get the job done; and a lack of meaningful recognition for one's efforts and accomplishments. It is important to note that the mere existence of the symptoms described above is not the crucial element in the identification of burnout. The frequency and magnitude of these symptoms are the crucial elements of burnout.

The rehabilitation administrator, supervisor, and counselor experience many situational conditions that precipitate burnout. Administrators can be genuinely overworked. Supervisors can easily feel tremendous pressures and demands from the agency, people they supervise, and their own genuine desire to improve the quality of service delivery. The counselor may be too idealistic, may be isolated from others in their work, and may be under agency

pressures to help the more severely disabled with
limited funds and resources.

The following 10 preventive/corrective measures
appear to be realistic strategies of minimizing
burnout:

1. "Know thyself."
2. Delegate authority.
3. Open relations with significant others.
4. Engage in recreation, hobbies, etc.
5. Establish realistic goals.
6. Engage in more group activities at work.
7. Supervisors and administrators should get
    out into the field and interact with
    clients.
8. Alternate work roles and functions.
9. Schedule physical activity.
10. Acknowledge and attend to the needs and
    feelings of other coworkers.

Emener, W. G., Luck, R. S., & Gohs, F. Z. A
   theoretical investigation of the construct
   burnout. Journal of Rehabilitation
   Administration, November 1982, 6(4), 188-196.
   The current political-economic climate has had a
negative impact on the effectiveness of pub-
lic-service agencies and providers. Individuals
associated with these agencies are experiencing the
impact of burnout at increasingly higher rates.
Because of the increasing numbers of burned-out
professionals, a project was developed to determine
the theoretical base for burnout. Purposes of the
study were to "survey and synthesize existing
literature to identify theoretical constructs of
burnout, develop an experimental instrument to test
the constructs and gather additional information,
use the instrument as a training stimulus with
rehabilitation professionals to gather experimental
information for comparisons to the theoretical
constructs, and to develop a synthesis of preliminary factors or categories which may possibly
further define the phenomena of burnout."

An operational definition of burnout encompasses
the following characteristics: loss of concern and

enthusiasm, pessimism, disenchantment, fatigue, boredom, discouragement, confusion, anger, and reduced physical health. These characteristics of burnout are perceived as harmful because they reduce an individual's potential to express concern, creativity, problem-solving, joy, or love.

The Emener-Luck Burnout Scale (ELBOS) was designed to determine burnout based on "seven theoretical constructs." The areas are: feedback, work environment, autonomy, expectations, affect/attitude, self-perception, and job mobility. Administration of the ELBOS was done in five states with 251 volunteers who were professional in the field of rehabilitation.

The study found that general work-related feeling "has the highest correlation with and therefore also the best indicator of the burnout measure, is essentially affective in nature." Individuals with satisfying work-related experiences tend to suffer less burnout than those with negative feelings about work.

Although the factors of the ELBOS influence burnout and its potential, they do not determine a definitive cause-and-effect relationship on burnout. The ELBOS is presently most useful as a training device and a research instrument. "Burnout appears to be more highly related to affective or emotional factors experienced about an individual's line of work than to physical or tangible rewards or punishments."

Flood, M. A. Kashka, M. S., & Tweed, S. Burnout, the inevitable, professional hazard? Kansas Nurse, June 1981, 156(6), 11-13.

The nursing faculty at the University of Kansas presented a workshop to explore parameters of burnout in the nursing profession. Common characteristics among nurses in regards to burnout were explored as well as the socialization to burnout inborn in nursing education and ways to correct it.

A model of the burnout syndrome was used which was developed by Jerry Edelwich, a social worker. This model described burnout as having four progressive stages: enthusiasm is the initial stage and is characterized by total commitment and voluntary overtime; stagnation is the experiencing of physical and emotional fatigue; frustration, which is the core of burnout and the condition most often identified, is characterized by a sense of powerlessness, anger, psychosomatic illness, and damage to personal and family relationships; the last stage, apathy, is characterized by emotional and physical withdrawl, often resulting in termination.

The results of the workshop identified consistent reasons for burnout among the nursing profession: excess paperwork, powerlessness, little money, and lack of appreciation from supervisors and physicians. Also identified was a need for greater communication and teamwork as a solution for feeling unappreciated by supervisors. To achieve this goal, the workshop suggested regularly scheduled meetings between doctors and nurses, the addition of nurses to hospital committes, and most important, the development of support groups for each individual.

Fooner, A. Teacher burnout: When you're beyond stress. Forecast for Home Economics, May-June, 1981, 26(9), 13-14.

This article deals with some specific remedies for teacher burnout that are more extensive than those commonly delineated in the literature. These remedies are necessary because in 1979 a study was conducted that reported that 70% of teachers are regularly abused verbally or psychologically by students while 1 in 20 had actually been attacked. Teachers are also exposed to the stresses of budget cuts and expectations of service beyond their training, such as counseling, social work, and parole officers. Many teachers experience high blood pressure, ulcers, cynicism, and detachment. There is lack of support from administration and from parents, as well as from students. Isolation, detachment, absenteeism, and use of tranquilizers are further indicators of too much stress.

To alleviate stress, the first step is to review successes and strengths. The next step is a detailed analysis of the sources of stress. The point is to be as specific as possible so that remedy is also defineable. The analysis begins with the specific list of stresses. Then one makes four columns labeled "who," "how often," "where," and "how much control" and then codes each one with letters to represent colleagues, students, administrators, and parents under the "who" column. Under the "where" it is necessary to code classrooms, halls, meetings, and home. Under the "how often," the teacher is to mark frequency with weekly, daily, or constantly. "How much control" is described with adjectives like some, little, or none.

The next step is to review the list and act on three of the items. Following the commitment it is necessary to look at all possible ways to make some changes--items which range from exercise to getting more sleep to taking a long bath. At this point the teacher is to choose two changes and stick with them. Finally the teachers are charged to be creative and come up with their own short and long-term coping strategies. The final suggestion is support from peers, a remedy which is probably the one recommended by the most stress alleviation programs.

Forney, D. S., Wallace-Schutzman, F., & Wiggers, T. T. Burnout among career development professionals: Preliminary findings and implications. Personnel and Guidance Journal, March 1982, 60(7), 435-439.

A relatively low percentage of professionals consider themselves to be effective in their work. The burdening responsibility to examine both the incidence and factors that contribute to this malady is long overdue. The study measured the discrepancy between what personnel want from their jobs and what they perceive as actually being offered. The interviews, equally crossbased between 24 professionals, were led through the use of five major categories including job content, work environment, work-nonwork relationship, self-awareness and energy level/burnout.

While there still remains no clear-cut definition of the term <u>burnout</u>, it is viewed as a two-dimensional aspect containing both attitudinal and behavioral components. The lack of enthusiasm and energy constituted the attitudinal response and deviations from the individual's normal behavior were used as the behavioral components. This study did reveal that there are three distinct levels of burnout that we should concern ourselves with. The first level, trait, considered a level of being totally wiped out; the state level included such factors as being drained during the recruiting period; and the functional level, such as being depressed from performing the individual career-counseling function.

Because burnout is influenced by internal and external factors, it is not appropriate to formulate universal solutions. Therefore, the thought of treating burnout by the usage of a formula approach is unrealistic. So, a major emphasis on the individual's nature is essential to both the person and the environment. While the symptoms of burnout are numerous, the warning signals associated with this problem are similar and recognizable. While repetition, lack of challenge, overextension, and insufficient time are some of the leading indicators of this malady, some of the above-mentioned circumstances can be prevented if properly diagnosed in time. Therefore, to reduce the potential or to maximize recovery, a primary goal becomes one of minimizing the uncontrollable aspects on both the internal and external levels. A major focus of this emphasis is to determine how an individual perceives himself and how the person deals with the reality. Personnel who were able to combat the burnout phase through the use of internal controls could see beyond the myth that their own profession was directly responsible for their reduced effectiveness. Rather, they gained insight and control over the potential of burnout by rationalizing their own concepts and problems into realistic terms of variety. The bottom line seems to be that accurate problem identification is the first step. Awareness

on both the part of supervisors and the personnel
themselves would lead to the next aid, that of the
knowledge and ability to implement intervention
strategies for the person seeking to meet his own
needs.

Francis, B.   A nursing network to battle burnout.
  Journal of Practical Nursing, Nov/Dec., 1980,
  30(11), 25-27.
  Nursing is a particularly high-stress occupation
due to the dichotomies a nurse operates under.
These include being compassionate and sympathetic
while treating the patient as an individual; another
is being warm and friendly and objective at the same
time. An added stress is cause by the atmosphere of
lights, alarms, and hurried activities of the nurses
themselves. High stress units, such as intensive
care, emergency units, and oncology units, are
especially responsible for adding to burnout among
nurses.
  There are several ways indentified for coping with
burnout. Some nurses try to battle it themselves;
however, a nurse who chooses this option loses the
support of others who have had to cope before and
may be able to aid her. Other nurses run away from
nursing, which may result in failure issues for her
at a later point. Seeking help is probably the most
productive, but is also constrained by the ability
of the sought-out person to be helpful. Family
members often are not aware enough of the particular
stresses of the job to offer constructive aid.
  Support groups of nurses who work in the same
hospital and especially the same unit are probably
the most effective means of coping with and alleviating burnout. These groups allow nurses to venti-
late and also offer objectivity on specific cases
because they know the facts about the patient
situation.

Freudenberger, H. J. Staff burn-out. Journal of
  Social Issues, 1974, 30(1), 159-165.
  To burnout is to become exhausted by making
excessive demands on energy, strength, or resources.

Physical signs include: exhaustion, fatigue, lingering colds, frequent headaches, insomnia, and dyspnea. Behavioral signs include: irritation, anger, loss of emotional control, cynicism, paranoia, and excessive use of drugs. In addition there are growing signs of rigidity, stubborness, and inflexibility. People act and seem depressed. They do less and less, consuming more and more time. Their jobs becomes their total lives. The 'helping professionals' know the difference between a mature, healthy involvement or commitment as opposed to one that reflects a personal need. An excessive need to give helps identify individuals who are prone to burnout. Suggested preventative measures include:

1. Helping your training staff to judge and evaluate the difference between a realistically committed person vs. an unrealistically dedicated person.
2. Avoiding sending the same staff member into the same job over and over.
3. Limiting the total hours a person can work.
4. Allowing members to take time off.
5. Promoting groups to work together and to watch out for each other.
6. Sharing your experience with others.
7. Taking time off to attend related by not emotionally draining activities, e.g., seminars and conventions.
8. Taking on more volunteers to reduce work.
9. Encouraging physical exercise.

Freudenberger, H. J. The staff burnout syndrome in alternative
    institutions. Psychotherapy: Theory Research and Practice, 1975, 12(1), 73-82.
The dictionary defines the verb burnout as to fail or wear out or become exhausted by making excessive demands on energy, strength, or resources. There are a number of personality types that are most prone to burn out in alternative self-help or crisis intervention settings. They include: (a) the dedicated and committed worker, (b) the staff member who is overcommitted and whose outside life is

subsatisfactory, (c) the authoritarian (d), the
administrator, and (e) the professional. There are
a number of physical, psychological, and behavioral
signs of burnout. Physical signs or burnout are the
feeling of exhaustion, being unable to shake a cold,
feeling physically run down, suffering from frequent
headaches and gastrointestinal disturbances. Loss
of weight, sleeplessness, depression, shortness of
breath, and a variety of other psychosomatic ailments are additional signs that depict the
burned-out victim. The behavioral signs of burnout
are the quickness to anger, instantaneous irritation, and frustration responses. The anger may also
be accompained by a suspicious attitude, a paranoia.
Linked to the paranoid-like state are feelings of
omnipotence, which may produce some alarming
risk-taking behaviors on the part of the burned-out
victim. With those individuals who are prone to
psychosomatic symptoms, an excessive use of tranquilizers and barbituates may come about. One of
the more serious personality manifestations that
emerge with burnout is rigidity, the person becomes
closed to any input. Change is threatening to an
exhausted person, the least little demand upon him
that involves a change becomes inconceivable to him.
Another personality indicator is a totally negative
attitude. The burnout becomes the "house cynic."
The burned-out staff member really just hangs
around. He works harder and harder, and longer and
longer, and does less and less. Careful observation
and evaluation has produced a number of preventive
measures.

1.   Utilize a training program to select
     volunteers offering help.
2.   Help your staff to judge and evaluate the
     difference between a realistically
     dedicated or committed person and an
     unrealistically dedicated person.
3.   Rotate job functions as much as possible.
4.   Limit the number of hours each person
     works.

5.   Extended time-out procedures should be employed.
6.   Groups should work as groups, and individuals within the group should be discouraged from advancing ahead and thus losing contact with the group.
7.   Share your experiences with others and see to it that your staff members share experiences with one another.
8.   Incorporate workshops and training sessions in your institution.
9.   Encourage staff and yourself to get in a lot of physical exercise.

Freudenberger, H. J., Burnout: The organizational menace. Training and Development Journal, July 1977, 26-27.

Burnout is described as a syndrome characterized by loss of productivity, energy, and interest by staff members in their jobs. Burnout strikes those staff members who originally showed the most enthusiasm and were the most devoted to their careers and to the organization. Burnout victims have not necessarily experienced any significant change in working or home conditions, but they gradually and usually imperceptibly find themselves easily fatigued, depressed, irritable, bored and overworked. When the symptoms are noticed, fault is placed on someone or something outside of the victims. Additional signs of burnout are inflexibility, working harder and longer, yet accomplishing less and less, cynicism and hypersensitivity to criticism or cross-examination, especially on matters concerning their deteriorating condition.
 Stated causes of burnout are linked to individual imperfections that exist from the start, but only later manifest themselves. Individual shortcomings in their personal lives produce a need to over commit themselves in their work so as to compensate for these past failures. A lack of gratifying relationships, social pursuits and hobbies lead to these misguided efforts in their work. The outcome of this is people who are becoming less productive

and less satisfied in an endeavor in which they most wish to prove themselves competent, namely, their work. Helping a burnout victim requires an indirect approach, e.g., gradual shifting of routine and responsibilities, or a possible vacation, if it can be suggested in an unobtrusive way. In addition, one may try to promote group participation, joint responsibility for work, and sharing of feelings of burnout.

Frew, D. D. Transcendental meditation and
   productivity. Academy of Management Journal,
   1974, 17, 362-368.
Proponents of Transcendental Meditation (TM) argue that the technique increases physical energy levels. This argument logically leads to the conclusion that TM increases productivity. However, the increases might be mediated by a motivational factor. Would the meditator necessarily be motivated to pursue company objectives with his expanded energies, or might he utilize those extra personal resources for some activity that essentially would be in opposition to organizational goals.
A three-page questionnaire was used as the research instrument. The questionnaire attempted to measure the independent variables-structure and organizational level-and the dependent or productivity variables.
Three different calculations of six measures of productivity produced significant positive correlation between the practice and the three research questions. The six variables measured were: job satisfaction; performance; turnover propensity; relationship with supervisor; relationship with peers; and motivation to climb. Three conclusions drawn from results include:
   1.   TM would appear to be positively related
        to productivity-meditators report that
        they experience more job satisfaction,
        improved performance, less desire to
        change jobs (turnover), better interper-
        sonal relationships, and a decreased
        climbing orientation.

2.   The data support the proposition that
     productivity gains are an increasing
     function of structural level. The higher
     the level, the greater the gain in produc-
     tivity. Meditators at higher levels
     reported that their gains in job satisfac-
     tion and performance, their reduced
     turnover propensity, and improved inter-
     personal relationships were significantly
     more positive than those of meditators who
     work at low levels of organizations.
3.   Gains in productivity would appear to be
     related to the type of organizational
     structure. The more democratic the
     structure, the greater the gains in
     productivity variables.

Gardell, B. Reactions at work and their influences
  on nonwork activities. Human relations, 1976, 16,
  885-904.
  This study has investigated the effects of feelings experienced by the individual (active behaviors, passive behaviors, spillover effects and
repercussions on mental and physical health) as a
sign of the powerlessness of the individual human
who is being rigorously directed and specialized.
Work is seen as leading to alienation and pathologi-
cal effects at both the individual and societal
level.
  Traditional ways of organizing work in industrialized societies are in conflict with basic human
needs related to creativity, influence, and growth.
This conflict affects work satisfaction, job and
labor market behavior, and participation in rewards
from nonwork activities such as organized cultural,
political, and educational activities.
  Developments in the job world must be subordinated
to social policy and to human life. Work is one of
the means for the creation of resources both mate-
rially and culturally, but it is unprofitable and
undemocratic if these resources are created such
that people risk their health and vitality. One
needs to see the connection between what happens in

the job world and the rest of society so that the
different sides of social life amplify one another.
  This research has shown that most people dislike:
authoritarian and detailed leadership; tasks that
seriously constrain the use of personal resources;
working conditions that put little if any premium on
responsibility and initiative; and tasks that allow
little scope for influence over work planning and
performance. The research also demonstrates that
the range of choices open to the individual at
different times of life should be broadened with
regard to working, family, and education. The
employment relationships that govern today's labor
market are too rigid and must be changed to make
them more flexible. We must continue the efforts to
make working life more humane and democratic and to
enhance the individual's economic security and
freedom. We must also strive toward a substantial
shortening of the working day as well as the size
and complexity of present day-work organizations.

Gardner, R. Guard stress. _Corrections Magazine_,
  October 1981, 7(5), 7-10; 12-14.
  Corrections officers in prisons and jails encounter dangerous situations each day as part of their
work. They are subject to verbal and physical abuse
from inmates daily. In order to tolerate the
difficult environmental situations of the correctional system, officers are learning relaxation
techniques. Many officers are learning these skills
through voluntary courses because many systems, such
as the U.S. Bureaus of Prisons, have no systematic
stress training for officers. The great amount of
stress in the correctional system has resulted in
annual turnover rates of 50% to 100%. It is believed that the stress training has resulted in
fewer absences and officers who are better able to
deal with stress.
  A study done by Cheek and Miller found that correc-
tion officers had a higher rate of heart attacks and
migraine headaches than police officers. Areas in
which stress is reflected are: absenteeism, sick
leave, early retirements, and denial of the impact

of stress. Conditions of the prison sys-
tem--overcrowding, antiquated facilities, overtime,
low pay-- are believed to aggravate stress. Officers perceive themselves to have a role "functioning
as a manager of violent, explosive men but not
recognized as a manager. He's only a guard, a
watcher. He's regarded as an individual functioning
at a low level. He's expected to go by the book,
but the book doesn't work. You can't control an
institution coercively, so what he does is to
bargain, negotiate. Consequently, a C.O. feels he
had a responsible managerial role. Yet he has no
input into the rules and no support in carrying them
out."
In an effort to confront the problems of burnout,
which are manifested in hostility, impotence,
alcoholism, chain smoking, and excessive coffee
drinking, officers should be given positive coping
techniques. These include: physical exercise,
hobbies, time off, a relaxation exercise, deep
breathing, use of imagery to control tension,
assertiveness training, and voice control. The
techniques focus on the individual and help him to
more accurately analyze the situation and resolve it
without conflict.

Gatre, S. H., & Rosenblum, M. L. Lighting fires in
burned-out counselors. Personnel and Guidance
Journal, November 1978, 158-160.
What began as workshops in leisure consciousness
to help counselors come to grips with an area of
their clients' life space that seemed to receive
little attention evolved into the development of
exercises to help counselors. These exercises
assisted counselors in becoming aware of their uses
of leisure time and its potential for life and job
enrichment.
Two exercises are described in which participants
discussed their value preference for a life devoted
to leisure activities. Participants also discovered
that for the most part they projected negative
feelings about work while projecting positive
feelings with regard to the concept of leisure.

This result was a contradiction to recent surveys showing that only semiskilled and unskilled workers find work so imbued with negative characteristics that they use leisure as an escape.

Leisure therapy is defined as the process of utilizing leisure activities for the purpose of increasing personal and professional effectiveness. Participants confront their own attitudes and values with regard to work and leisure. This experience culminates in an exercise called "individual introspection" in which participants list 20 activities that they find enjoyable, meaningful, and in some way contribute to making their lives worth living. Once this list is compiled, the following aspects are analyzed to assist participants to make the first step toward influencing their environments at work: activities, date since last done, expense, other persons, job, physical-secondary time, years of employment left in activity.

A single interpersonal relationship cannot be expected to fulfill all of one's needs for relating; a single vocation cannot be counted on to fulfill every need for personal identity, mastery, and achievement. Counselors must diversify their activities to the extent that it becomes possible to focus on other needs. A new "consciousness of leisure" becomes essential. If unmet needs cannot realistically be addressed by modifying a work situation, the creative use of leisure time becomes mandatory to achieve a wholeness of spirit. Enthusiasm and zest for life are contagious and valuable allies to the therapeutic process. Similarly, boredom, routine, and lackluster attitudes are easily transmitted to others.

Geist, G. O., & Backes, R. G. Job attitudes of union versus N.R.C.A. members. Journal of Applied Rehabilitation Counseling, 1978, 9(3), 116-119.

After a review of state vocational rehabilitation agency counselors becoming involved in the labor union movement and attitudes of professionalism and extrinsic rewards, the article examined the hypothesis that counselors affiliated with either N.R.C.A.

or the union did not differ in their attitudes toward professionalism or extrinsic job rewards.

Results indicate that the two organizations have an attraction based on different, but overlapping appeal to the counselors, such that the professional association, while important, is sufficient only insofar as the counselor finds the job to hold adequate extrinsic job rewards for the work required. The union member apparently expresses dissatisfaction with the job rewards by the act of joining the union. However, it seems reasonable to conclude from the results that fear of a lack of sympathy for the ideals of professionalism, or a lack of concern for client welfare, as a concommitant of union membership is unfounded.

Genevay, B., & Simon-Gruen, D. A group approach to working with stress. Social Casework, 1979, 60(6), 368-371.

This article traces the development and process of a series of groups formed to teach people how to cope with stress. Entitled "Learning to Live with Stress," these learning groups have included a broad base of the local community population, ranging from middle-management executives to homemakers, teachers, and children. The groups were designed to serve persons who would not consider themselves as needing traditional counseling, but could use some basic human-relations skills for dealing with issues that bring others to a family agency.

The group procedure was outlined in a series of five sessions, with each session having particular activities associated with it. Persons participating in these groups were then asked to complete a written evaluation of the stress class. Most people indicated that the classes were worthwhile, and the following concepts the most helpful: (1) body awareness, (2) relaxation and breathing techniques, (3) the concept of choosing whether or not to take on stress, (4) the concept of power within oneself, (5) acceptance, and (6) pleasuring.

The authors believe the most significant accomplishments of the stress classes were: (1)

establishing the concept that change is possible, (2) helping family members and individuals reduce and accept stresses, and (3) teaching specific skills to reduce stress.

Girodo, M., & Stein, S. J. Self-talk and the work of worrying in confronting a stressor. <u>Cognitive Therapy and Research</u>, 1978, <u>2</u>(3), 305-307.
     Anticipatory problem solving and mentally rehearsing coping strategies for dealing with a stressor can partially inoculate a person against severe emotional duress. This constructive worrying was explored by assessing cognitive events during a 10-minute wait period and while confronting the stressor.
    Subjects were randomly assigned to four treatment groups based on the following: description of film to be seen, film description plus teaching, subjects denial and intellectualization statements, and control subjects were given no preparation before viewing the film. In addition to assessing subject arousal on five 10-point scale items (administered four times during treatment), subject heart rate was also monitored continuously.
    These tentative conclusions were made from the results: beneficial coping with a stressor occurs when active rehearsal and planning of a coping strategy takes place, and rehearsal may result in subjective anxiety. For subjects taught to emit internal feelings, there was more worry and apprehension during the actual waiting period than during the actual viewing of the film. Heart rate was not associated with coping success or failure.

Glaser, E. M. State-of-the-art questions about quality of worklife. <u>Personnel</u>, 1976, <u>53</u>, 39-47.
    The article addresses the term "Quality of Worklife" (QWL), identifying the essential component of any QWL program as being "real and ever-present opportunity for individuals or task groups at any level to influence their working environments, to have some say in what goes on in connection with their work." The author goes on to say that this in

turn requires an organizational climate structure
that really encourages, facilitates, and rewards
questions, challenges, or suggestions related to
improving the existing modus operandi in any way.
It also requires the expeditious, respectful, and
appropriate responses to such inputs. The author
continues to identify other necessary components of
a QWL program including:

1. Style of management that invites participation.
2. Systematic feedback.
3. Commitment from management to an open
   nondefensive style of operation.
4. Affording opportunities for continued
   growth.
5. Breaking down the traditional status
   barriers between management and production
   or support personnel.
6. Evaluating and analyzing results, including failures, leading to revised efforts
   to continual improvements.

Grater, H. A., Kell, B. L., & Morse, J. The social
service interest: Roadblock and road to
creativity. Journal of Counseling Psychology,
1961, 8(1), 9-13.

The apparent lack of creative research being done by
counseling psychologists is a concern of the profession itself. In order to determine the nature of
this lack of research productivity, the role of
nurturance as a primary motivating force behind the
social service interest was considered.

It is hypothesized that the nurturant need arises
in the human being as a consequence of a conditional
affection and approval given by significant persons
in the individual's life. Therefore, a child learns
to give in order to receive a sufficient supply of
parental response. Nurturance achieves not only a
gratifying emotional response but in addition, the
assurance that this emotional response will not be
withdrawn. It is assumed that an interest in
counseling psychology is one extension of the
nurturant need, i.e., nurturance is a basic need of

the individual and a prerequisite for job satisfaction. Although counseling psychology is chosen because of the need to take care of and be close to other people, the counseling relationship is basically unilateral and not reciprocal. The counselor cannot expect any return in the counseling relationship.

The hypothesis is held that the nurturant individual is a conforming individual and therefore fears creative thought that might separate the individual from others. Since counseling itself is already an isolating experience for the counselor, doing research is then seen as a further threat to relationships with other people.

One alternative to the isolation of doing creative work is researching in groups. The group can provide a sense of sharing to the extent that the anxiety of creating is outweighed by satisfaction and comfort in the intimacy of producing together. In addition, team productivity and motivation can yield more work than individuals working alone.

Greenberg, O. S.   Stress, relaxation, and the health educator. Journal of School Health, November 1977, 47(9), 522-525.

When the mind is affected, so is the body. Researcher Hans Selye described stress as the "nonspecific response of the body to any demands made upon it." Selye found that though the source of the stress may vary, the physiological response stayed the same. He called the response General Adaptation Syndrome (G.A.S.). The three stages of G.A.S. are: 1) alarm reaction, 2) stage of resistance, and 3) stage of exhaustion. The body's homeostasis is thrown out of balance and the body attempts to correct it. This process begins when the pituitary gland discharges andrenocoritcotrophic hormone (ACTH) and thyrotrophic hormone (TTH). Secretions of ACTH, corticoids, TTH, thyroxin, and adrenalin create the "fight or flight" response. The physiological effect causing the heart to beat faster, the blood pressure to rise, muscles to tense, breathing rate to increase and the digestive system to become inactive.

"Selye believes that each man possesses a limited amount of 'adaptive energy' and that this energy cannot be replenished. When this energy is gone, Selye believes, so soon is the man." Physical disorders that accompany frequent stress are: tension headaches, colitis, diarrhea, constipation, ulcers, and allergies. It is believed that stress plays a very important role in the conditions of: hypertension, coronary heart disease, stroke, and cancer. Estimates believe one third of the population suffers from hypertension which is a factor in stroke and heart disease and is associated with stress.

In the study of coronary heart disease a particular personality type proved to be more prone to heart disease. This personality type subjects himself to stress through aggressiveness, free-floating hostility, and a sense of time urgency. It is believed that stress plays an important role in causing cancer. The immune system defenses are lowered due to stress which allows cancer cells to grow. It is also believed that stress increases the blood's coagulability, which causes fibrin to form on blood vessel walls and snag cancer cells. The cells then accumulate and begin growing in the tissue around the blood vessels.

Health educators are concerned with teaching people to reduce the stress present in their lives. Four basic methods allow the individual to deal with stress in a healthy manner. Meditation-Transcendental Meditation or the relaxation response- allows the meditator to lower his metabolic rate, respiratory rate, oxygen consumption, and blood pressure. Ideally meditation should be done for 20 minutes in the morning and late afternoon. Progressive relaxation combats the effects of stress through alternating tensing and relaxing of muscles. Autogenic training is described as autohypnotic. It uses imagery and suggested feelings of heaviness and warmth in the limbs to create the state of relaxation. Autogenic training increases the alpha brain waves-which are found when a person is in a relaxed mood. Biofeedback measures physiological events in the body. This methods allows the participant to learn the relaxation response with more speed than other techniques.

Grossnickle, D. R. Teacher burnout. Clearing House, 1980, 54(1), 17-18.
Teacher burnout is caused by increasing reports of physical assaults on teachers, public criticism of schools and teacher performance, lax discipline procedures and enforcement, talk about declining enrollments and the need to reduce the teaching force, increasing curricular pressures such as the minimum competency and back-to-basic movements, court decisions that cause fear of any teacher decision that may cause reprisals, suggested teacher incompetency and early retirement requirements, unrealistic teacher evaluation practices, too much talk of shortage of funds and teacher budget cuts, low pay with comparison to factory and "unskilled workers," and the increasing frequency of students who disrupt the class and verbally abuse the teacher.
This reveals several issues in the problem: there are indeed problems that affect teacher morale and teaching climate. Complaining may compound the problem; talking about the problem will not make it go away; catharsis may help. It appears that collective griping has succeeded in raising the level of public conciousness and people talking about teacher burnout. Teachers seem no longer content because they do not derive satisfaction from teaching.
Collective teachers voices and teaching unions are providing a means of counterattack toward finding help to solve their problems. But parents, legislators, courts, and communities must help.

Gruneberg, M. M. Understanding job satisfaction. New York; The MacMillan Press, Ltd., 1979.
This book intends to introduce the manager and the student to the complex topic of job satisfaction and

to consider what job satisfaction is and how it might be improved, and to cover the major factors that affect and are affected by job satisfaction.

The reason for the study of job satisfaction is that most individuals spend a large part of their lives at work, so that an understanding of factors involved in job satisfaction is relevant to improving the well-being of a large number of individuals in an important aspect of their lives. Another reason is the belief that increasing job satisfaction will increase productivity and the profitability of organizations.

The definition and measurement of job satisfaction are discussed in light of the variety of ways job satisfaction is defined and measured. A list of nine different operational definitions, each based on a different theoretical orientation and each resulting in different measures, is provided. The major differences between definitions is in terms of the different ways in which aspects of job satisfaction are combined. When the relationship between job satisfaction for different aspects of the job and overall job satisfaction is analyzed, considerable differences in the extent of the correlation is found. One measure, the Cornell Job Descriptive Index (JDI), is regarded by many workers as the most carefully developed instrument for measuring job satisfaction.

The chapters in this book include:
1. Introduction
2. Theoretical Consideration
3. Job Satisfaction and the Job Itself
4. Job Satisfaction and Context Factors
5. Job Satisfaction and Individual Differences
6. The Consequences of Job Satisfaction and Dissatisfaction
7. Job Satisfaction and Job Design
8. Concluding Remarks

In the studies on job satisfaction, a distinction needs to be made between a common-sense explanation and a reasonable explanation. Explanations given after the event are invariable seen as reasonable.

It is reasonable to account for the fact that there is no relationship between job satisfaction and productivity by pointing out that people often derive satisfaction in work from aspects of the job that have little to do with productivity, such as social interactions. If people are asked what they think is the likely relationship between satisfaction and productivity before they examine the actual relationship, the great majority will hypothesize that the greater the satisfaction the greater is the productivity. The common-sense approach is clearly at variance with what actually happens.

A discussion of research problems involved with such stories reveals that part of this can be attributed to unsatisfactory design and interpretation, the complexity of the phenomenon, and demanding precision of the natural sciences.

Even though many of the studies done have not shown correlations between job satisfaction and productivity, the practical value of these studies is that they have led to job enrichment, job redesign, and pay-satisfaction resolutions that have enhanced productivity. The extensive application of job satisfaction studies to real life problems, together with the eight job satisfaction studies shown, and understanding of the individual's well-being at work, surely justifies continued rigorous study, despite the problems pointed out by critics.

Gruneberg, M. M., Startup, R., & Tapsfield, P. The effect of geographical factors on the job satisfaction of university teachers. Vocational Aspects of Education, 1974, 26, 25-29.

Research has been examined concerning the effects of environmental factors on job satisfaction. It shows a significant positive correlation between the attractiveness of the town and overall job satisfaction, as well as a significant relationship between satisfaction with the location of the town and overall job satisfaction.

Data was obtained through a two-part questionnaire administered to 189 university teachers. Contents included biographical information concerning age, faculty, status, and a wide variety of topics likely to be related to job satisfaction of university teachers. In addition, an analysis was made of the contribution of geographical factors of a local and national nature to job satisfaction.

The results indicated a 73% positive contribution of the local environment to job satisfaction due to pleasant and attractive surroundings. This was compared to 9% who were dissatisfied due to feelings of isolation such as academic isolation, inadequate library facilities, and isolation from other colleagues elsewhere. The effect of geographical satisfaction and dissatisfaction indicates that only where the geographical factor contributes a great deal to dissatisfaction is there a negative direction effect on overall job satisfaction. Individuals satisfied with their jobs are more likely to be satisfied with all aspects of life.

Hackman, J. R., & Oldham, G. R. Development of the job diagnostic survey. Journal of Applied Psychology, 1975, 60(2), 159-170.

This article concerns the development of a measurement tool, the Job Diagnostic Survey (JDS), which is designed to:
1. Diagnose existing jobs to determine if (and how) they might be redesigned to improve employee motivation and productivity.
2. Evaluate the effects of job changes on employees.

To accomplish this purpose the instrument is based on a theory of how job design affects work motivation and provides measures of:
1. Objective job dimensions.
   a. Skill variety.
   b. Task identity.
   c. Task significance.
   d. Autonomy.
   e. Feedback from the job itself.
   f. Feedback from agents.
   g. Dealing with others.
2. Critical psychological states.

       a.   Experienced meaningfulness of the
           work.
       b.   Experienced responsibility for work
           outcomes.
       c.   Knowledge of results.
   3.   Affective reactions to the job.
       a.   General satisfaction.
       b.   Internal work motivation.
       c.   Specific satisfactions.
   4.   Individual growth need strength.
       a.   "Would like" format.
       b.   "Job choice" format.

The reliability and validity data was summarized
for 658 employees on 62 different jobs in 7 organizations.

In addition, there were several issues and cautions
that should be recognized when using this instrument. They are:

   1.   Respondents to the JDS must be moderately
       literate. It is not recommended for
       individuals with an eighth-grade or less
       education.
   2.   The instrument is readily fakable, and
       probably should not be used for selection
       or placement purposes.
   3.   Related to the above, it probably is
       preferable for employees to take the JDS
       under conditions of anonymity.
   4.   The instrument is not recommended for use
       in diagnosing the jobs of single individu-
       als.

Hamner, C. W., & Tosi, H. L. Relationship of role
   conflict and role ambiguity to job involvement
   measures. Journal of Applied Psychology, 1974,
   59, 487-499.

Measures or role conflict, role ambiguity, and
various job involvement variables were obtained for
61 high-level managers. Role conflict was negatively related to the amount of reported influence and
positively related to the amount of perceived threat
and anxiety, while role ambiguity was negatively
correlated with job satisfaction and influence and

positively related to job threat and anxiety. It is suggested that organizational level be taken into account when studying the relationship of role stress factors with job involvement measures.
The specific purpose of this research was to examine the relationship of role conflict and role ambiguity to various job involvement variables. This study also examines the relationship of role conflict and role ambiguity to propensity to leave the organization. Role conflict was not significantly related to either job satisfaction or the propensity to leave the organization. There was, however, a trend toward a negative relationship to the amount of reported influence (participation), while role conflict was positively related to the amount of perceived threat and anxiety. Role ambiguity, on the other hand, was negatively correlated with job satisfaction and was positively correlated with job threat and anxiety. As with role conflict, role ambiguity was not significantly correlated with the propensity to leave the organization. Job satisfaction tended to relate negatively to the perceived threat and the anxiety produced by the job and was positively correlated with the amount of upward influence perceived by the employee. While job satisfaction was not significantly related to the propensity to leave the organization, the executives who had the least influence were the ones who expressed a greater propensity to leave the organization. Job satisfaction did not correlate with either role conflict or the propensity to leave the organization. The executives who had the least influence in the organization were the ones who expressed the greatest desire to leave.

Hanson, J. E. Job satisfaction and effective performance of school counselors. Personnel and Guidance Journal, 1968, 46, 864-869.
This study concerns the relationship between job satisfaction and the quality of the performance of first year school counselors.

The Job Satisfaction Inventory was mailed to 122 counselors in the state of New York. The 92 counselors who replied had their administrator and two coworkers rate their effectiveness in 6 job activities, as well as having their clients rate them in 3 aspects of the counseling relationship.

The results show a positive relationship between job satisfaction and counselor satisfaction in regards to their future security, advancement in the job, interest and liking for the job, knowledge and training in the field, and their working conditions. Those counselors who were rated more effective by their clients, coworkers, and administrators regarded their jobs as lifetime careers.

Hassett, J. Teaching yourself to relax. Psychology Today, August 1978, 28-40.

High blood pressure or hypertension is a very common disease with a growing number of treatments. One out of every three American adults has high blood pressure. More than 90% are diagnosed as "essential hypertension." Most doctors accept the evidence that stress is the key factor in the syndrome. Blood pressure is the force of the blood moving away from the heart pushing against the artery walls. Blood pressure is expressed as two numbers: systolic pressure (the maximum value when the heart beats) over diastolic pressure (the minimum value between beats). Normal blood pressure is somewhere around 120/80 mmHg. Blood pressure varies constantly under stress. When blood pressure goes up and stays up, the medical condition is called hypertension. It is a primary cause of stroke and increases the risk of suffering heart attacks and coronary-artery disease.

Five to 10% of hypertensives have clearly an identifiable physiological problem, i.e., kidney malfunctions, the majority however, have their cause related to lifestyle and while it cannot be cured, there are a variety of treatment approaches to maintain it at normal levels.

Treatment approaches range from drugs to meditation techniques. The following is a list of current treatments:

1. Drugs such as diuretics and vasodilators
2. Biofeedback training to reduce blood pressure directly. Training to reduce muscle tension via EMG (electromyogram) which produce a general state of relaxation.
3. Autogenic training, often used in conjunction with EMG, is a set of convert mental exercises producing mental relaxation.
4. Shavasam. A yoga technique that produces relaxation.
5. Jacobson's progressive relaxation technique. A series of exercises in which people tense and then relax every major muscle group of the body.
6. Condition relaxation. A series of tape-recorded exercises in which a metronome clicks every second and a voice instructs the patient to "relax . . . let go."
7. The relaxation response. A specific physiological relaxation response is elicited through a concentration mental technique.
8. Diet, exercise, and changes in life styles.

Today's researchers need to determine not just which treatment will produce the largest immediate effects, but which treatment is best suited for the patient, i.e., which treatment will people use. Thus far, compliance to any medical regimen has been tantamount to the treatment of high blood pressure.

Hauenstein, L. S., Kals, S. V., & Harburg, E. Work status, work satisfaction, and blood pressure among married black and white women. Psychology of Women Quarterly, Summer 1977, 1(4), 334-349.
     In Detroit during 1968 and 1969 a survey was made of 508 married women. A random group was selected

whose ages were between 25 and 60; all married and
living with their spouses; with relatives around
their own age living in the Detroit metropolitan
area; composed of the predominant race of the census
tract they lived in. The respondents lived in four
areas of Detroit: a black high-stress area; black
low-stress area; white high-stress area; white
low-stress area. A definition of high stress is a)
low socioeconomic resources, b) residential instability, c) family instability, d) high crime
rate, and e) high population density.

A nurse of the same race as the respondent approached individuals selected for the random sample.
A hour and a half interview was composed of standard
survey questionnaire items with precoded response
categories about the women's medical history,
financial and educational status, and other demographic variables. The women's attitudes and
perceptions about themselves and their life situations were included in the questionnaire, as well
as such things a skin color, size and crowdedness of
dwelling, and cooperativeness. During the interview
the nurse took three blood pressure measurements in
the first half hour.

The blood pressure levels of married women in
relation to work-related variables such as work
load, satisfaction with work, reported strain, and
evaluated performance were examined. The conclusions were: "a) Differences in work load were
unrelated to blood pressure levels. Currently
unemployed working women had lower levels. b)
Housewives reporting tension about housework and
being critical of own performance had higher blood
pressure. c) Working wives with a strong commitment
to the work role had higher blood pressure levels,
as did those women who were relatively low on
indicators of job achievement." The premise studied
is that stress may play an important role in blood
pressure levels and that chronic exposure to a
stressful situation may lead to chronically elevated
levels of blood pressure. The work and attitudinal
variables studied concerned work load, satisfaction
with housework and job, and indicators of job

history and job motivation. The results found that
those women committed to the work role had higher
blood pressure levels. Higher blood pressure levels
were related to low job achievement.

Hendrickson, B. Teacher burnout: How to recognize
  it; What to do about it. Learning, 1979, 7(5),
  38-39.
  This article presents some ideas for coping with
and/or avoiding burnout. The author, a freelance
writer and former teacher, lists 16 specific tasks
to employ in combating burnout. She also presents
brief case studies of teachers who have utilized
some of these strategies for avoiding or coping with
burnout.
  Carol S. combats burnout by incorporating change,
making her teaching program different each year.
Another of her secret weapons is an outside activity, tennis, as well as carefully protecting her
out-of-classroom life from encroachment by her work.
  Michael L. became burned out but didn't realize it
until three years later after taking another job out
of desperation. The point in this case is that it
is important to realize that it is not always your
fault when you are burning out. Some factors are
under your control and some are not. The ability to
separate the two can facilitate coping with burnout
and making the decisions of how to go about it.
  The case of Nancy F. focuses both on the advantage
of a team approach and the underlying motivation of
of a common extracurricular activity which keeps
them interested and involved even when the going
gets tough. Some of the tactics listed by the
author include:
  1.   Retreats with your colleagues to get away
       from the source of the problems and
       develop a "staff approach" to your common
       problems.
  2.   In-service programs in areas of interest
       that are not directly related to classroom
       responsibilities. The greatest defense
       against burnout is personal growth.

3.   Change, try a new curriculum, it will
     challenge you.
4.   Change grade levels.
5.   Team teach.

Holland, R. P. Special educator burnout.
  Educational Horizon, Winter 1982, 60(2), 58-64.
  Stress is defined in the article as "a positive or
negative reaction occurring when there is a substantial imbalance (perceived or real) between environmental demands and the response capability of the
individual." Stress leads to burnout in the areas
where negative stressors increase a lack of
self-worth and loss of concern for clients. Symptoms include detachment from students or clients,
physical reactions, inability to cope, cynicism, and
personal and professional problems. Holland delin-
eates first-degree burnout, which is mild and
results in fatigue and irritability. Second-degree
lasts two or three weeks and is moderate, while
third-degree has stress-related physical complications such as insomnia, hypertension, back pain,
arthritis, allergies, sexual problems, cancer, and
diseases of adaptation.
  There are various indicators of burnout among
special educators: time spent recruiting, hiring
due to turnover; role confusion, resentment and
problems between teachers, administrators, and
special educators; and resistance to bureaucratic
regulations and procedures for handicapped students.
  Stress and burnout drain good teachers from the
system and lower the quality of education for the
students. Teachers become isolated and often
exhibit the side effects of alcohol abuse, mental
illness, absenteeism, and depression. Other physical problems include heart problems, headaches,
ulcers, and kidney problems.
  Special causes of stress among special educators
are inadequate pay, lack of mobility, budgets,
paperwork, lack of adequate training, lack of
rewards, violence, lack of administrative support,
lack of perceived student success, and pupil loads,
as well as interactions with parents. One study

felt that the best predictor for burnout was the discrepancy between the teacher's perception of the role and other's expectations of the role.

There are various prevention strategies for burnout. Some are environmental changes involving administrative plans, attitude changes, negotiating job specifications, new teacher orientation and support, job transfers, and support staff. Other ways to prevent or alleviate burnout occur in the personal area. These include advance knowledge of the job situation, realistic goals, planning, work delegation, team teaching, workshops, support groups, exercise, and hobbies. Meditation, retreats, and stress counseling are also advocated. Special educators are under more pressure than other teachers to curtail their burnout because the students they teach are not as flexible as other students and are more detrimentally affected by an ineffective teacher.

House, J. S. <u>Work stress and social support.</u>
   Addison-Wesley: Reading, MA: 1981.
   There are four broad classes or types of supportive behaviors or acts. These four classes should be considered as potential forms of support. Emotional support, which involves providing empathy, caring, love and trust, seems to be the most important. Instrumental support is the most clearly distinguished form emotional support, at least in theory, involving instrumental behaviors that directly help other people do their work, take care of them, or help them pay their bills. Informational support means providing a person with information that the person can use in coping with personal and environmental problems. Appraisal support, like informational support, involves only transmission of information, rather than the affect involved in emotional support or the aid involved in instrumental support. However, the information can be explicitly of implicity evaluative. Social support, then, is a flow of emotional concern, instrumental aid, information, and/or appraisal (information relevant to self-evaluation) between people.

A wide range of evidence from laboratory and field studies of both animals and people indicates that the presence of social relationships, especially if they are characterized by supportive behavior, can reduce the experience of stress, improve health and/or buffer the impact of stress on health.

Although a great deal is not known about what makes some work environments more supportive than others, researchers have identified a set of factors that seem important. The supportiveness of supervisors, coworkers, or other informal sources of support at work is a function of both the characteristics that individuals bring with them to their work role and those that are acquired and reinforced in the work setting. There are a number of organizational attributes that affect the levels of support available. The structure of the organization and of the jobs in it can enhance or inhibit the potential for support. Some empirical evidence indicates that specialization and fractionation of jobs and the creation of highly isolated work roles is deleterious to levels of both supervisor and coworker support. The converse appears to foster social support. It is clearly possible to train supervisors, union stewards, and employees themselves in giving and receiving social support. The extent to which the organizational, technological, and personnel policies of an organization tend to foster or dampen levels of support appears to be largely a function of the goals and priorities of the organizations' top management and the larger economic system. The major determinants of the socially supportive inputs provided to individuals by others are (1) their ability and motivation to provide support and (2) the degree to which the larger interpersonal and social context condones and supports such efforts. Nonwork support appears to vary as a function of (1) the general level of social and family integration in an area, (2) the characteristics of specific family and friendship networks, and (3) the degree to which the work roles of people facilitate or hinder the development of nonwork relationships.

If social support is to be effective in reducing stress, preventing health problems, and increasing workers' ability to adapt to the irreducible stresses at work, all people must be able to obtain support from persons with whom they routinely work--superiors, subordinates, and coworkers or colleagues. Making individuals more supportive toward each other involves:
access, training, rewards, reinforcement, and combining research and practice.
The Table of Contents includes:
1. Work stress, social support, and health: the promise and the problems.
2. The nature of social support.
3. Effects of social support on stress and health I: of mice, men, and women.
4. Effects of social support on stress and health II: the work setting.
5. The determinants of social support.
6. What should and can be done?

How to deal with stress on the job. U.S. News and World Report, March 13, 1978, pp. 80-81.
Stress is a health problem that has come under scrutiny in various occupations. A certain bank has a psychiatrist come in monthly to help employees deal with stress. Nurses in a California hospital have a "wake" to deal with their grief after the death of a patient. School administrators in Michigan are learning relaxation techniques while Stanford University has added a course on coping with stress to its graduate business program.
There are both positive and negative results of stress. Some workers thrive on tension; it gives them a sense of excitement about their jobs. Others get high blood pressure, heart attacks, and insomnia, which often result in absenteeism, termination, or even accidents.
One cause of stress that occurs in several of the most stress-producing jobs (laborer, secretary, machine operator, and laboratory technician) is the lack of input about how the job is performed. A cause of stress might be the piped-in music, which

some people love and others hate. Another cause
that produces ambivalent reactions is the lack of
walls, which is supposed to promote togetherness but
eliminates privacy for some. Other sources are the
loss of a sense of value in work well done and lack
of communication on the job.

There are certain remedies that are commonly
suggested. One is exercise of any type, as long as
it takes place regularly. Yet another is job
termination, but a problem with this is that it
reinforces a lack of problem solving and may reoccur
as a solution. A realistic cultivation of interests
outside the job may be the most effective way to
treat stress.

Hulin, C. L., & Smith, P. C. Sex differences in job
   satisfaction. Journal of Applied Psychology,
   1964, 48(2), 88-92.

Several research studies seem to conclude that
higher job levels and higher wages generally contribute to higher satisfaction; that the type of
leadership has certain effects on job satisfaction,
but these effects are modified greatly by situational factors; that age and tenure seems to be positively related to job satisfaction; and that job
satisfaction seems to be related to a general life
adjustment-maladjustment factor.

The findings concerning sex differences permit no
neat cogent relationship. In the area of satisfaction with teaching, women report being more satisfied than men, yet women were more poorly adjusted
than male teachers. Other contradictory findings
concerning sex difference and job satisfaction
center around women generally earning less money and
more frequently being found in lower-level jobs.
The hypothesis was that female workers should be
less satisfied than male workers. The study found
female workers significantly less satisfied than
their male counterparts.

Sex per se is not the crucial factor leading to
either high or low satisfaction. It is, rather, the
entire constellation of variables that consistently
covary with sex; for example, pay, job level,

promotion opportunities, societal norms, etc., are
likely to be causing the difference in job satisfaction. In each of the samples the women were receiving less pay and were working on lower level jobs
than the men.

Humphrey, R. D. Are you a stress carrier? Training
and Development Journal, February 1978, 32(2),
38-41.
The rate at which technology has outstripped the
ability to adjust to the environment is of significant concern. Many people in management positions
are carriers of stress-producing styles and are
unaware of the impact this has on subordinates,
peers, and the effective operation of the organization. Yet others are aware that they are stress
carriers and do not have the willingness or capacity
to change, or have decided to continue with their
present management style because they are unwilling
to pay the price that change always brings about.
Being a stress carrier gets in the way of individual and organizational effectiveness. Not only does
the organization suffer but so does the individual.
The family and friends bear the burden of the
frustration and torment. Once the destructiveness
of certain styles is made apparent to a manager and
he is willing to face up to it, the manager begins
to realize that if he elects to continue with this
style he is actually undermining the business. Most
of the managers who are confronted with this option
usually decide that no matter how painful the change
process, it's worth it. Along with the manager's
responsibility to change is the obligation of the
staff to work him through the discomfort and the
conflict that change always presents.
People possess the capacity to reduce the amount of
stress they carry; through reflection, awareness,
decision to change, willingness to risk, practice of
the new style of behavior and a continual pursuit of
personal growth.

Hyson, M. "Playing with kids all day": Job stress
in early childhood education. Journal of the

National Association for the Education of Young Children, January 1982, 37(2), 25-32.

One of the unusual stresses in early childhood education is the presence of too much variety, which creates too much stimulation resulting in psychological overload. Children are unpredictable and their methods and manners of response to what the teacher plans can either be acceptance or uproar. Because there is much unstructured time in an early childhood educational setting, it is hard for the teachers to measure progress. The resultant ambiguity concerning their own role performance augments stress.

Colleague relationships can be stressors because everyone must work together cooperatively despite personal idiosyncracies. Societal pressures to achieve status do not give much recognition to people who "play with kids all day." Another source of stress is the grief/loss syndrome at the end of each school year when the teachers "lose" the student to whom they have become close.

Burnout is evidenced in increased anger, apathy, blocking, depression, helplessness, headaches, and loss of resistance to disease. Some coping methods need to be brought into play in order to begin to recover the physical and psychological effects of stress. Further, education, curriculum planning, changes in room layout, and new structures for feedback might all be considered. Assertion and direct confrontation are other options to effect changes. Finally, personal commitment to exercise, good nutrition, meditation, and support groups can round out a program of burnout recovery.

Ivancevich, J. M. Effects of goal setting on performance and job satisfaction. Journal of Applied Psychology, 1976, 61(5), 605-612.

Locke's theory of goal setting has been extensively tested in a laboratory setting. The purpose of this research report is to test the hypothesis in a field setting. Four general objectives are set by the authors: first, it tests three hypotheses of

implied superiority of the participative over
assigned goal setting; second, investigates how
sales personnel react to formal goal-setting
training; third, sets multiple hard-performance
goals simultaneously; fourth, approximates time
after formal training at which decreases in
performance and/or satisfaction occur. Data was
collected for the project at three month intervals
after the initial training.

Similar studies were discussed and a description
of this research was outlined. The results of this
study did show support for the Locke theory. The
statement can be made that setting specific goals
is more productive than not setting goals. The
study showed that Locke's theory can be applied to
field studies of sales personnel. It also concluded, however, that as the training period dissipated
into the past, there was less improvement noted,
particularly at the 12-month interval after training.

Jenkins, C. D. Recent evidence supporting
   psychologic and social risk factors for coronary
   heart disease. New England Journal of Medicine,
   1976, 294, 987-994; 1033-1038.

Studies of coronary disease have shown such
variables as elevated blood pressure and serum
cholesterol, cigarette smoking, obesity, diabetes,
and family history of coronary disease to be
factors predictive of elevated risk of incidence of
this disease in groups and in individuals. However, not all of the standard risk factors are valid
predictors of coronary disease in all cultural
settings.

Although much is known about the precursors of the
disease, at least an equal amount remains unknown.
Psychosocial and behavioral variables offer the
possibility of accounting for at least part of the
causes of coronary disease remaining unexplained.
Personality and stress may also be involved in the
pathogenesis of coronary disease. Sociological
influences, habits, and personality structure all
are decisive in the development of coronary disease.

The empirical research dealing with psychological, social, and behavioral factors associated with the risk of coronary disease involves sociological indexes, social mobility and status incongruity, anxiety, and neuroticism.

It was found that there are differences in coronary disease incidence and mortality between populations of different countries. The highest rates in all age groups were found in Finland and the United States. Early in the process of urbanization and industrialization, the upper socioeconomic classes are at a higher risk of coronary disease, whereas towards the end of the process the lower economic classes have higher risks. Problems and conflicts in the areas of financial, family, work, coworkers and superiors were all associated with development of angina pectoris.

Social mobility and status incongruity may be valid predicators only in certain places and eras, only for certain presentations of coronary disease, or only when other variables are also present.

Depression, anxiety, and somaticizing have all been associated with coronary disease, but neuroticism is nonspecifically related to general morbidity. Various psychological defenses and reactions to challenge have been associated with risk of coronary disease. The central nervous system is an important factor in coronary disease. There has also been much evidence in the last five years by several nations that gives strong support to the position that the coronary-prone behavior pattern, type A, is associated with prevalence of coronary disease in a variety of populations. The studies of the type A behavior pattern are greater in number and in consistency of positive findings than any study of the major categories of psychosocial variables.

Johnson, J. L. The ministry can be hazardous to your health. Leadership, Winter, 1980, 1 (1), 25-30.

Some of the results of the long hours and hectic schedule that most ministers choose to follow are:

colitis, diverticulitis, migrane, chest pain, high blood pressure, and heart disease. One factor in pastoral abuse of time is that the pastor feels that since he is working for God he should be able to do more than other humans. The pastor is expected by the congregation to be at every meeting of every group, to do everything from janitorial work to writing well-thought-out sermons. He is also evaluated by every person in the congregation based on each person's individual standards and is told regularly when he does something that does not please someone. One suggestion for a new look in the pastorate is to set up an authority structure and follow it. In that way the pastor can begin to delegate authority and call for accountability from the people he works with.

There will probably always be strain in the ministry, but there are ways to prepare for it. One is to plan medical checkups a year in advance and follow the doctor's orders. Another is to clear one whole day of church activities and relax. Daily exercise is another method of dealing with stress. One of the most difficult, but effective methods is to learn to say "no" to events the pastor does not need to attend. Another is to learn business management principles. Cultivating a personal friend in the church and setting aside time for family are two final steps in dealing with the omnipresent demands and stresses of the ministry.

Johnson, J. W. More about stress and some management techniques. Journal of School Health, January 1981, 51 (1), 36-42.

A large amount of stress in life today is due to change--in society, in values, in physical environments, in organizations, and in our personal selves. All change progresses in the following manner: change = psychological loss = anger = depression. Morever, as change promotes stress, stress promotes illness. A stress-quotient rating scale and children's rating of stressful events are included   in   tables.

The Morale Curve (developed by Menninger at the

Center for Applied Behavioral Sciences) suggests
looking at change and stress as a process. This
process includes the arrival period when one is
anxious and enthusiastic; the engagement period,
when one realizes the loss of what was left behind;
the acceptance period, when one is angered and
eventually reassesses; and the reentry period, when
one once again becomes anxious at the change, yet
satisfied with completion.   The engagement period
is based on the premise that as change becomes
intense, one reaches out for familiar roots.

The capacity to deal with stress varies from
individual to individual. One response is the
traditional fight or flight response which may lead
to sleeping more or arguing more.   Illness is
another response and although dangerous, can
provide long-term positive benefits if one recog-
nizes the need to stop and take inventory to solve
the problem.   In addition, adaptive responses can
include psychological defense mechanisms which may
surface as regression to childlike behaviors.   In
general, defense mechanisms are largely unconscious
and tend to be used in combinations.

These mechanisms, however, act only to relieve
stress, but do not act to remove the causes and
accumulation of stress. The author suggests taking
inventory of things that are causing stress,
including societal, situational, or personal and
personality-linked causes. It is only after this
process that one can develop appropriate management
techniques. Although the Menninger Foundation is
cautious about simple solutions to complex stress
problems, the following suggestions are offered:

1.   Talk/share (get feedback).
2.   Anticipate stressful situations and be
     prepared.
3.   Find enjoyment (if jogging is boring,
     find another technique).
4.   Sublimate (use agressive energies to hit
     a racquetball instead of a dog).
5.   Exercise to rid self of aggression.
6.   Develop a philosophy of life (religion
     may offer support that rational answers

are not always possible for complex
problems).

Jones, M. A., & Emanuel, J. The stages and
  recovery steps of teacher burnout. Education
  Digest, May 1981, 46(3), 9-11.
The avoidance of the burnout syndrome is a
problem facing many in the helping profession.
This article examines the steps teachers go through
during burnout and possible steps for avoiding or
remediating the symptoms.
  The burnout syndrome can be experienced through
three stages: heating-up, boiling, and explosion.
The heating-up stage brings about dissatisfaction,
isolation, and feelings of rejection with little
positive reinforcement. Being a teacher is no
longer a thrill, the whole atmosphere has faded.
In the boiling stage the teacher experiences
helplessness, intense frustration, and begins to
question his usefulness.   In the last stage,
explosion, the individual begins to feel one of two
ways: either as a robot who chooses to escape
frustration and disenchantment by mechanically
performing the task of teaching, or the individual
may explode in open rebellion against the whole
teaching profession and leave it.
  The burnout recovery process involves taking a
serious look at the self, realizing the feelings of
frustration and isolation, and taking the risk to
express one's personal needs openly. Secondly it
involves a more active professional investment,
assuming personal initiative and conducting inservice at school. The last stage involves the
ability to cope with the explosion stage; professional counseling is suggested.
  All of the recovery stages assume a deep and real
concern for the professional commitment of the
individual. They also assume that professional and
personal competency contributes to issues of
self-worth and job satisfaction. Nevertheless, the
alternatives are examined that demand a commitment
and a life-style change. It is necessary and
important that the burned-out individual not see

himself as a casuality, but view his decision as a major strength.

Justice, B., Gold, R. S., & Klein, J. P.   Life
   events and burnout.   Journal of Psychology, July
   1981, 108, 219-26.
Burnout is viewed as a primary problem of the helping profession, especially since one of it's most important features appears to be a loss of concern for the people who look to the helping professionals for support and help.

There are many signs and symptoms that may appear in regard to burnout, which are categorized into four areas: emotional, behavioral, somatic, and defensive. There also exist several factors in which burnout may result: change in one's life, a lack of fit between an individual and one's job, and a conflict between one's own values and those required by the job.

A survey of 54 males and 134 females, most of whom were in direct service positions of a counseling and social work nature, were given a battery on tests, including a measure of burnout, life events, and items concerning satisfaction with work and life in general. The higher one's score on the burnout scale, the less satisfied the individual tends to be.

Results from the data report that little differ-ence was indicated in the likelihood of burnout for men and women or between those filling any particu-lar job category. While many differences exist in the nature of these job settings, the influence of life events are significantly related to the probability of burnout. There also exists a significant difference in the likelihood of burnout between those in public sector jobs and those working in the private sector.

The only differences in total life-change scores between these two groups were the significant differences in the number of positive events reported. The negative events make their impact on burnout more severe, but the positive events reduce the likelihood and severity of burnout. It it does

not appear to be the case that burnout is strictly
related to what happens on the job but that it is
related to other factors as well.

Kahn, R. L. Conflict, ambiguity, and overload:
  Three elements in job stress. Occupational
  Mental Health, Spring 1973, 3, 2-9.
The productivity of organizations and the affect
of organizations on individuals were the bases of
research at the Institute for Social Research at
the University of Michigan. The variables studied
in the research were objective environment; psychological environment; response; criteria of mental
and physical health and disease; enduring properties of the person; and interpersonal relations.
The goal of the research was to develop a "theory
of mental health as it is affected by the contemporary environment of the individual, taking into
account the facts of genetic endowment and personality insofar as necessary to make sense of the
environmental effects."
Six projects were given as examples to show the
differentiation of the stress concept. The con-
flict-and- ambiguity intensive study focused on 53
persons to examine the degree of conflict, harmony,
ambiguity, or clarity required in their vocational
roles. A national survey included 1500 respondents
in an effort to examine role conflict and ambiguity
in work situations. A sales office study resulted
in data that demonstrated how disagreement affects
performance. Secondary- analysis-role-conflict
data was administered to NASA employees and students to differentiate the concept of role conflict. The Goddard Space Flight Center Study
studied the factor of overload as a form of role
conflict and a source of stress in certain jobs. A
Kennedy Space Center Study included measures of
strain in a longitudinal base.
Individuals were consistently found to have lower
job satisfaction, greater job-related tension and
less confidence in the organization when subjected
to high role conflict. Persons with poor interpersonal relations as well as those in positions

requiring creative problem-solving, such as managerial or supervisory, also experienced role
conflict.

Personality and interpersonal relations were
influenced by role conflict. Those persons who are
anxiety prone had a more intense reaction to
conflict than others. Introverted individuals
tended to have more tension and greater deterioration of interpersonal relations when they experienced role conflict. Some individuals reduced role
conflict through distortion of what they perceived
to be managerial and supervisory expectations.
Role conflict also influenced role overload which
is: "the amount of pressure felt to do more work,
the feeling of not being able to finish one's work
in an ordinary day, and the feeling that the amount
of work interferes with how well it gets done."
Quantitative load (the amount of work) and qualitative load (the difficulty of the work) were found
to be related to job tension and self-esteem. In
some administrators quantitative overload was
related to self-esteem. A large ratio of individuals in highly technical fields were found to have
symptoms of strain with quantitative overload and
lowered self-esteem when under a qualitative
overload.

When a person does not have enough information to
perform a task adequately but still must execute
the task he is experiencing role ambiguity.
Commonly, the individuals experience feelings of
confusion about what is expected of them by colleagues and supervisors. Many of the negative
feelings-- sense of futility, low self-confidence--
resulted from a need for structure that was not
available. Some ambiguous job-related feelings
included: threat to physical or mental well-being,
job dissatisfaction, and lack of utilization of
skills and knowledge.

Kahn, R. L. Job burnout: Prevention and remedies.
   Public Welfare, Spring 1978, 61-63.
   Dr. Kahn offers definitions, remedies, and
interesting correlations between stress and

burnout. He begins by defining burnout as a
syndrome of inappropriate attitudes toward clients
and towards self, often associated with uncomfortable physical and emotional symptoms ranging from
exhaustion and insomnia to migraine and ulcer.
Deterioration of performance is a frequent additional element in the syndrome.

Laboratory studies and research findings are
presented to show the relationship between stress
and burnout. The lower a person is on the
socioeconomic scale of occupations, the more
evidence of physical and emotional strain. Heavy
physical demands produce physiological signs of
strain while difficult mental tasks cause similar
strains. Evidence shows a high level of strain in
those who are responsible for the reward or punish-
ment of all participants in a situation, including
the one made responsible. One of the most prevalent job-related stresses is that of role conflict.
The most frequent type of stress is job overload,
which means too much to be done within a short
period of time and with limited resources. The
physical effects of overload were found to include
elevated cholesterol levels, elevated heart rate,
higher rate of peptic ulcers, hypertension, diabetes, etc.

It is not always possible to select an employee
who will be resistant to stress and burnout. Rigid
personalities are found to suffer less from role
conflict but their behavior is not an asset in some
stressful jobs. Instead of selecting resistant
employees, many organizations are reducing the
stress in the workplace. The work day is
shortened, work assignments are varied and reduced;
part-time employees are used more frequently and
direct involvement with clients is reduced.

The author sees the ultimate support to relieve
stress and burnout in service organizations. By
increasing the linkage between professional service
agencies and networks of social support, the
employee rate of burnout would be reduced in the
helping professions.

Kalleberg, A. Work values and job rewards: A
 theory of job satisfaction. American
 Sociological Review, 1977, 42, 124-143.
Of great interest to social scientists is the
concept of job satisfaction as the result of a
personal-value system which assumes that work that
satisfies one's needs furthers the dignity of the
human individual. Work that does not satisfy one's
needs limits the development of personal potential
and is, therefore, negatively valued.
The objectives are to conceptualize and empirical-
ly examine the relationship between job satisfaction and the work values and job rewards associated
with dimensions of work: intrinsic, convenience,
financial relations with coworkers, career opportunities, and resource adequacy.
The data were obtained through personal interviews
coming from the quality-of-employment survey that
is representative of the national employed civilian
labor force. The data consist of perceptions of
these individuals regarding characteristics of
themselves and their jobs.
It has been found that rewards have a large and
positive effect on job satisfaction while values
have a smaller significance. Rewards also have
positive net effects on job satisfaction while
values have a smaller significance. The highest
level of job satisfaction will be experienced by
those workers with high rewards and low values,
while the lowest levels of job satisfaction will be
experienced by those workers with low rewards and
high values. Both values and rewards have independent effects on job satisfaction. The extent to
which workers are able to obtain perceived job
rewards is a function of their degree of control
over their employment situations. The failure of
workers to achieve their values with respect to the
content of the task itself is the prime cause of
their dissatisfaction with their jobs.
Factors associated with the intrinsic dimension
have the greatest affects for producing overall job
satisfaction. The financial dimension has the
second-greatest affect on job satisfaction, since

wages, fringe benefits, and job security constitute the major sources of access to almost all goods and services. Convenience and relations with coworkers have small net affects on job satisfaction.

Workers in an industrial society have little control over the distribution of rewards to positions, but they do have a certain amount of control over their attainment of these positions. Workers with a relatively wide range of opportunities should be able to find jobs that provide greater rewards than workers whose range of choice is relatively restricted. Workers with more resources should have greater power obtaining job rewards than workers with fewer resources. In reality, people do not attain rewards, they obtain jobs.

Kanner, A. D., Kafry, D., & Pines, A. Conspicuous in its absence: The lack of positive conditions as a source of stress. Journal of Human Stress, December 1978, 4(4), 33-39.

Variety, autonomy, self-actualization, and success are all examples of positive conditions that, for many, are the most crucial in life. The absence of these conditions would be a source of great stress, often leading to a sense of failure, alienation, disappointment and distress. The absence of positive conditions could constitute a unique source of stress and a failure to consider this source would be a serious omission. Two hypotheses have been generated by this line of reasoning: (1) the absence of positive conditions and the presence of negative conditions are both substantial sources of stress, and (2) the two sources of stress are independent of each other.

In a study of 289 subjects, employed in a variety of occupations including business, science, art, human services, homemaking, and clerical work, tedium and the lack of positive features were researched using a 21-item questionnaire. The questionnaire was designed to reflect the subjects' appraisal of three aspects of tedium: physical, emotional, and attitudinal exhaustion.

The overall results indicate the (1) tedium in life and work is substantially and independently affected by the presence of negative and the absence of positive life and work conditions, (2) life satisfaction/ dissatisfaction is strongly related to positive conditions but is only modestly related to negative conditions, and (3) in sharp contrast to tedium, work satisfaction/dissatisfaction is exclusively a function of positive conditions.

The positive and negative conditions function differentially as sources of stress, depending on which type of outcome is being examined and, especially in regard to the satisfaction/dissatisfaction data, on the settings in which the outcomes occur.

Most stress research looks only at the presence of negative conditions, thereby obscuring the possibly mitigating influence of positive conditions.

Karasek, R. A., Jr. Job demands, job decision latitude, and mental strain: Implications for job redesign. Administrative Science Quarterly, June, 1979, 24, 285-307.

Strain develops from job demands in conjunction with job- decision latitude. This study indicates that a redesign of work processes may allow more decision latitude, thus reducing mental strain without affecting job demands. Psychological strain is seen as an outcome of work environment combined with decision- making freedoms. It is the constraints in decision-making that affect the executives as well as the workers with low-class jobs and little freedom for decision-making. The worker who can't make job decisions, or makes few in his job while pressure is maintained for output, is most subject to job strain. Also pointed out is that the more active jobs are more satisfying (with high-decision latitude), and depression is reduced, even though demand is great. Passive jobs (low demand and decision latitude) are dissatisfying. It appears that strain is minimized by more decision latitude, independent of work-load demand. It must be noted, however, that increasing decision latitude in existing comfortable jobs can be detrimental, especially when those jobs already have some degree of decision latitude. For low status jobs, more decision latitude can relieve strain.

Kasl, S. V. Mental health and work environment: An examination of the evidence. Journal of Occupational Medicine, June, 1973, 15(6), 509-518.

This study examined the link of mental health and the impact on work performance and the accompanying variables. The categories of mental health include: functional effectiveness, well-being, mastery and competence, and psychiatric signs and symptoms. The categories form the general basis of the definition of mental health. The meaning of work is characterized by: effort, purpose, economic gain, and cyclical nature. Though the concept of work, as given, is limited, it applies to most activities that give a source of income.

A study was conducted of working men and retired men. Most working men stated that they would continue working even if they were financially able to stop. Among professionals work was found to be a source of status, which increased with job level. Individuals who have creative or intrinsically interesting work may have a greater association with the value of work in relation to their psychological well-being.

Factors influencing job satisfaction and mental health are varied. Low job satisfaction is related to: conditions at work, job content, work group (coworkers), supervision/decision making, the organization, wages, and promotion. To help rectify the above conditions, job enlargement is believed to increase job satisfaction.

Although evidence has previously attributed job satisfaction as an index of motivation, it is more probable that a positive relationship occurs when "good performance is followed by extrinsic (pay and promotion) or intrinsic (use of valued skills) rewards." It also has been found that absenteeism and performance are not as strongly indicative of vocational adjustment as had previously been thought.

Individual differences are critical in achievement motivation and aspirations. Evidence suggests that individuals "with high need for achievement will be more dissatisfied regardless of how high a job level they have reached." Poor mental health has been linked to individuals with high educational level and relatively low occupational level. Older workers have been found to have higher job satisfaction and better attendance records because they are not as concerned with promotion and job security. Some influencing factors are: occupational level of siblings, age, societal barriers, health, etc.

Some conclusions drawn concerning what affects mental health in relation to work are: the work environment and job demands, the person's abilities and needs, and the discrepancies between job demands and personal abilities. It is difficult to determine what an individual needs in terms of satisfaction and self-image in relation to employment because the studies are unable to adequately measure such variables.

From studies done in the area of worker mental health in relation to employment, it is evident that few cause-and-effect relationships can be positively identified. There is strong evidence that there is a definite relationship, but other variables have to be studied before definitive results can be obtained.

Kehl, D. G. Burnout: The risk of reaching too high. Christianity Today, Nov. 20, 1981, 26 (20), 26-28.

Burnout is analagous to a flashbulb exploding, to a tool that stops with a shower of sparks, and to a motor that grinds to a smoking halt. People burn out in similar fashion. High, unrealistic aspirations coupled with a lack of visible results often result in burnout. The gap between expectation and reality can produce a feeling of fatigue and depletion as well as physical ailments, anger, detachment, and depression.

Christians are susceptible to burnout because of their high expectations and goals, which can be coupled with the work ethic that does not regard relaxation or vacations as good use of time.

There are some noneffective ways of coping with burnout: excessive work, materialism, divorce, gambling, sex, and chemical abuse. However, there are some positive ways of coping, beginning with a real sense of self-awareness. People need to set realistic goals, accepting their own limitations in the process. If false motivation provokes burnout, then Christians need to be motivated by the love of Christ and not looking to men for all approval. Another source of coping is renewal at all levels-- physical, emotional and spiritual. These might include exercise, relaxation, sports, reading, hobbies, and conversation. The key to a healthy whole life is balance in all areas. Burnout occurs when reality and aspirations are out of balance.

Keller, R. T. Role conflict and ambiguity: Correlates with job satisfaction and values. Personnel Psychology, 28, 1975, 57-64.

This article is a summary of a research grant testing the Kahn theory of role dynamics and to expand on the theory. The Kahn theory found decreased job satisfaction where role conflict and ambiguity existed. The author was also able to support Kahn's predictions through a review of the literature, which he summarized.

Fifty-one subjects participated in the study. Role conflict and ambiguity were tested through two scales developed by previous researchers. The Job Description Index measured job satisfaction and the Study of Values test was used to evaluate values related to personality.

In the final analysis, the author mentions that his study partially supports the Kahn theory and in comparison with other research on the topic, opposite results were found.

In conclusion, implications for personnel practices were discussed. Recommendations were made
that role expectations should be made clear to the
employee, since lack of clarity can cause conflict
and lead to decreased satisfaction and poor job
performance.

Klerman, G. L. The age of melancholy. Psychology
   Today, 1979, 4, 37-42, 88.
A series of data is examined as evidence that a
pervasive mood of anxiety is giving way to depression and despair as dominant moods in modern
man. Depression is also looked at as an evolutionary phenomenon for our species. Though the capacity
to become depressed seems not to be an exclusively
human one, it has been a part of our evolutionary
heritage and has played a biologically adaptive
function.
This study intended to show a correlation between
depression and the effects of disruptions of
attachment bonding on human beings by looking at a
sample of 370 persons (185 clinically depressed
individuals and a random sample of 185 normal
individuals).
Both samples were interviewed for the presence or
absence of various types of life stress. When
patients and those in the control group controls
were compared, there was no statistically significant difference between them regarding entrances,
but there was a dramatic difference with regard to
exits. The depressives had experienced far more
episodes of loss and separation in the 6 to 12
months prior to the interviews than did the control
group.
The proposition is made that the sharp separation
of old and new attachment bonding is a relatively
new experience in that most of the social-support
systems on which our forebears relied until recently have emphasized some degree of stability and
continuity. The three most common social support
systems have been the family, the church, and the
immediate neighborhood, which acted as buttresses
against disruptive emotional states. These support

systems are in various degrees of disarray.

The limits to the theory that all or most depression can be explained as a reaction to loss and
separation are: 1) loss and separation are not the
antecedent events in all clinical depressions; 2)
not all individuals who are exposed to loss,
separation, or dissolution of attachment bonds
become depressed; and 3) loss, separation, and
disruption are not specific to depression.

The factors of stress seem to result in a general
propensity for illness, perhaps more so for depression, but in the evidence, their influence is
not conclusive and cannot explain the clinical
phenomena by itself. Some factors offered are
genetic: early life experiences in which the
individual became sensitive to loss, lowered
self-esteem, changes in the social-support system,
the absence of the extended family, and the inability to make friends or develop group supports.

Knutsen, E. J. On the emotional well-being of
    psychiatrists: Overview and rationale. American
    Journal of Psychoanalysis, Summer 1977, 37(2),
    123-129.

It is very important and necessary for a psychiatrist to have a stable emotional state and to be
competent. There are extensive ramifications
relating to the emotional well-being of psychiatrists. Physicians, in general, have a higher rate
of suicide, and at an earlier age, than the male
population as a whole. The next most serious
mental health problems are: alcohol and drug
abuse, depression, paranoia, and psychotic disorga-
nization. Problems that may afflict the emotional
well-being of psychiatrists include: anxi-
ety/depression, psychosomatic manifestations,
questioning and doubting, and questions about
personal and professional growth.

Broad categories that specifically affect physicians and psychiatrists and their emotional
well-being are examined: 1) causes of ill-being:
are physicians subject to certain stresses or
emotional difficulty? 2) prevention of ill-being

and the enhancement of well-being: are constructive coping behaviors being used to maintain a
positive emotional state? 3) case finding and
referral: the physician and medical community have
an obligation to be accountable to their patients
and colleagues: if a physician needs help for
himself he should be responsible to himself and his
patients and seek the needed treatment; 4) treatment: physicians frequently have difficulty
accepting/following the recommended treatment for
their health problems; 5) disciplinary actions:
what is the best procedure for disciplining an
impaired physician--sanctions or therapeutic
handling? 6) ethical and legal issues: how does
the legal community distinguish between issues that
could have legal implications but are also ethical
issues among their colleagues, when is the doctor-patient relationship ended?
The assumptive world affects the professional and
his sense of well-being. The assumptive world
guides a person's perceptions and behavior and is
an interacting set of values, expectations, and
images of oneself and others. An individual is
entitled to the following in his assumptive world:
1) to recognize his own uniqueness and to provide
for his own self-care, 2) to develop a stance of
continual learning whatever the source of learning,
3) to recognize the necessity of continuing experiences of personal validation, 4) to legitimately
raise questions concerning values and the meaning
of life. When the assumptive world will not allow
for questioning and violates individual humanity,
it generates feelings of ill-being within that
person.

Kobasa, S. C. Stressful life events, personality,
    and health: An inquiry into hardiness. Journal
    of Personality and Social Psychology, January
    1979, 37(1), 1-11.
The rate of illness, the personality, and the
stressful life events are examined in relation to
the probable precipitation of somatic and psychological disease. Research has shown that

individuals experiencing frequent stressful events
are more likely to suffer serious illness. A
stressful life is one that causes changes in an
average person's normal routine. For the average
individual living in a modern, urban society, it is
difficult to avoid stress and the possible opportunities that accompany it. In order to avoid
stress, a better, or more successful life may be
lost to an urban resident.

Researchers have studied probable reasons why some
individuals under high stress remain healthy while
others under low stress may become ill. Some
researchers have tried to link onset of illness and
stressful life events to the theory of Hans Selye.
According to Selye, factors that influence a
person's ability to handle stress are: physiological predisposition, early childhood experiences,
social resources, and personality. The author
chooses to define as hardiness the personality
feature that insulates high-stress individuals from
illness. A hardy personality is characterized as
possessing "the belief that they can control or
influence the events of their experience; an
ability to feel deeply involved in or committed to
the activities of their lives; anticipation of
change as a challenge to further development."

Based on the study, it is likely that some individuals are able to stay healthy under stress
because of their personality. A hardy individual
is able to face life changes with "a clear sense of
values, goals, and capabilities, and a belief in
their importance; a strong tendency toward active
involvement with environment; ability to evaluate
the impact of a transfer (or new situation) in
terms of a general life plan with its established
priorities." Physiological status is believed to
be related to hardiness in maintaining the body's
resistance to illness. Psychologically negative
effects of illness may be reflected by responses on
personality questionnaires. Some individuals found
to be low in stress and high in illness "showed
personality scores midway between low illness/high
stress and high stress/high illness groups."

Kobasa, S. C., Hilker, R. R. J., & Maddi, S. R.
  Who stays healthy under stress? Journal of
  Occupational Medicine, 1979, 21, 595-598.
  Stressful life events are either positive or
negative. In either case, there is as a result,
the threat of illness. Any type of readjustment
that must be made as a result of stress can produce
negative physical consequences. The belief is that
following routine is best. This presents no major
changes, thus reduces the chance of illness. In
short, it is believed that stress, positive or
negative, should be avoided.
However, another problem often arises. It is
impossible to avoid stress completely. The belief
has not been proved viable that the individual who
does not have to work avoids stress. Though
experienced in different degrees and handled
differently, stress is experienced by all. The
individual who continues in an attempt to avoid
stress has already failed.
Stressful events do not produce the same results
with everyone. Some are able to cope; some are
not. The author believes that constitution and the
nature of social-support systems are factors to be
considered. Further, certain personality dispo-
sitions deter the debilitating effects of stress.
Three hypotheses are considered as to the type of
personality that escapes ill health as a result of
stress. First, it is believed that those persons
who are committed to diverse aspects of their lives
are less prone to ill health as a result of stress.
Research has proven that individuals who experience
high stress and high illness are more hostile than
high-stress/low-illness individuals. The second
hypothesis states that of the persons who experience a considerable amount of stress, those who
believe that they are still in control of their
lives are usually more healthy. To confirm this
hypothesis, the study proved that
high-stress/low-illness individuals are less
passive than high-stress/high-illness subjects.
Lastly, the hypothesis was explored that among
individuals who experience a significant amount of

stress, those who search for new and challenging
experiences will, more often than not, continue to
be healthy.   It has been confirmed that
high-stress/low-illness subjects enjoy a change of
pace, endure, and achieve more than the
high-stress/high-illness individuals.
This study provided only a few ways one can handle
stress without the resultant ill-health effect.
Viewing stress as something that can be controlled
instead of something that controls reduces the
threat of oncoming stressful events.   Stress cannot
be avoided.   However, when regarded in this way,
many of the debilitating effects can be avoided.

Kovecses, J. S. Career guide: Burnout doesn't
   have to happen. Nursing, October, 1980, 10(10),
   105-111.
With the majority of the helping professions
experiencing burnout, nursing is no exception.
Nurses who have been in nursing for a few years
will have to deal with the warning signals in
themselves, their coworkers, and even their supervisors.   But no one is expected to fight burnout
alone; therefore empathic support and protection is
available from the nursing management.
Through various helpful steps provided by the
nursing management, burnout prevention and solving
are worked through.   Burnout solving includes:
relief periods, encouraged vacations, supervisor
support, assignment rotation, and opportunities for
yoga and meditation.   Burnout prevention includes:
the ability to say no without any guilt, looking
out for oneself, contingency help, and inservice
education programs.
However, it is all too clear that the answers to
burnout have not been found yet.   Knowing the goals
and needs of individual nurses, and management
doing its best to meet these needs, is a benefit to
all.

Kuna, D. J. Meditation and work. Vocational
   Guidance Quarterly, June 1975, 23, 342-346.
   Increasing interest has risen among Americans in

the area of meditation. In particular, Transcendental Meditation is being practiced more and more. Generally speaking, meditation provides a means for individual and social change. Some use it as a relaxation technique. Still others connect spiritual growth to meditation. Whatever the reason for the uprising, meditation is worth looking into.

Transcendental Meditation is an uncomplicated technique. It consists of "an attempt to restrict awareness to a single, unchanging source of stimulation for a definite period of time." In so doing, it expands the capacity of the conscious mind and permits one to use his or her full potential in all areas of thought and action. The ease in which TM can be performed has made it widely known.

Research has proven many positive effects of TM. In relation to work, TM is known to reduce high anxiety levels. Businessmen note that a lower anxiety level results in increased productivity. TM improves the ability to focus attention. It also speeds up reaction time, resulting in a relative increase in alertness, improved mental and physical coordination, and improvement in one's efficiency in perception and performance. Further, those individuals actively seeking employment could improve their mental and physical coordination in the interview process.

Kyriacou, C., & Sutcliffe, J. Teacher stress: Prevalence, sources, and symptoms. British Journal of Educational Psychology. June, 1978, 48(2), 159-167.

Teacher stress is a response syndrome of negative effects resulting from the teacher's job. More and more teachers are experiencing stress, and severe stress is being experienced by more teachers.

A questionnaire survey was used among 257 school teachers in 16 medium-sized, mixed comprehensive schools in England. It was found that about 20% of the respondents rated being a teacher as either very stressful or extremely stressful. Female teachers age 45 or older found low status of the teaching profession less stressful than their colleagues. They also found several items regarding pupil misbehavior greater sources of stress than their male colleagues, whereas the latter reported greater stress for administration and paperwork.

The results also indicated that there is little association between self-reported teacher stress and the biographical characteristics of sex qualification, age, length of teaching experience, and the position held in school. Some of the sources of stress reported were: pupil misbehavior; poor working conditions; time pressures; and poor school ethos, the most frequent of which was exhaustion and feeling frustrated. The symptom that contributes most to the awareness of stress symptoms is a feeling of being very tense, since higher levels of arousal associated with stress reactions are experienced.

Labovitz, G. H., & Orth, C. D. III. Work conditions and personality characteristics affecting job satisfaction of student interns in extended health care facilities. Journal of Applied Psychology, 1972, 56(5), 434-435.

A pilot study involving 58 college students was conducted to gather information in order to understand better the working environment within extended health care facilities. The goal was to alter more accurately that environment in order to increase job satisfaction and reduce turnover rates of college-educated part-time employees.

Data collection included scores from the Allport-Vernon Lindzey (AVL) Study of Values and the Thematic Apperception Test (TAT) for motivation. In addition, daily logs were kept to record the type of activities a student engaged in, the time allotted to each, and reactions to various activities based on a satisfaction index. Significantly high AVL social and low political economic scores were found among the interns as compared to the test populations. The TAT scores were

inconclusive and indicated only somewhat higher
affiliation scores over power scores. Analysis of
daily logs, interview notes, and debriefing tapes
indicated that student interns were more satisfied
by direct patient care. Conversational or highly
personal interaction with patients was cited as the
factor that made less desirable elements tolerable.
Although policy, salary, and other context factors
were seen as not satisfying, job satisfaction was
linked to content factors such as direct patient
care. Apparently, job restructuring that permits
and enhances interaction and complete responsibility for a few patients can add measurably to job
satisfaction.

Lamb, H. R.   Staff burnout in work with long-term
   patients. Hospital and Community Psychiatry,
   June 1971, 30, 96-398.
This article discusses how the seeds of staff
burnout are planted when mental health professionals who work with long-term patients do not recognize that such patients vary greatly in their
potential for rehabilitation.
Due to the increased priority to serve severely
disabled patients, many mental health agencies and
most other community and social agencies have
enlisted large numbers of new staff to provide
services. Many of those staff do not have a
realistic conception of what they can expect to
accomplish and are without a sound underlying
conceptual framework for the long-term patient's
care or understanding of the patient's varying
needs and capabilities.
The failure of mental health staff to recognize
and accept these differences creates major problems. Some of these are discrediting rehabilitation for a number of reasons: the slow pace and
length of time before any progress is shown,
failure to set realistic goals for normalization
and staff understanding of severely disabled
person's capabilities, social and administrative
pressure for quick results, and pressure on
long-term patients to be socially and vocationally

rehabilitated by unrealistic, enthusiastic staff.
   Mental health staff must also become aware of
their own motivation for working in the helping
professions. They must be able to resolve their
own sense of self-gratification without trying to
consciously or unconsciously have patients meet the
needs of the staff.
   Another significant factor in staff burnout is
confusion about the extent to which nurturing
patients and meeting their dependency needs is
desirable and appropriate. Staff must become
comfortable in gratifying dependency needs and
realize that all patients need some degree of
support. Such support can be given without undermining the client's push toward whatever level
of autonomy he or she is capable of reaching.
   The author recommends that staff must have a
realistic view of long-term patients and of the
wide variations in their needs and potential. The
staff should not be subjected to administrative
pressure to accomplish the impossible. They must
be able to make clear, open decisions about their
willingness to work with long-term patients. Then
they will not be as likely to become frustrated and
burned out and either abandon long-term patients or
unwittingly drive them away.

Lammert, M. A group experience to combat burnout
   and learn group process skills. Journal of
   Nursing Education, June 1981, 20(6), 41-46.
   Like any other professional, nurses are susceptible to the symptoms of burnout. They have been
given greater responsibility for understanding
group processes and operating competently in
groups. Some undergraduate curriculums require
that nursing majors and other students enroll in
one course that deals with group and organizational
behavior. It is true that nurses engage much of
their career lives in different types of groups.
Nevertheless, they too have to deal with stress and
burnout symptoms.
   Nurses are involved in group activities, which can
add considerably to burnout because of the

frequency of involvement. It is suggested that a
group experience be considered to combat burnout.
The group experience would involve self-disclosure
and feedback. Individuals would have the opportunity to be open and honest about their feelings
on particular issues. In order to be successful in
dealing with stresses in human services organizations, group members must possess the ability to
develop mutually supportive relationships with
colleagues. They must be in touch with their
needs, feelings, etc., so that they can take care
of themselves.
  The group experience is outlined in a step-by-step
procedure. This process helps professionals in
human services to acquire the necessary characteristics mentioned above that will assist in
combating burnout. This procedure, however, will
not prevent all from experiencing burnout or its
related symptoms. Nevertheless, it can serve to
introduce nurses to significant professional
concerns which can add to the growth and well-being
of their careers.

Lantos, B. Metapsychological conderations in the
    concept of work. International Journal of
    Psychoanalysis, 1952, 33, 439-443.
  The acceptance of the work principal as a direct-
ing motive in its activities is a special activity
of the adult ego, achieved by a long and dull
development.
  It's not the object of skill of the activity that
makes the difference between work and play, but the
participation of the superego, which changes play
activities into work activities. What is felt as
the urge to work is really the voice of the superego, the inner representation. Work makes ego
activities, serving self preservation and distin-
guishing that from play. But work has to be done
in order to obtain all possible means from the
environment for satisfaction which is not provided
by activities within the instinctual sequence.
  Work is not primarily a psychological but a
sociological concept characterized as an essential

human activity. The ultimate motive is not pleasure but self-preservation mediated by intelligence
and reinforced by conscience. With the specific
work pleasure being the relief from tension, the
agreement between the ego and superego is achievement.
  However, to gain pleasure by work and to enjoy
one's work is considered a happy, but not a guaran-
teed, state of affairs. We look upon work as an
obvious necessity, a proof of good adaption.

Laron, C. S., Gilbertson, D. L., & Power, J. A.
   Therapist burnout: Perspectives on a critical
   issue. Social Casework, Nov. 1978, 563-565.
   Burnout is the therapist's failure to muster the
reserves necessary to remain effective on the job.
It is the byproduct of working within an environment that places constant demands on its professionals without allowing for a balancing of experiences within that environment that may contribute
to the therapists' differentiation, identification,
and growth.
  The avoidance of burnout demands a restructuring
of the mental-health attitude and environment to
incorporate a concern for therapist differentiation
and nurturance. Therapists must learn to differentiate and to explore all facets of their needs
within their professional and personal environment.
There is a need to set limits on the demands of
others, the need to balance work and social needs,
the need to foster self-respect, and the need to
reject the notion of being all things to all
people. Caseloads should not be to an overloading
point. They should not overlook the implications
of working with a large percentage of severely
disturbed patients or with patients for whom they
are not personally or professional well-suited.
  A superhuman attitude seems as much the cause of
burnout as the product of training and anxieties.
The work atmosphere should encourage a balanced
caseload, geared to differing professional preferences and abilities. Although appropriate at
times, the incorporation of the attitude that all

problems have answers may inadvertently set the stage for feelings of personal inadequacy and failure when the best plans and intentions fail to produce the desired results consistently.

With the frequent emotional drains upon the therapist, burnout inevitably takes its physical tolls. Routine work breaks should occur in each work day. Burnout is hastened when the therapist works in isolation. Therapists tend to isolate themselves routinely and to accept this as neces- sary condition for getting work done. So- cial-support systems should not be dismissed as "goofing off," but rather should be viewed as an effective way to combat the growth of the burnout condition.

Mental health managers must be willing to allow, to encourage, staff to work within a nuturing as well as functional environment. It is up to the mental health manager to structure the work en- vironment to allow for staff differentiation. The scheduling of regular staff meetings, group train- ing, and group athletics or luncheons are subtle ways to promote group identification and avoid therapist isolation.

Training seminars, research projects, and atten- dance at professional conferences will encourage individuality and the opportunity for self-expression. If management encourages indi- vidual and group solutions to everyday program operations, problems of burnout and poor productiv- ity will be removed.

Lattanzi, M. E. Coping with work-related losses. Personnel and Guidance Journal, February 1981, pp. 350-351.

As a helping profession, counseling as a career choice implies a desire on the part of an individu- al to work with people to attain the best possible level of health and functioning. In certain institutions and settings, the accomplishment of this goal may be difficult or may cause the indi- vidual to redefine personal expectations and values. Work-related stress and professional burnout can be related to personal expectations, coping responses, and available support.

Counseling, as a profession, tends to attract individuals who are often idealistic and have a high need for job satisfaction and self-actualization. The vision or desire to make things better versus helplessness and situational reality can result in insidious loss for the counselor in some settings.

Career and job choices involving work in stressful settings, such as Hospice, are best made if the individuals have questioned why they desire to work in a particular field or situation. The delivery of care and services, and an interdisciplinary team approach provides a network of mutual support and learning available to all involved. This approach prevents the isolation and individual withdrawal that often arise when working with the dying. Careful selection of individuals to work in a program, either as paid professionals or as professional volunteers, is crucial. Individuals need successful experiences, outside supports, and a clear sense of their strengths and skills.

Lazarus, R. S. (Interviewed by Goleman, D.)
    Positive denial: The case for not facing
    reality. Psychology Today, November, 1979, pp.
    44-60.

Stress is a generic term describing situations that produce physical and mental reactions, the reactions themselves, and numerous intervening processes.

Psychological stress resides neither in the situation nor in the person; it depends on a transaction between the two. It arises from how the person appraises an event and adapts to it. Stress is what occurs when the demands of the environment, in the person's eyes, clearly exceed the resources of the person to handle them. Foremost among those functions is how the person construes the situation: does he or she judge it as threatening, or as a challenge?

A current popular view is that stresses at any

given time can be added up to get a single stress score. But the correlation between such a single index of stress and a person's health is extremely small. The constant minor irritants may be much more important than the large, landmark changes.

Most people handle the garden-variety of stress through two main varieties of coping. One is problem-solving, the other is emotion focused. Problem-solving coping refers to efforts to change the troublesome situations for the better. This coping strategy is very effective except that not all stress is something you can do anything about. There are some realities you just cannot change. Emotion-focused modes include things you do or say to yourself to make yourself feel better, which do not alter the actual relationship between yourself and the environment. These modes include denial, thinking of something else, and joking or making light of a situation. The people who get into psychological trouble under stress probably ap-proach coping in a rigid way. They use the same strategy, whether or not it is productive.

Lazarus comes around to the view that denial (refusing to face the facts) and illusion (false beliefs about reality) have their usefulness in coping with stress and indeed may be the healthiest strategies in certain situations. In severe crises, denial buys preparation time; it lets the person face the grim facts at a gradual, manageable pace.

Lecker, S. How to get ahead young--without burning out. McCalls, 105, March 1978, 94.

To be successful in this life, one must accept stress as a part of everyday life--the sooner, the better. Stress control and the coping strategies utilized determine the distance one can go.

To cope with stress and prevent burnout, one must be aware of the source of stress. The basic formula: (pace of life) x (complexity of tasks) x (number of tasks) = stress. It is important that one be aware of and adhere to limits in order to keep self in control. By setting a winning pace, putting priorities in order, and using deadlines, one can become a "hyperachiever" without burning out.

Leffingwell, R. J.   The role of the middle school counselor in the reduction of stress in teachers. Elementary School Guidance and Counseling, April 1979, 13(4),   286-290.
Teachers of adolescent children face a particular kind of stress.   The adolescent faces a transition period that influences all stages of his life as well as his day-to-day interactions with others. The manner in which the adolescent handles himself affects the manner the educator approaches teaching.
Physiological, psychological, and social dimensions of life are sources of stress in teachers of adolescents.   Stress is likely to occur when a teacher is physically fatigued, has no free time to unwind, and desires to maintain complete control of student behavior.   A general sense of helplessness may arise as the teacher tries to meet the needs of too many people.   Teachers often label these feelings as negative and try to rationalize them away.   The overuse of defense mechanisms results in the reduction of problem-solving behavior.
The following eleven points were found to facilitate problem-solving behaviors:
1. Provide an environment of support and confidentiality in which the teacher can discuss feelings and ideas.
2. Clarify the point that feelings are real and not necessarily bad.
3. Disclose personal experiences with frustration and effective problem-solving techniques.
4. Believe that solutions do exist to problems, and that the ability to seek solutions is healthy.
5. Identify and accurately label the type of stress and the effect it is having on the individual.

6.   Clarify the source and degree of stress. The more information, the greater the probability of finding solutions.
7.   Search for alternative solutions to problems, recognizing that there is no one solution that will work in all cases.
8.   Make a commitment to plan of action, knowing that if it is not successful there will be reasons for the lack of success and forces can be grouped to search for alternate plans.
9.   Provide an ongoing support base to assist in the indentification and clarification of accurate labels and alternative solutions when original solutions are inadequate.
10.   Train the teacher to cope with stress in positive ways, such as through relaxation techniques.
11.   Recognize that there are no panaceas to happiness.

There are no simple solutions to becoming happier and more productive in life. There are some basic principles that affect behavior, and these are vital to know if one wishes to facilitate growth processes in people. The most important factor in implementation of the principles of learning is the genuine, warm, empathetic understanding of the facilitator.

Lenhart, R. C. Faculty burnout and some reasons why. Nursing Outlook, July 1980, 28(7), 424-425.
Faculty members of colleges nationwide are suffering stress and burnout at an alarming rate. The reasons are politically, economically, and socially based. Economically, instructors are teaching at schools with reduced budgets, with reduced enrollment, and even reduced faculty. Instructors have to worry about retaining their tenure and maintaining high credentials to remain on staff. The ability of the instructor to play politics sometimes becomes more important than the ability to teach students.

College instructors are also faced with teaching a heterogeneous group of students. The enrollment often reflects a variety of backgrounds and ages as well as educational training. Some college re- cruiters have attracted students under false promises and lowered admissions standards. Remedi- al programs are then offered to bring deficient students up to a higher level. These factors cause instructors to face the added stress of teaching to a nonhomogeneous group that may have some members below level and not capable of mastering the subject.

Added to this are the problems generated by students raised in a permissive society. These students often except preferential treatment. Frequently this is expected in the form of a passing grade because tuition has been paid. The pressure to retain a student regardless of compe- tency negatively affects the professional standards of the school. Instructors have met resistance when they insisted on higher admission standards, maintaining current standards, or when they have tried to dismiss an incompetent student.

As a result of the above factors and their often negative influence, many instructors have given up. They no longer fight to maintain standards. When enough faculty members have left the system and it collapses, the public will be the losers. When students take state board examinations and cannot pass them, it reflects negatively on the school and faculty. The solution seen to resolve this con- flict is pressure from faculty to maintain the professional standards of the organization. When learning institutions and professions are account- able to students and society, the negative effects of burnout on instructors may cease.

Levi, L. Preventing work stress. Reading, Mass.: Addison-Wesley, 1981.

Stress denotes a force that deforms bodies. In biology, however, the term stress often takes on a different meaning, being used to denote stereotyped physiological strain reactions in the organism when

it is exposed to various environmental stimuli
called stressors.

The following is a list of the working-life
situations that are general stress-evolving conditions:

1. Over- and understimulation.
2. The person-environment misfit.
3. Role conflicts.
4. Shift work.
5. Piece work.
6. Mass production.
7. Automation.
8. Noise and vibration.
9. Machinery and tools.
10. Building and premises.

Principles for protection and promotion of workers' health and well-being should be based on the
following:

1. A comprehensive view of human beings and
    their environment, i.e., equal and
    intergral consideration for physical,
    mental, social, and economic aspects.
2. An ecological strategy, i.e., consid-
    eration of the interaction between the
    entire individual and the entire environ-
    ment (physical, chemical, psychosocial)
    and of the dynamics of the complex
    system.
3. A cybernetic strategy, with continuous
    evaluation of the effects of different
    working environments and of changes in
    them, and with a continuous adaptation
    and reshaping of the working environment
    in the light of these various types of
    change.
4. A democratic strategy, giving individuals
    the greatest possible influence over
    their own situation and direct, efficient
    channels of communication to the various
    decision makers.

Improving the work processes involves some of the
following recommendations: greater independence
and responsibility; autonomous groups to break down

complex production systems into smaller units;
information input that facilitates understanding
and processing for optimal decision making and for
avoidance of fatigue; optimal design of shift work;
rest breaks; social support systems; living with
less work (e.g., reduce working hours and lowering
retirement age) and; improve person environment
fit.

Table of Contents:
1. Occupational stress--a bird's eye view
2. Impact of modern technology
3. Stress and distress
4. High-risk situation
5. High-risk groups
6. Stress reactions at work
7. Improvement of work environment to prevent
   mental stress
8. Improving the work processes
9. Disease prevention and health promotion:
   possibilities and constraints
10. Summary and conclusions
11. Recommendations for consideration at
local, national, and international levels

Lipton, M. Stress and the specter of the law.
  Management World, July 1981, pp. 14-15, 44.
    A striking increase in the rate at which employ-
ees have taken legal action against their employers
with stress-related claims is a growing concern.
Employees charge that occupational stress can be
physiologically damaging. The Massachusetts
Superior Court recently stated that "a mental or
emotional disorder causally related to stressful
incidents at work is a personal injury arising out
of and in the course of employment," thus making
workers eligible for workman's compensation.
  Historically, individuals were not able to collect
compensation for stress on the job due to the
inability to provide "specific events" (as opposed
to gradual wear and tear) that precipitated the
illness. But, in the Massachusetts case, a direct
connection was established between the individual's
working conditions and emotional disorder. The

evidence included three incidences of the individual removing (upon direction of a superior) benefits previously granted other workers, an action that was consequently humiliating and stressful to the individual. The fourth incidence aroused physiological symptoms in the individual and rendered him unable to work afterward. Change is perhaps the greatest stressor in life.

Court cases in New York and Michigan have supported employer liability existing regardless of the illness being deep-seated or underlying if it is aggravated, increased, or initiated by any condition of employment. The organization's structural characteristics, its communication patterns, its leadership styles, its decision-making and goal-setting processes are now realized to influence not only productivity, but occupational health as well. Management must protect itself against false liability in the event of employee stress by examining these issues. The courts need to truly examine the individual causes of stress and consider underlying factors as well as those that trigger, aggravate, or bring out symptoms.

Lubin, M. Faculty fight burnout with weekly seminar. A P A Monitor, December, 1982, 13(12), 24.

In an effort to reduce the frequency of faculty burnout and academic stagnation, the Illinois School of Psychology instituted weekly seminars. The goals of the seminars were to "promote faculty development and cohesion, and to combat isolation and burnout." The seminar format allows each individual to have an active part either by presentation or critique and suggestion. Participation allows faculty members to learn from each other as well as to encourage cohesiveness among the group. At the seminar, faculty members learn what their colleagues are teaching and their philosophical approach. In addition, some faculty members felt that standards were developed and maintained concerning teaching techniques and grading procedures. Most important was the development, among

faculty members, of a support system that is
willing to offer help backed by experience.

The administration supported the seminar program
because it improved communication and fostered good
feelings between faculty and administration. The
quality of instruction improved because the critique process was also used to evaluate current
programming for any needed changes. This is
important when budgets are constantly in jeopardy.
Faculty and administration are able to air complaints at the seminars, which helps reduce the
sense of distrust between the two groups. In
addition, the seminar process encourages contact
between the dean and individual faculty members.
These meetings initiate continuous evaluation of
performance, which offers a better understanding of
the values and emphasis of the instructional
program.

Lunn, J. A. Absenteeism an occupational hazard.
  Nursing Mirror, May, 1975, 65-66.
  Nursing is a very demanding occupation, both
physically and mentally. The majority of young
people can cope adequately with challenging and
demanding work if the necessary support is provided, not only at work, but also in off-duty hours.
It is in this latter respect that problems arise
because of the special circumstances of nursing.

Those who spend most of their time caring for sick
people have a natural tendency to be over anxious
about illness and to be unduly conscious of symptoms which are minor, but which create association
with serious illness as often observed in patients.
The stress and anxiety produced is essentially
occupational in origin. Doctors who have the
responsibility for the care of nurses in training
are acutely aware of this problem. During the
early months of training clinic attendance is
generally higher. Insecurity and unhappiness tend
to increase in those nurses who become uncertain
about continuing their training and this is also
reflected in a higher rate of sickness.

The group morale of a nursing set can be important

in providing support for any one nurse in moments
of stress. It is important that there is an
opportunity to talk over problems and worries.
When no opportunity exists for this release of
tensions, individual stress and anxiety is more
likely to develop. There is a definite increase in
depression and anxiety among those who are more
isolated in their accommodations.

The more demanding a job is, the more essential it
is for personnel to have relaxation and recreation
in off-duty hours. Unfortunately, the duty hours
of most nurses make it difficult to take part in
activities outside the hospital. Evening clases
and weekend sports tend to be precluded. Many
nurses are also far from their own homes and miss
the benefit and companionship of being part of a
local community. Much more attention must be given
to remedying these defects through the provision of
recreational facilities and social links, especially in large district hospitals. There is little
doubt that loneliness and boredom may be far more
important in producing unhappiness and depression
among student nurses than many of the problems they
meet in their work. While nurses are in training
it is necessary to change wards frequently. It is
accepted that such changes are necessary, more
awareness of the effect of stress on nurses can
help to prevent the problem.

The introduction of multispecialty wards, despite
their other advantages, has contributed to decreased staff morale. The older ward system,
despite its disadvantages, created a sense of unity
and loyalty among the nursing and medical staff. A
sense of belonging helps nurses through periods of
stress.

Caring for patients who are psychiatrically
disturbed creates far greater demands on nurses
than any other form of nursing. Unless nurses
themselves are particularly sure and confident when
they become involved with these patients, marked
stress and depression can result. During the first
year of any new group of nurses, it becomes apparent which of them have less resistance to stress

and tension.   Some of them may be well advised to
avoid psychiatric training where it is optional.
Those who are familiar with treating behavioral
problems among nurses in training will be well
aware of the dangers of adding further stresses and
tensions created by psychiatric training.
   The majority of women who take up nursing are
leaving school and home for the first time and
starting their first job.   For most young people,
these are major events.   This, along with the
demands of nursing, make the provision of understanding and support even more important.

Lustman, P., & O'Hara, D. J.   Biofeedback: A new
   strategy for coping with stress.   Management
   World, July 1981, 12-13.
   Biofeedback refers to any procedure that measures
bodily functions of which a person is not normally
aware.   Individuals learn to act in a particular
way when they receive feedback about the consequences of their behavior.   This is first accomplished through using electronic equipment to
detect and amplify body conditions such as blood
pressure or muscle tension.   These readings are
then reported auditorily or visually to the individual, thus allowing the person to recognize and
regulate body responses not normally under conscious control.   Relaxation skills can then be used
to quiet the hyperactive bodily process in order to
cope with a particularly stressful situation.
   In stressful situations, individuals tend to
become tense, generating greater amounts of electrical activity in their muscles, thus leading to
tension headaches, anxiety, and irritability.
Electromyographic (EMG) biofeedback helps the
person to detect and decrease the electrical
activity and therefore relax the muscles.   An image
exercise is suggested for the subject to try to
demonstrate the potential value in using
biofeedback.
   Biofeedback has also been used effectively with
individuals suffering from hypertension, insomnia,
stuttering, headaches, ulcers, spastic colitis,

chronic pain, and other stress-related difficulties. Supervisors who conduct job performance
appraisals to identify employees' inadequate coping
mechanisms will find biofeedback useful as employee
assistance programs become more prevalent.

Lutz, F. W., & Ramsey, M. A. The voodoo killer in
  modern society. Personnel, 1976, May-June, 30-38.
  The article deals with the issue of stress in
modern society's complex organizations and how it
relates to the ancient practice of voodoo. An
explanation of the phenomenon of voodoo, death, or
illness in primitive societies is given to illustrate the impact of psychological stress on the
physiological process of the nervous systems.
Further illustrated in this article is the means by
which insensitive administrators in complex organizations are often directly or indirectly responsible for this same type of phenomenon in modern
society.
  Four cases are given in the article to illustrate
the voodoo effect in both primitive and modern
society. This is followed by suggested antidotes
to the voodoo effect in modern society. Suggestions given for the organization's change agents
are:
  1.   Identify those whose skills or orga-
       nizational behavior are not commensurate
       with the organization's new goals.
  2.   Confer with these persons.
  3.   Provide inservice training opportunities
       where possible.
  4.   Provide some form of systematic reeval-
       uation and guidance.
If it is determined that such individuals must
leave, the organization should:
  1.   Help the person perceive the problem as
       not one of "poor" skills.
  2.   Do as much as possible to help the
       individual find another job with another
       organization.

Lyons, T. F. Turnover and absenteeism: A review

of relationships and shared correlates.
Personnel Psychology, 1972, 25, 271-181.
The problem of absenteeism and turnover as
behavioral criteria in industrial research is
discussed. Little attention has been given to the
relationship between absenteeism and turnover.
Three common assumptions have been made about this
relationship:
1.   Absenteeism and turnover can be discussed
     together since the worker who is absent
     is simply making a temporary decision
     similar to the one he will make when he
     decides to quit.
2.   Absenteeism and accidents are forms of
     organizational withdrawl that are engaged
     in as an alternative to turnover.
3.   Absenteeism and turnover differ not from
     the stimuli that prompt one type of
     withdrawl over another but from the
     consequences from these two forms.
The conclusions reached by the review of the
literature were that 16 out of 29 independent tests
of the relationship between absenteeism and turnover were significant and positive, and one was
significant and negative. The second question
(i.e., regarding a progressive alienation) was also
supported but the sample from which this finding
was taken was quite small (and possibly unrepre-
sentative). The last question, searching for
common factors affecting both absenteeism and
turnover, was examined by investigating 92 variables. Absenteeism and turnover both were significantly related to only 8 common factors. Therefore,
the support for common correlates is quite weak.

Macy, B. A., & Mirvis, P. H. A methodology for the
   assessment of quality of work life and
   organizational effectiveness in behavioral-
   economic terms. Administrative Science
   Quarterly, 1976, 21, 212-226.
This paper describes the development and implementation of a standardized set of definitions,
measures, and costing methods of work performance

as well as the broader concept of effectiveness and ways to express this in financial terms. The paper illustrates their use in assessing a quality-of-work-life experiment.

Employee behavior at work results from the choices made.   It assumes that workers remain with a company if they obtain satisfaction from their job and if they expect rewards for harder, more efficient work. Behavioral definitions were created to distinguish behaviors like absence for jury duty, funerals, and maternity leave, from those related to the work environment. Behaviors like alcohol consumption were omitted. Four variables were selected for member participation: absenteeism, tardiness, turnover, work stoppages, and strikes. Six variables reflecting role performance were chosen: productivity, quality, grievances, accidents, job-related illness, downtime and excess inventory, material, and supply-use variances.

Voluntary and involuntary absenteeism were distinguished and reported separately. Turnover was defined as movement across the membership boundary of the company. This was distinguished by two groups as to whether the employee initiated the action or not. Strike days were compared with the total number of available working days.

Productivity is best regarded as a family of measures comparing a set of work inputs with a set of work outputs. Productivity indicators measure product quality below standard, downtime, material, supply, and inventory-utilization variances all in comparable dollar terms.

Malone, H. N., & Falkenberg, D. Ministerial burnout. Leadership, Fall, 1(4), 1980, 57-60.

When ministers burnout they become boring and pedantic; they lose enthusiasm. In the church, burnout is also seen as a spiritual failure with a negative stigma, despite the fact that it occurs in all other types of helping professions without the stigma. One concept that is probably not clear to many church members is that a particular pastorate is a job, while the ministry is a career. Other careers often are formed in the process of a number of job changes. The ministry can certainly be conceived of in this way. For instance a pastor could leave a particular church to become a hospital chaplain or could take an administrative job in the church hierarchy and still be in the ministry.

If a pastor stays in his congregation beyond the time when it is exciting for him, he tends to slow down the growth in ministry in that place while the congregation is equally responsible for slowing down the pastor. It is possible for a pastor to assess his work and skills and interests and make some decisions in a new direction. There are four dimensions to job success: interest in the work, demands of the job, skills required, and fulfillment provided. No job will have all these areas to an equal degree, but it is helpful for the pastor to assess what he needs and wants at a given time. Sharing doubts with a small group is an excellent way to grow and be renewed.

Margolis, B. L., Kroes, W. H., & Quinn, R. P. Job stress: An unlisted occupational hazard. Journal of Occupational Medicine, 16(10), 1974, 659-661.

Research shows that occupational stress is a causal factor in disease. For example, research has found that air traffic controllers had four times the rate of hypertension and twice the rate of peptic ulcers and diabetes mellitus as second class airmen, and that railway dispatchers lived about 16 years less than normal.

The purpose of this research is to identify the association between strain and six different types of job stress.

In 1973, 1,496 employed persons were interviewed about job stress, work, and attitudes towards work. The six stress measures were: role ambiguity, underutilization, overload, resource inadequacy, insecurity, and nonparticipation in decisions that affect one's job.

The results showed nine out of ten strain indicators were significantly associated with job stress.

In all cases, increased stress was associated with poorer physical and mental health. Nonparticipation correlated the highest of all stresses with eight of the strain measures. Self-esteem correlated with all six stresses. The data reported provided further evidence that psychological stress can affect physical and mental health.

Some suggestions for intervention are that good in-service training for staff and supervision could help improve both morale and performance; that administrators devote some attention to clarifying goals, objectives, and responsibilities in areas such as mental health consultation and education where high ambiguity interferes with staff performance. Job satisfaction may also be increased by job redesign; but there are constraints on this due to federal, state, and local funding.

Maslach, C. Burned-out. Human Behavior, September, 1976, 5(9), 16-22.

This study discusses the correlation between work in the health and social-service professions and burnout. The sample includes 200 professionals in California in poverty law, physicians, prison personnel, social-welfare workers, clinical psychologists and psychiatrists in a mental hospital, child-care workers, and psychiatric nurses.

The findings of this study show that professional groups tend to cope with stress by a form of distancing that not only hurts themselves, but is damaging to their clients. Some of the ways this is demonstrated are by a shift toward cynical or negative feelings about people, thinking of clients in more derogatory terms, and suppression of emotions. In addition, stress that is not resolved on the job is resurrected at home. These changes correlate with other damaging indexes of human stress, such as alcoholism, mental illness, marital conflict, and suicide.

The verbal and nonverbal techniques used to achieve detachment were, using a change in terms to make clients appear more object-like and less human, describing things as precisely and scientifically in more intellectual and less personal terms, and making a sharp distinction between job and personal life. Another technique for cooling emotions is to minimize physical involvement by standing farther away, avoiding eye contact, and by communicating in impersonal ways or simply spending less time with clients.

Maslach, C. Job burnout: How people cope. Public Welfare, September 1978, 36(2), 56.
Burnout is a condition, or syndrome, observed among a wide variety of helping professionals. Working closely with people in an emotionally charged environment results in a gradual loss of caring about their clients; a kind of emotional exhaustion sets in. Burnout is the emotional exhaustion resulting from the stresses of interpersonal contact. The syndrome seems to manifest in stages; certain responses occur in patterns. First, emotional exhaustion is seen specifically as a loss of positive feelings sympathy and respect for clients or patients. Secondly, a cynical and dehumanizing perception of clients occurs. As the condition advances, the emotional stresses are dealt with less effectively. Finally, the burnout victim may resign from his position; possibly the profession. The abuse of alcohol and drugs may occur, with some victims seeking counsel or psychiatric treatment. Correlations between burnout and low morale, absenteeism, high job turnover, and reports of increased marital and family conflict have been found. A state of ignorance is further aggravated by the helping profession's own historial image of being cool, calm, and collected. The emerging theme from research is that there are not bad people as much as there are bad situations.
Presently, people have been seen to cope with burnout by:
1. Intellectualizing.
2. Psychological withdrawal, avoid becoming emotionally involved.
3. Take short breaks when things grow critical, e.g., leaving the room,

counting to 10.

   4.   Hiding behind policy rules.

A clear separation must be kept between job and home life. This separation allows for a switching of roles, which has been found to be crucial in avoiding high burnout rates. Various daily time-out activities are recommended. Situational factors are also important; work breaks, quality of client contact, and caseload will have a bearing on the professional.

Maslach, C. The client role in staff burnout. Journal of Social Issues, November, 1978, 34(4), 111-124.

The intense involvement with clients required of professional staff in various human-service institutions includes a great deal of emotional stress, and failure to cope successfully with such stress can result in the emotional-exhaustion syndrome of burnout, in which staff lose all feeling and concern for their clients and treat them in detached or even dehumanizing ways. This paper focuses on the role that clients themselves play in staff burnout.

One crucial aspect of the staff-client interaction that can have a major determining influence on the level of emotional stress is the particular role played by the client. Important client factors include the type and severity of the clients' problems, the prognosis of change or cure, the degree of personal relevance for the staff member of the clients' problems, the rules governing staff-client interaction, and the clients' reactions to the staff members themselves.

A possible alleviation of staff-client conflict discussed is earlier analysis of the clients' dependent stance, which can facilitate making clients more self-reliant. If clients took a more active and initiating role in their interactions with staff, the relationship could come closer to being one of equals. Staff and clients could function more as partners in problem resolution and share in the decision-making responsibility.

Secondly, a great deal of misunderstanding and upset arises from the mismatch between client and staff expectations. This could be avoided if both staff and clients were explicit about their expectations at the outset, clarified the relationships possibilities and limitations, and considered each others perspectives.

Clients may sometimes have unrealistic ideas about the extent of personal warmth and caring they can legitimately expect from professional staff, and clients and will often not grant professionals the range of feelings they allow in others. A recognition by clients of the limits to the comfort they can expect in addition to their services might ease these misunderstandings.

Staff-client contact could also be improved by socializing between both participants to provide positive feedback to each other when justified, rather than taking accomplishments for granted. Staff need to know explicitly from clients when things have gone well and when they have not. In addition to face-to-face feedback, regular client ratings of staff performance could begin to give clients a greater sense of input into, and possible control of, the institutions that are supposedly serving them.

It is important to keep in mind that there are two participants in this relationship who shape and direct the interaction and the thoughts and feelings arising from it. Just as staff can dehumanize clients by processing them in a standardized way, ignoring their pleas and demands, and judging them as somehow less capable and worthy than themselves, so too can clients dehumanize staff by failing to acknowledge their presence, failing to follow their advice or guidance, and failing to provide positive instead of exclusively negative feedback. These dehumanization processes are interrelated and can gradually escalate in intensity and frequency.

Maslach, C., & Jackson, S. E. Lawyer burnout. Barrister, Spring 1978, 5(2), 52-54.
There is a growing concern over the high turnover

in legal services. The turnover rate in 1976 was
approximately 33 percent. The average length of
stay was slightly over two years for attorneys.
Lawyers list the causes of turnover as the lack of
professional growth, lack of salary prospects, and
poor management. However, the most commonly stated
reason was burnout.

Burnover in lawyers is thought to be characterized
by emotional exhaustion and attitude shifts. The
quality of service deteriorates as lawyers process
people as if they were machines. It appears to be
caused by the intimate involvement in the psychological, social, and physical problems of the
clients they serve. The burnout victims include
the client, the individual, and the family. It
shows up in the home life and in the work environment of afflicted persons.

It occurs because the lawyer is under the pressure of providing service to large numbers of
people. Lawyers have to have training in how to
deal with people on a continuing basis. The
emotional drain frequently proves too much for the
individual to handle.

The authors suggest job solutions for job stress
through support groups, time-outs, and positive
escapes. Work breaks, spent in doing something
completely removed from work, and the setting of
personal boundaries have also been demonstrated as
beneficial in burnout situations. Other solutions
include the examination of goal expectations and
clarification of realistic objectives.

Maslach, C., & Jackson, S. E. Burned-out cops and
    their families. Psychology Today, May 1979,
    12(2), 59-62.

Police work is highly stressful and it is likely
that a large number of people in a public-opinion
poll would consider this type of work the most
stressful because of the physical dangers involved.
Research has suggested that the stress is due more
to the psychological than physiological risks.
This study of 130 police couples in California in
1977 sought to examine any correlation between high

job stress and marital discord and family difficulties.

The responses of the husband and wife were
measured and the findings showed that high burnout
scores are associated with domestic strains that
are absent or mild in the families of low raters.
Younger officers, who scored higher than others on
burnout, seem to be in the greatest jeopardy.

Some of the aspects of police work discussed in
relation to stress are coping with the painful
aftermath of crime in terms of the victim's loss,
suffering, or even death. Also, the police officer
usually has to deal with people under adverse, even
tramatic, circumstances. The way some of the
officer respondents deal with this emotional
conflict is through a process of habituation. This
unemotional response is carried over into family
life by distancing from spouse and children, by
becoming more tough and aggressive when dealing
with family, by appearing to mistrust and becoming
less capable of getting emotionally involved with
family, and by holding little or no discussion of
the job.

Wives report their husbands as distant and
isolated in the higher ratings of stress. Some of
the coping methods employed by policeman and their
families are use of alcohol and tranquilizers and
involvement in sports or other physical exercise.
Eighty % of the wives seek out organized activities
as a source of help and social support, but only
10% of the men do.

Larger police departments, in recognizing the
need for assistance to their officers, have psychologists on staff for the development of
stress-reduction programs and for counseling police
officers and their families. These services appear
to be underused unless there is assurance that word
of the visits will not leak back to their fellow
officers, supervisors, or onto their records.

Acknowledging that the burnout syndrome is a
common frailty of many people whose jobs require
them to give too much and too often to other people
can perhaps begin a reexamination and restructuring

of the job itself to better control the intensity
and exposure to emotional stress. Additionally, the
public recognizing the potentially destructive
impact of job burnout on the people who serve some
of our most basic needs may be instrumental to the
solution.

Maslach, C., & Pines, A. Burnout: The loss of
  human caring. In: Pines, A. & Maslach, C.
  (Eds.). Experiencing Social Psychology. Random
  House, 1978.
People in the various health and service professions are often confronted with constant emotional arousal, which is a very stressful experience for any human being. Over time, learned
techniques of detachment (techniques that allow a
degree of objectivity without sacrificing the
capacity for caring) are weakened, resulting in
burnout. This loss is characterized by negative
self-concepts, negative job attitudes, alienation
from people they work with, low morale, poor
performance, absenteeism, high job turnover, and
poor delivery of health and welfare services.
  Five detachment techniques are:
  1.   Semantics of Detachment. Using terms
       that omit an emotional or human element.
  2.   Intellectualization. An attempt to deal
       with situations in their abstract qual-
       ities, avoiding the human ones.
  3.   Situational compartmentalization.   A
       sharp separation is made between work
       life and home life
  4.   Withdrawal. To minimize one's physical
       involvement with other people by main-
       taining a physical distance from client
       through impersonal communication, spend-
       ing less time with the patient, poor
       performance to assure fewer referrals,
       and hiding behind rules to avoid tasks.
  5.   Social techniques. Solicit advice and
       comfort from staff members. Humor is
       often used.
  Six remedies for burnout:

1. Ratio. Research on child care workers suggested a high ratio (1:12) of staff members resulted in poor quality of services, more rigidity, and sense of powerlessness. A low ratio (1:4) allows more time to focus on the positive, more involvement, and higher quality of services.
2. Time-outs versus escapes. Opportunities to do less stressful work while another staff member steps in vs. going AWOL.
3. Amount of direct contact. Job rotations, lateral job changes, sharing of difficult cases and even establishing part-time positions.
4. Social-professional support. Formal or informal programs to discuss, give advice, support, and analyze job stress.
5. Analysis of personal feelings. Burnout rates are lower for professionals who actively express and share feelings with colleagues.
6. Training in interpersonal skills. Research findings to date indicate a need to have special training for working closely with other people.

Maslach, C., & Pines, A. The burnout syndrome in the day care setting. Child Care Quarterly, 1977, 6(2), 100-113.

In many health and social-service organizations, professionals are required to work intensely and intimately with people on a large scale and on a continuous basis. Due to the number of situational pressures, many professionals are unable to maintain the caring and the commitment needed in human-service professions. This loss of caring that is characterized by an emotional exhaustion in which the professional no longer has any positive feelings, sympathy, or respect for clients or patients is called burnout. The professional who burns out is unable to deal successfully with the overwhelming stresses of the job. This failure to cope results in impaired performance, increased absenteeism, drug abuse, marital conflict, and mental illness.

The dehumanizing process is defined as a decreased awareness of human attributes of others and a loss of humanity in interpersonal interactions. This process involves psychological mechanisms such as intellectualization, denial, withdrawal, and isolation of affect. There are four classes of situations in which dehumanization is likely to occur: socially imposed dehumanization, dehumanization of self-gratification, dehumanization as a means to an end, and dehumanization in self-defense. There are five techniques that have been observed during field observations of professional staff coping with job stress. They include the use of certain types of language, compartmentalization, intellectualization, withdrawal, and social techniques.

In an extensive questionnaire and interview study of 83 staff members of several day care centers, statistically significance comparisons of the following are found; staff-child ratio, hours of work, time-outs, staff meetings, and program structure with the burnout phenomenon. The research identified several factors in the day-care setting that could either reduce the amount of stress, or aid the staff member in successfully coping with it. These factors involve reducing the amount of direct staff-client contact, improving or implementing social-professional support systems, sharing of personal feelings among staff, and training in interpersonal skills.

Mason, J. W. A historical view of the stress field. Journal of Human Stress, 1975, 1, 22-36.

This study presents selected aspects of stress theory. There have been two historical types of stress research: psychosocial and physiological. These two concepts of stress grew out of research done in the 1930s. Because this research included emotional stressors along with physical and psychological factors, there has been a widespread

assumption that psychological stress merely represents one component of a large unitary category of
biological   stresses   which   include   common
integrative mechanisms and are organized according
to common principles. The lack of specificity has
been a factor in the ambiguity associated with this
concept.

Nonspecific responses, believed to be common to a
wide variety of evocative agents, is known as
stress.   There has been a need for a considerable
time to check the research done with different
chemicals and methods to make sure that the right
answer was found.

Beginning in about 1960, an increasing body of
knowledge from experimental data began emerging
largely from the field of endocrinology.   This
raises questions about the nonspecificity concept
of stress.   One of the major developments in stress
research is the discovery of the sensitivity of the
pituitary-adrenal cortical system to psychological
and social influences, even those of a relatively
subtle nature.   Emotional stimuli rank very high in
prevalent stimuli that cause stress.

When special precautions are taken to prevent
psychological reactions in the study of physical
stimuli such as, heat, fasting, and moderate
exercise, it appears that the adrenal-cortical
system is not stimulated by nonspecific stress.

Twenty years ago, stress was regarded as a negli-
gible factor in comparison with physical factors.
Today,   the   burden   of   proof   lies   with   the
physiologists who must prove that physical factors
cause stress.   They must prove that physical
factors   influence   the   hormone   secretion   of
endocrine glands   The implication of this is that
early stress research was wrong.

The search for physiological first mediators of
stress responses has continued to remain largely
unproductive up to this time.   This is why there is
research being done in the field of endocrinology.
The unrecognized first mediator may have been
emotional arousal.   Emotional arousal is the most
nonspecific reaction common to a great diversity of

situations involving stress.

Matlin, M., & Stang, D. The pollyanna principle.
 Psychology Today, March 1978, 3, 56-59; 100.
  This study asserts that humans are an incor-
rigibly optimistic species. The preference for the
pleasant appears to predominate, leading the
authors to the Pollyanna principle. This principle
holds that we process pleasant items more accurately and efficiently than less pleasant items.
  The authors have listed 22 experimental results as
generalizations and the five following in detail to
support their hypothesis of incurable optimism.
1.   Word frequency. The findings were that
     people are as Pollyannaish in there
     spoken language as in their written
     language, and children and adults to the
     same degree.
2.   Size judgments. Researchers found that
     the more valued the stimuli, the larger
     the representation.
3.   Spew order. In results of a study of
     college students in listing pairs of
     personality traits and then circling the
     more pleasant member of each pair, the
     authors found positive relationships
     between pleasantness and spew order.
4.   Recall. A significantly greater number
     of pleasant events were recalled than
     unpleasant ones.
5.   Happiness. According to the studies of
     happiness, people are more likely to call
     themselves optimists than pessimists.
     College students were asked to compare
     themselves with their notion of the
     average person in the classroom on a
     variety of characteristics, one of which
     was happiness. Seventy-five percent
     rated themselves as happier than average,
     while only 8% rated themselves as less
     happy than average.
  The selective information-processing model is
favored as the explanation for pleasantness

predominating. It is argued that cognitive processes are selective, favoring some kinds of
information over others. Selectivity is needed
because of our limited capacity to deal with the
great mass of material available for processing.
Cognitive control processes located in long-term
memory seem to favor the processing of pleasant
information rather than neutral or unpleasant
information.

Further, it is proposed that selectivity operates
at many different stages in information processing.
Thus, selectivity in favor of pleasant information
is not limited to perception, language, or memory.
Instead, it seems to be inherent in the way humans
handle all information.

The authors propose that the products of cognitive
processes may be very concrete; but the explanations remain elusive.

Matteson, M. T., & Ivancevich, J. M. Straining
   under too much stress. Management World, July
   1979, $\underline{8}$(7), 4-6.

The negative effects of job stress--ill health
and poor performance--have resulted in the development of numerous programs to curtail it. Nonethe-
less, many are unaware of the causes, effects, and
cures of job stress.

In studies conducted by the authors, it was shown
that there is a definite relationship between job
stress and poor physical health. Some researchers
believe that 80% of all illnesses are stress
related. Further, the cost to the American industry for stress-related problems ranges well over a
billion dollars a year.

Everyone experiences job stress, though some
people are more susceptible than others. Whenever
one has an experience whereupon he reacts outside
of his normal behavior, he is subjected to stress.
These experiences may be varied. Thus, there are
several factors/conditions that can contribute to
job stress. The hard-driving, competitive individual who enjoys a challenge in work and social
situations (Type A person) is more prone to job

stress than one who is not. In short, job stress at one time or another can be expected to be experienced by all. What makes the difference is the amount of exposure to job stress and how it is responded to.

It is important that employers and employees be aware of the signs of job stress. Attention should be given to personality and behavior changes. It is normal for everyone to experience some type of change in personality and behavior some of the time. However, when changes become frequent and intensified, there is reason for concern.

McCarley, T. The psychotherapist's search for
  self-renewal. America Journal of Psychiatry,
  March 1975, 132(3), 221-224.

The normal stresses of middle age added to the emotional demands of being a psychotherapist can lead to depression. Because of feelings of embarrassment at the thought of being a patient and due to social relationships with colleagues to whom one might go for therapy, another source of help is indicated.

The annual institute of the American Group Psychotherapy Association (AGPA) allows practicing psychotherapists an opportunity not only to learn something about group therapy, but also to receive some attention for their personal emotional needs and conflicts. The dominant theme that emerged each year concerned the participants oppressive feelings of being overwhelmed by the responsibilities of caring for psychiatric patients and their feelings of discouragement.

The opportunity to explore their feelings periodically in a supportive, therapeutic atmosphere of a group may be very desirable, not only for the therapist's personal comfort, but also for improved functioning in the role as therapist.

McConnell, E. A. How close are you to burnout?
  RN, May, 1981, 44(5), 29-33.

It is the individual who believes it can't happen to me who becomes a prime candidate for burnout.

This individual is usually very dedicated, confident, and takes on more responsibility than he is capable of handling. Fatigue, depression, irritability, distancing, denial, and recourse to drugs or alcohol are a few of the many signs of burnout. It is a wise individual who heeds these warning signals before burnout occurs.

Nurses often set themselves up for burnout. More often than not, they have unrealistic, and therefore unmet, expectations for themselves and their patients. When burnout symptoms surface, nurses may be caught relating to patients or staff in a stereotyped, dehumanizing way. Relationships with coworkers may be distant and cold. It is important, therefore, to be aware of personal expectations and how realistic they are to help reduce the chances of burnout.

To prevent burnout, one must be able to recognize the stressors. Some experts indicate that keeping communications open with people around you is the best burnout-prevention strategy. To control burnout in oneself and others, the following coping mechanisms may be utilized:

1. Develop your problem-solving skills.
2. Get help.
3. Socialize.
4. Develop assertiveness skills.
5. Develop managerial skills.
6. Appreciate others.
7. Develop altruistic egoism.
8. Take a vacation.
9. Vary your job.
10. Practice relaxation techniques (yoga, aerobics, etc.).
11. Participate in physical activity.
12. Develop outside interests.

McKenna, D. Recycling pastors. Leadership, Fall 1980, 1(4) 18-24.

There often exists the attitude among church members that it is better for their pastor to wear out rather than rust out. However, if a pastor wears out he might not be repairable. A plan to

provide some realistic options for pastoral development is included in this article. Goals must be
set in all areas. Personal goals might include
physical fitness, economic planning, family relationships, hobbies, travel, and friendship building.
Other goals might include professional goals
within specific pastoral roles. Some goals will be
to reinforce strengths and others to aid in remedying weaknesses. Professional goals might include
inservice training that challenges the pastor
intellectually. Spiritual goals would also be set.
 Recycling pastors have to take into account their
individual variations. Some relax by taking a
five-minute nap, others need a day of complete
isolation after a hectic 80 hour week, yet still
others can work intensely for six months, but need
three weeks vacation time. One recommendation is
that vacations match the person's age: three weeks
in the 30s, four weeks in the 40s, etc.
Vacations are for physical relaxation and renewal.
Intellectual and spiritual renewal might be met by
offering sabbaticals. Another prospect for growth
is a formal evaluation based on specifics so that
pastors do not have to succumb to quirks.

McLean, A. A. Work Stress. Reading, Massachu-
    setts: Addison-Wesley, 1979.
    Stress defines a process or system which includes
not only the stressful event and the reaction to
it, but all the intervening steps between. The
stressor is a stressful event or stressful condition that produces a psychological or physical
reaction in the individual that is usually unpleasant and sometimes produces symptoms of emotional or
physiological disability. The stress reaction
concerns the consequences of the stimulus provided
by a stressor. Responses to stressful situations
at work have been measured by psychological
self-ratings, performance appraisals, and biochemical tests as well as the usual clinical studies of
employees presenting symptoms. There is a common
denominator to most occupational stress, and that

is change. All change involves loss of some kind. One of the greatest changes to which we all must adapt is the changing nature of work: the stressor. The stressors in the work setting are pervasive but are perceived differently by each person exposed to a given situation.

The physical setting, the health and safety practices of the employer, management attitudes toward employees, morale, the employee participation in decision making processes--these factors and many more are vital elements of the context in which we work. The broad social context in which an individual reacts in a healthy or unhealthy way is in part determined by such conditions as the state of the national and local economics. A number of rapid changes are occurring in industrialized society which have direct consequences on the work scene.

The research into stressful events and stressful conditions is ambiguous at best. But strong and cogent arguments clearly establish that the need to adapt to change at work is stressful, that the increasing pace of technological change calls for the need to adapt, which may not be done without breakdown, and that there are conditions that are obviously associated with an increased incidence of stress reactions and with higher-than-expected rates of stress-related disease. But there is other compelling evidence that suggests that occupations or events alone do not determine these stress reactions and these stress-related diseases. Rather, all those antecedents that go to make an individual a laborer or a physician, a shift worker, or one on steady daylight hours form a substrate that is the more important determinant of reaction to life's stressors. It is these characteristics that are far more important in determining possible stress reactions. Individual vulnerability, then, continues to be the most important of the three variables (individual vulnerability to stressors, the environment in which that vulnerability is exposed to stressors, and the resulting behavioral symptoms).

Research into stressors at work bears out the notion that literally anything can be termed stressful if the individual's vulnerability is extraordinarily high and if a supportive environment is unavailable. The following is a list of some of the important factors that have been found related to job stress:
1. Quantitative and qualitative overload.
2. Role ambiguity and role conflict. 3. Career-development conditions
   (frustration).
4. Organizational structure and climate.
5. Personal relationships at work.
6. The degree of responsibility for people.
Researchers increasingly find support for the idea that the more dangerous effects of occupational stress on health may be sharply reduced by social support. People are said to have social support if they have a relationship with one or more persons that is characterized by relatively frequent interactions, by strong and positive feelings, and by an ability and a willingness to give and take emotional and/or practical assistance in times of need. Support systems for the individual in the organization stem from the fundamental policies, the economic success, and the administrative practice of each work organization.
Table of Contents:
1. The stress of work
2. The dynamics of psychosomatic reaction
3. Context, vulnerablity, and specific stressors.
4. The broad social context
5. Ever-changing individual vulnerability
6. Stressful events and conditions at work
7. Social support systems
8. Personal stress management
9. A method of self-assessment

McMinn, S. Burnout. Nephrology Nurse, May-June, 1979, 1(3), 8-10.
Since the existence of chronic out-patient dialysis facilities, burnout and high staff

turnover have become very real problems occurring within nephrology nursing. It also occurs in other health care professionals as well, on an individual basis and among entire groups of staff members. Excessive demands on energy strength or resources cause these very special nurses to resign or seek another area in nursing.

For nephrology nurses, burnout usually begins somewhere between the first six months and the first year of employment. This is during the time period when the nurses have become comfortable with the technical aspects and become more aware of the stressful situations that chronic dialysis presents. Stress may develop into physical and/or behavioral systems of burnout including: fatigue, depression, sleeplessness, frequent headaches, hopelessness, negative and suspicious attitudes, mood change, and increased rigidity.

Preventative measures have been taken since the recognition of the burnout syndrome in relaton to employee turnover rates in dialysis units. In attempting to help nephrology nurses who have become victims of this syndrome, recognizing individual feelings along with the offering of support is of great importance in minimizing or alleviating the problems.

Meadow, K. P. Burnout in professionals working with deaf children. American Annals of the Deaf, February 981, 126(1), 13-22.

The Eastern Regional Conference for Educators of the Deaf was the site for the majority of this research study, while the rest of the subjects were associated with the demonstration school at Gallaudet College. These professional educators were given the Maslach burnout inventory to complete, demographic information and four extra questions related to job satisfaction. The results of the study were that teachers of deaf children were more likely to experience burnout than teachers of nonhandicapped students. Another result was that work role or job classification was another significant factor in burnout. The most compelling results were found among teachers who deal with the academic achievement of the deaf students, resulting in frustration and self-doubt and ultimately burnout. Teachers in demonstration schools experience the greatest amount of burnout while teachers in religious settings experience the least amount of emotional exhaustion.

Amount of time in teaching correlates to burnout in that the teachers with under two years and over 11 years have the least exhaustion while those in the middle of that span have the most. Presumably the newer ones are still enthusiastic and the older ones have adjusted. People with personal association with deafness experienced lower stress levels. People who were able to influence their own work situation had less burnout than others who were more rigidly employed. As a result of the survey, some suggestions for prevention and cure were developed. Developing support systems seemed to be the primary step to be taken. Other changes teachers can consider are change in pace, pattern, location, and approach. Another suggestion was to remember the reasons for entering the field in the first place and to maximize achievements or plan creative programs to implement. Finally, suggestions such as time out during the day, supportive staff meetings, and the use of a mental health consultant for short-term or ongoing programs were offered.

Mechanic, D. Stress, illness and illness behavior. Journal of Human Stress, 1975, 2, 2-6.

This paper is a discussion of some of the conceptual differences in the measurement and definition of stress, and an exploration of some of the alternative perspectives for continued research on the relatonships between life stress events and the health status of populations. It is the intervening factors that help explain why persons facing comparable stress react differently.

It is not enough to know the challenge that a person faces. The capacities of that person must also be taken into account if true measurements of stress are to be obtained. Exercises that help the person develop coping tecniques and reduce defense mechanisms for protection from negative arousal are more effective.

There has been significant confusion in the terms illnness and illness behavior. One refers to a definition, the other refers to a behavior. It is one thing to demonstrate that stress influences morbidity. It is another to show that stress may result in different responses to the occurrence of illness and ways of seeking assistance. This confusion results in part from the population that researchers use to study stress, and from the perspectives that guide their assumptions and research. The individual's motivations, skills, and defensive capacities do not develop in a vacuum, but rather, reflect the social context in which the person was reared and in which he or she develops social experience. Psychological stress does not deveop unless that individual is facing a threat or failure. Yet the loss is dependent on what society says is valuable. What helps to insulate people against stress is an intimate support system of friends and family. This has been shown to reduce depression significantly.

Miller, L. A., & Roberts, R. R. Unmet counselor needs from ambiguity to the Zeigarnik effect. Journal of Applied Rehabilitation Counseling, Summer 1979, 10(2), 60-65.

Professional rehabilitation counselors experience two kinds of work-related tension. The first is tension arising from work roles that require judgments and actions in situatons that do not permit clear-cut guidelines or a clear formula for performing many tasks. Instances or situations that stimulate this kind of tension are termed ambiguity tension. The second kind of tension arises from not being able to complete or get closure from tasks--closure tension. The Zeigarnik effect results from a situation involving the tension of always having incomplete tasks competing for your attention in the present. It seems the counselor is continuously under this effect insofar as closure is an essential and never-ending aspect of the rehabilitation process.

Five coping remedies counselors might try include: reducing contact time with clients, providing more structure, and directed interviews; ignoring paperwork that is not critical/audited; reducing or even eliminating placement contacts, follow-up, interaction with other agenices; and utilizing only the rehabilitation agencies resources. Additional recommendations for corrective attempts to aid the practicing counselor include the continuation of education and general training levels particularly in continuing education. The idea of personal growth should be emphasized through workshops that provide meditation, awareness, and self-actualizing experiences. Relevant, useful models for aiding the counselor in performing key tasks should be developed. The utilizaton of the direct, personal supervision model that educators employ in graduate training programs might be employed. Finally, the counselor resource procurement tasks provide a fertile ground to examine for possible ideas that might improve counselor closure and performance.

Miller, M. E. What the doctors say about stress. Supervisory Management, November 1981, 26(11), 35-39.

Executive stress has existed since the first executive. Concern has grown as society has become aware that there is both good and bad stress. The number of anxiety-ridden executives has spawned workshops designed to help business people deal with stress. One such workshop was held by Hahnemann Medical College and Hospital in Philadelphia. The following are the results of interviews with members of Hahnemann's medical staff.

The body reacts in various ways to stress. The higher the position an executive holds, the more likely he or she is to blow up at insignificant problems. When our body reacts to stress, the end result is a discharge of catecholamines, which are

adrenalin-like substances that enter the blood-
stream and cause physical distress on the already
distraught executive. This process affects the
cardiovascular system. Hypertension is a common
ailment of this system.

Some common ways harried managers can protect
themselves against the ravages of stress are:
exercise (a well-regimented exercise program wll
help the body build up a resistance to
catecholamines and other maladies); quit smoking
(after two years of cold turkey, the reformed
smoker faces no greater likelihood of heart attack
than someone who never smoked at all); have frequent checkups (one per year); and don't crowd your
schedule (schedule important meetings before 3
P.M.).

In addition to cardiovascular problems, another
common occurrence is Irritable Bowel Syndrome,
which is often confused with ulcers. IBS is not a
serious disease, as far as long-term repercussions
are concerned, but it is virtually uncontrollable.
However, recognizing IBS when it occurs can provide
the manager with some emotional relief.

Executive stress is an emotional as well as a
physical problem. The most common sources of
emotional stress among executives are changes in
personnel, interpersonal and social differences,
changes in office procedures and regulations, and
home and family problems that interfere with the
manager's schedule.

Some simple steps a person can take to reduce
stress are: increase communication with employees
and colleagues; plan a retreat or vacation; fix a
drink (providing you didn't have drinks for lunch
or are planning on drinking later); and seek
counseling (many large companies now employ resident psychologists).

Mirkin, G. How to cope with job stress. Nation's
    Business, January 1979, pp. 69-72.
Many individuals suffering from job stress can
reduce or eliminate it by changing factors of their
employment or engaging in activities that bring

enjoyment.   Some   stress-induced   illnesses   are:
stomach   ulcers,   migraine,   chest   pain,   heart
palpitations,   colitis,   diarrhea,   nasal   congestion,
muscle weakness, skin rashes, and impotency.

Job stress is not the only source that results in
stress-induced illness. Changes in lifestyle such
as marriage, vacation, birth of a baby, death of a
spouse, and being fired from a job can all cause
illness to occur. To make the reader more aware of
actions that can result in distress, thirty-one
danger signs were given. The signs are as follows:

1. General irritability, hyperexcitation, or depression.
2. Pounding of the heart.
3. Dryness of the throat and mouth.
4. Impulsive behavior, emotional instability.
5. Overpowering urge to cry or run and hide.
6. Inability to concentrate.
7. Feelings of unreality, weakness, and dizziness.
8. Predilection to become fatigued.
9. Floating anxiety.
10. Emotional tension and alertness.
11. Trembling and nervous ticks.
12. High pitched nervous laughter.
13. Tendency to be easily startled by small sounds.
14. Stuttering and other speech difficulties.
15. Grinding of the teeth.
16. Insomnia.
17. An increased tendency to move without reason.
18. Sweating.
19. Frequent urination.
20. Diarrhea and cramping.
21. Migraine headaches.
22. Premenstrual tension or missed periods.
23. Pain in the neck or lower back.
24. Increased or decreased appetite.
25. Increased smoking.
26. Increased use of legal drugs.
27. Alcohol and drug addiction.

28. Nightmares.
29. Neurotic behavior.
30. Psychosis.
31. Accident proneness.
If an individual has several of the above symptoms
and a physician can not relate them to an organic
problem, the following suggestions are made:
1. Know your limitations.
2. Exercise more.
3. Pursue activites that you enjoy.

Mitchell, E. How decision makers can beat stress.
  Computer Decisions, 1979, 11(6), 30-36, 102.
  An interview with Edgar Mitchell, astronaut to
the moon, deals with fighting stress and techniques
adapted from the space program. Mitchell feels
that in addition to our present generation being
under more stress, our communicatons are so good
that stresses are surfacing that have never been
apparent before. Moreover, he suggests that our
economic, political, and business problems are
interacting in far more aggravating ways.
  While the amount of stress factors seem to be
increasing, the damage such as heart attacks,
ulcers, alcoholism is also increasing. He believes
that our maladies are becoming more associated with
mental and emotional problems rather than physical
problems.
  As with other stress theorists, Mitchell believes
that some people thrive on various amounts of
stress, while others fail to cope. Stress comes
from finances, personal situations, and marital
situations with family situations probably creating
more debilitating stress than job stress, which is
more impersonal and objectively viewed.
  Mitchell suggests that people can always
choose--either to get out of the stressful situation or to change their view of that situation so
that it does not stress them. Keeping oneself
detached emotionally from potential stressful
situations is recommended (need vs. preference).
When dealing with a supervisor who creates stress,
one can quit, transfer, detach oneself from the

problem, or confront the boss with the
stress-inducing behavior.
To mentally deal with a stressful situation, one
can either imagine the problem to its most painful
end (desensitization) or on the other hand, think
of a quiet, relaxing, happy experience. Although
Transcendental Meditation, Zen, prayer, jogging,
group therapy are common ways of dealing with
stress, Mitchell feels that they all have strong
limitations.
Stress can be detected in coworkers and employees
by observing any changes in normal behavior:
frequent medical problems, increase in drinking, or
an inability to make decisions. Managers can
improve communication and interpersonal relationships, treat humans as human beings, and, perhaps,
give time off if needed to help reduce stressful
situations. In addition, counseling or recreational areas may be helpful. Giving people better
decision-making tools is also useful in breaking
down stress. Properly trained intuitive decision-making ability can result in decreasing
stress.

Moracco, J. C. Burnout in Counselors &
   Organizations. ERIC Counseling and Personnel
   Services Clearinghouse, ERIC/CAPS, School of
   Education, The University of Michigan, 1981.
   Counselor stress is defined as an adverse response that is often associated with pathogenic
physiological and biochemical changes as a consequence of aspects of the counselor's work and
mediated by the appraisal that demands made upon
the counselor present a threat to his self-worth
and that current coping mechanisms are inadequate
to diminish the perceived threat.
Burnout is an inadequate coping mechanism used
consistently by an individual to reduce stress.
Subsumed under burnout are such coping mechanisms
as drug use (abuse), withdrawal, sarcasm, loss of
humor, and a sense of paranoia. Often burned out
individuals adopt a tunnel vision and a set of
rigid attitudes that prevent the development of any

creative adaptation to stressors. A cycle is set whereby the burned out individual is less able to cope with stress, which in turn increases the frequency of stressful situations. Burnout is thus a collective term for a set of ineffective coping mechanisms to deal with stress.

The manifestations of stress and burnout in counselors include peptic ulcers, cardiovascular diseases, depression, anxiety, deterioration in work performance, and deterioraton in interpersonal relationships. In addition, the individual is easily fatigued, bored with work, and quick to anger.

Ineffective coping techniques include the agreement not to discuss work related topics at home, the utilization of jargon in a clinical but depersonalized manner, both physical and emotional distancing, and an increase in rigidity.

System strategies include the use of social-professional support systems, time-outs, and the rotation of job duties of counselors. Individual strategies include the use of self-observation and a greater self-awareness, vigorous exercise, relaxaton techniques, and cognitive restructuring (monitoring self statements for appropriateness and restructuring them with more realistic ones).

Organizational burnout is characterized by low employee morale, low rates of productivity, high levels of absenteeism, ineffective and infrequent communication among workers, and frequent job turnover. Conditions leading to burnout are lack of funds, lack of organizational flexibility, lack of decison-making power of middle managers, little recognition for staff efforts, and the nature of the client population.

Preventing burnout in organizations involves the providing of opportunities for organizational self-assessment, using a consensus approach to problem solving, giving feedback and rewards to members, providing time-outs for members experiencing burnout, and the screening of potential employees carefully.

Moracco, J. C., Danford, D., & D'Arizenz, R. V.
   The factorial validity of the teacher
   occupational stress factor questionnaire.
   Educational and Psychological Measurement, 1982,
   42(1), 275-283.
Studies have been conducted for the last fifty
years on the relationship of teacher stress,
anxiety, and mental health. Over the years, the
percentage of teachers experiencing stress has
increased to a reported level in 1976 of 78 percent
of teachers stating that they experienced moderate
or higher levels of stress.
 A study was conducted to determine the validity of
a scale when used with a large sample. The sample
group consisted of 644 teachers from 49 schools of
a school district with an enrollment of 121,000
students.
 Some survey items were considered to be loaded for
various factors. Another study, subsequent to the
one mentioned above, identified the factors of:
administrative support, working with students,
financial security, relationships with teachers,
and task overload. Although both lists of factors
represented stressful areas for the respective
groups sampled, the settings are believed to
influence responses given.
 The lack of administrative support was found to be
a major source of stress. This is due to the
teachers' perception that they have little or no
support from the principal, little authority,
little recognition, and too many responsibilities.
The second factor, teaching conerns, results in
stress because teachers feel inadequate in their
ability to improve student motivation, improve
student discipline, or involve parents in the
educatonal process. Results of the third factor
indicate that teachers feel they are not paid a
salary commensurate with their responsibilities,
and that the job did not provide them financial
security. Factors four and five indicated that
some teachers experience stress when they have to
interact with their colleagues and/or they have a
certain amount of work to accomplish.

Moracco, J. C., & McFadden, H. The counslor's role
in reducing teacher stress. Personnel and
Guidance Journal, 1982, 60(9), 549-552

Teachers are encountering increasing amounts of
stress, which is believed to affect their behavior
and effectiveness. By using the training of
counselors it is believed that the stress can be
reduced. The definition of stress is an alteration
of psychological homeostasis resulting from aspects
of the teacher's job that are perceived as threats
to the individual's well-being or self-esteem.

The model of stress which is used incorporates
cognitive aspects which allow for several intervention points. The categories of stressors which
are considered include: societal, occupational,
and home. Individual interactions with society,
home, and family, and occupation will determine in
part the extent of stress experienced or encountered. Individual belief systems, perceptions, and
coping mechanisms are also important in reducing
the effect of stress.

Counselors are able to assist the teachers who are
experiencing stress because of their position.
Counselors have a school-wide perspective which
becomes a factor in: knowledge of special programming for the school, flexible schedules, special
training, and position within the authority hierarchy. In order to reduce stress in teachers a
strategy should be used that includes inservice
training and support groups. As part of the
inservice training, coping mechanisms such as time
management and relaxaton exercises should be
examined. An important component of a stress
workshop for teachers is learning to think differently in certain situations, thus altering the
influence or effects (cognitive restructuring) of
those situations.

The goal of inservice training-assessment scales
and examination of behavior is to formulate a
workable and individualized stress-prevention plan.
This plan would incorporate variables that should
be actively used daily to reduce stress. Another
part of the plan may include a professional support

group. These groups offer teachers: an opportunity to analyze problems without endangering their
jobs; a source of new ideas and suggestions that
are of use both professionally and personally; a
feedback system to ward off stress; and a group to
belong to that will confirm the self-esteem and
value of its members.

Newman, J. E., & Beehr, T. A. Personal and
   organizational strategies for handling job
   stress: A review of research and opinion.
   Personnel Psychology, Spring 1979, 32(1), 1-43.
   The purpose was to explore what can be done by a
person or an organization in the way of productive,
constructive, and adaptive responses to stress. A
review of the literature was presented, beginning
with a definition of job stress: "a situation
wherein job related factors interact with the
worker to change his or her psychological and
physiological condition such that the person is
forced to deviate from normal functioning."
   The primary concerns of the authors are with
strategies that enable employees to enjoy good
physical and mental health, the implications of
such strategies for human effectiveness in the work
place, and hence, for organizational effectiveness.
   People may adopt strategies for handling job
stress; they may focus on the personal condition
and or the environmental condition that caused the
stress.
   Strong positive relationships have been demonstrated between TM and productivity based on
self-report questionnaires. It has also been
concluded that TM was also an effective way to
handle stress. The doer and the target would be
the focal point, the adaptive action would be the
20 minute periods in the morning and in the afternoon. The adaptive response could be considered
both curative and productive.
   In psychological withdrawal, the employees felt
that certain job situations would demand that the
employee withdraw himself or herself psychologically to minimize the effects of the stressful

situation.

Another strategy is to plan ahead: an individual who thinks about forthcoming events, and the potential stresses for those events, can make an adaptive response.   Research has indicated that planning ahead is an effective strategy.   Personal strategies aimed at changing one's phys-ical/physiological conditions include behavior modification.   Evidence is presented that behavior modification is a stress reducer.   However, the authors state that no hard evidence was provided to substantiate the claim of behavior modification, so the effectiveness cannot be evaluated.   Other methods mentioned were: desensitization and participation in social groups.

Strategies aimed at changing the person and the environment were also provided.

Nicholson, E. A., & Miljus, R. C.   Job satisfaction
   and turnover among liberal arts college
   professors. Personnel Journal, November 1972,
   51, 840-845.

Many colleges and universities in the United States have experienced a relatively high rate of faculty turnover during the last twenty-five years. While turnover has some advantages for both faculty members and colleges, a high rate of turnover in some colleges can result in a faculty of limited commitment, ineffective curriculum development, and faculty unrest.

From the point of the individual faculty member, although he wishes to be upwardly mobile, he also seeks to gain meaningful experience and satisfac-tion as he climbs the ladder.   He wants to be mobile only as a result of a better offer, not as a result of dissatisfaction with his present posi-tion.   Turnover is needed in a college to prevent stagnation, but a high rate of faculty turnover can be costly both to the reputation of the college and to the well-being of the students.   The task of the administration is to avoid or remedy situations that result in undesirable faculty turnover, while at the same time providing opportunities for faculty advancement and professional growth.

To control faculty turnover, it is important that personnel policies and practices be based upon a thorough knowledge of the attitudes, values, and aspirations of the faculty member.

The purpose of this article is to look at those factors or conditions of employment with which faculty members are the most satisfied or dissatisfied, for we assume that academic people make employment decisions based upon their personal aspirations.

During the academic year 1968-69, questionnaires were sent to all faculty members at 21 liberal arts colleges in Ohio, requesting both biographical data and attitudinal data.

Faculty respondents were asked to indicate how satisfied or dissatisfied they were with each of 46 factors. They were especially satisfied with the nature of their work, class size, courses taught, teaching load, and academic freedom. Congenial and competent colleagues appear to be a significant source of satisfaction for the liberal arts professors. Also cited frequently were favorable conditions of service, including flexible teaching schedules, pleasant associates, and longer summer terms for study and travel. They were much less satisfied with the tangible reward of the system, especially salary and promotion considerations.

Salary differentials within the college, criteria for promotion, and the procedures for determining salary increases and promotion are apparently the most dissatisfying aspects of employment as liberal arts colleges. The comments of the respondents' attest to their dissatisfaction with promotion procedures.

The most striking aspects of the data is that those who intended to leave were less satisfied than their colleagues who were remaining, with 45 of the 46 factors. Turnover most often results from conditions that produce general alienation and not from dissatisfaction with a single concern.

Promotion and salary policies and administrative practices appear to be the very core of the turnover problem.   This is true, not because faculty are first and foremost economic people, but like other employees they seek tangible evidence of achievement, desire organizational recognition for their accomplishments and seek consistent and equitable treatment from their superiors.

The amount of dissatisfaction with salary and promotion factors, even among those faculty members who intend to stay, suggests that administrators need to review their policies in a justifiable manner.   Faculty should be made fully aware of what is expected of them, how they are evaluated, the criteria for evaluation and salary increases, and who determines promotions and salary levels.

Experience leads us to believe that administrative secrecy pervades many small colleges partly as a result of tradition, but in a great part because some of the practices could not survive close scrutiny.

Notarius, C. I., & Levenson, R. W.   Expressive tendencies and physiological response to stress. Journal of Personality and Social Psychology, 1979, 37 (7), 1204-1210.

While the study of overt emotional expression and the physiological response is one of old standing, this paper deals with only the expressions of the face.   The debate over whether or not facial display is important in an emotional response is moot, but no accord has been reached on whether or not this effect attenuates or augments response to emotion-arousing situations.

An observer watched a subject on a video screen and tried to decode the subject's emotional response based upon the subject's facial responses. The subject's respiratory responses were monitored. When facial expressions are controlled and kept to a minimum, the accuracy of the observer's evaluation of the subject's emotional response is reduced.

As results in other studies have varied with the results presented here, there is great difficulty in assessing the overall responses in a uniform manner. There is some conflict presented by the instructor as to the tone and presence that he may offer the subjects.

The basic findings of this report indicate that expressive subjects were significantly less physiologically reactive to an emotional stressor than were nonexpressive subjects. The report cannot prove that facial expressions function as a causal agent.

All in all, further studies will have to be done in order to simplify the assessment needs and the overall judgement of the accuracy that facial expressions render.

Organ, D. Meanings of stress. Business Horizons, 1979, 22(3), 32-48.

Stress has become the latest phrase to catch the attention of the masses. It is the rationalization of the failure and the glory of the successful. Any behavior, no matter how bizarre, cruel, or apparently irrational, is suddenly understandable if we imagine the individual as operating under stress conditions. Any act of love or benevolence is somehow tarnished if it did not create stress for the actor or was not born out of the very crucible of stress.

Stress has become a watchword of the time that comes as close as any word to expressing the subjective tone of the world view. The word functions more and more to express than to denote. So the word becomes more susceptable to usage when it can be neither proven or disproven.

People are forced to act the role of aggressive, assertive, energetic, ambitious individuals who are naturally geared to operating at a high adrenalin level. This causes more physiological stress on people than nature meant for them to operate under. Part of that demand may be the very effort to maintain performance in the presence of simultaneous competing demands from the environment, such as unpredictable noise, information overload, fatigue from illness, or even distractions by sexually arousing stimuli. Because of stress, many business men become "hooked on adrenalin."

Osborn, R. N., & Vicars, W. M.   Sex stereotypes:
  An artifact in leader behavior and subordinate
  satisfaction analysis. Academy of Management
  Journal, 1976, 19(3), 439-449.
  Women compose over 50 percent of the population
and 38 percent of the work force, yet only 18
percent of management positions. Two questions are
considered to determine management potential of
women: 1) Do female managers behave differently
toward subordinates than male managers? And 2) do
female managers have a different effect on subordinates than male managers?
  Arguments against women in management positions
include sex-role stereotyping, i.e., men are
naturally superior to women and aggressive and
competitive enough to gain follower respect.
Differences were found, though, in studies of
short-term, artificial situations and field
studies. In artificial environments, sex stereotyping detrimentally affects evaluations of
females in selection and promotion decisions and in
performance ratings (even when all female raters
were used); leadership descriptions depended on
leader sex. In field studies, however, where
leaders and subordinates have had an ongoing,
long-term relationship, no significant differences
in leader behavior between males and females was
found.
  Related demographic characteristics such as age,
education, or experience differences may in fact
contribute to differences in leader behavior. The
association between leader sex and leader behavior
and employee satisfaction in two mental-health
institutions was investigated in this study.
Although a statewide survey of mental-health
institutions was done, only two facilities were
used in this study since in the others, only the
lowest management levels have sufficient females to
constitute an adequate sample. Upper-management
posts were held almost exclusively by males.
  Results were that across both institutions, female

leaders are reported as having somewhat higher
consideration and initiating structure.   Although
there are scattered significant results for the
association between leader demographics, employee
sex, and employee demographics, leader sex does not
appear to have a consistent influence on leader
behavior.   In addition, no significant association
between leader sex and employee satisfaction was
found.

The results, however, are in conflict with lab
findings where leader sex was found to be associated with leader behavior and employee satisfaction. This discrepancy between lab and field seems
to come from subjects responding based on available
stereotypes in lab settings; in field settings,
extensive interpersonal contact provides subjects
with a more realistic basis for their behavior.
Proper technical training and accumulated time on
the job can mediate any sex stereotyping that does
exist.   It was recommended that longitudinal data
are needed to verify these results.

Pacinelli, R. N., & Britton, J. O.   Some correlates
   of rehabilitation counselor job satisfaction.
   Rehabilitation Counseling Bulletin, June, 1969,
   12(4), 214-220.
The recent expansion of the federal-state vocational rehabilitation program has created a shortage of counselors.   In the 91 state agencies more
than 850 new counselors are needed each year.   Of
this number, 300 counselors are needed to fill job
vacancies due to the turnover rate.   One way to
decrease the turnover rate is through improvement
of job satisfaction.   The degree of satisfaction
which an individual receives from his or her job
depends upon an interaction between the counselor
and various job-related factors.   The literature
suggests the importance of studying individual job
satisfaction in relation to supervisory behavior
and background of the worker.   No research in a
rehabilitation setting has been reported concerning
the relationship between job satisfaction of the
counselor and supervisory leadership behavior.

The purpose of this study was to examine the relationship between counselor job satisfaction, the counselor's perception of the supervisor's leadership style and selected background factors of the counselor. The areas of leadership behavior were consideration and initiating structure.

In reviewing the literature the data indicates that consideration and initiating structure leadership behaviors are related to rehabilitation counselor job satisfaction with almost equal importance. This is not surprising since consideration behavior is indicative of mutual trust, friendship, respect, etc. The findings of this study suggest that improvement of supervisor leadership style could have a positive effect on counselor job satisfaction. Rehabilitation administrators should consider training programs for supervisors that emphasize leadership style.

The findings were conclusive that age of the rehabilitation counselor was the most important background factor correlated with satisfaction variables. Older counselors rated themselves higher than did the younger counselors. This suggests that counselor expectations of the job differ with age, also, that present agency policies and practices are geared toward the older counselor. Older counselors tend to have a more varied work background and this knowledge of the work world may contribute to their job satisfaction. Younger counselors tend to be more idealistic and may find the agency lacking in several respects, such as job prestige, professional stimulation, professional freedom to express ideas, and the underuse of skills. It is, therefore, of vital importance to increase the job satisfaction of younger staff members and indirectly help to influence their decision to remain with the state agency.

The findings indicate that supervisory staff training should be given indepth consideration by rehabilitation administrators. Administrative and agency policies and procedures should be evaluated periodically and changed to meet the needs of present staff and to attract to the agency those individuals who are interested in rehabilitation counseling as a career.

Parkington, J. J., & Schneider, B. Some correlates of experienced job stress: A boundary role study. Academy of Management Journal, June 1979, 22(2), 270-281.
Employees of service organizations tend to experience job stress due to role ambiguity/role conflict. This is increased when perceived management and customer demands are in conflict. Frequently this conflict is related to employee feelings of job dissatisfaction, frustration, lack of confidence in the organization, and a propensity to leave the firm.
Action that tends to cause negative results is the bureaucratization of service organizations. This changes the function of the organization from service to system maintenance, which causes people to feel unneeded. By using an "enthusiastic orientation to service," which is client-centered, managers can reduce the negative effects of role ambiguity/conflict. The purpose of the study was to determine whether customer evaluation of service directly influenced employee work.
Results of the study indicate that "service orientation discrepancy and role stress perceptions are related to organizational dissatisfaction, intention to leave the organization, frustration, and feelings that the quality of service being offered to customers is low." To change perceptions it was suggested that use of an intervention strategy (personnel selection) may be needed. Selection of employees holding an orientation similar to that of management may profit the organization in terms of improved quality of service.

Parrina, J. J. From Panic to Power: The Positive Use of Stress. New York, John Wiley & Son, 1979.
This self-help book uses scientifically derived principles and techniques for identifying, monitoring, and controlling stress for more productive

work and more effective personal living. Case
studies of three people, who have become nonfunc-
tional because of stress, are used to demonstrate
the concepts detailed in the chapters.
The physiological functioning of the body under
stress is explained using the Human Response System
developed by the author. Information is provided
concerning the integration and application of
biofeedback, self-control, self-regulation, and the
physiological aspects of stress.
The application of this data is intended to
relieve stress and assist one in developing a
personal feedback system to gain some control over
one's psychological and physiological destinies.
The chapters included in this book are as follows:

The appendices detail the results of maladaptive
coping, provide a relaxation technique called the
muscular relaxation response, and include a behavior profile in the form of a 30-item analysis to
determine one's level of stress.

Patrick, K. S. Burnout: Job hazard for health
  workers. Hospitals, November 16, 1979, 87-90.
    Burnout may be manifested in a variety of ways,
but it has basic, consistently identifiable elements: emotional exhaustion, shift toward negative
attitudes, and sense of personal devaluation that
occurs over time in response to continuous
work-related stress. Many of the first symptoms of

burnout are physical. These include increasing levels of fatigue, easy tiring, sleep distrubances, low levels of energy, changes in appetite, lowered resistance to infection, or a variety of physiological dysfunctions such as gastrointestinal disturbances and headaches.

A number of dramatic effects of burnout occur in an employee's psychological functioning. These include:

1. Negative changes in attitudes toward clients, patients, and their families occur. These attitude changes may generalize to coworkers, supervisors, peers, managers, and the employment setting.

2. Emotional exhaustion or fatigue becomes frequent, thereby adversely affecting interpersonal contact between the employee and patient.

3. A key outcome of burnout is a drastic change in the employee's self-image. He may develop self-deprecating attitudes and may begin to make negative statements about himself.

4. Depression, anger, or withdrawal are not uncommon emotional changes that accompany the burned-out employee.

5. Rigidity increases as the employee tries to maintain order and control over his surroundings.

Causes of burnout can be either self-generated or system-generated. The self-generated causes are: (a) highly stressful patient care; (b) repeated decision-making situations; (c) lack of self-awareness; (d) self-imposed restrictions; (e) stresses in personal life; (f) job overload, too many hours of work; (g) adversive work setting, i.e., high noise levels; (i) lack of support systems for employees; and (j) isolation caused by job responsibilities.

The goals of burnout-care programs include prevention, intervention, and management. These include: (1) alterations in problem-solving and

decision-making approaches, statements about oneself, and attitudes; (2) develop or modify coping capacities, change ways in which emotions are expressed, and enhance growth potential; (3) the individuals' communication skills should be improved and strengthened; (4) the importance of health care should be emphasized; smoking, excessive drinking, or poor diet habits should not be overlooked by the employer in assuming responsibility for change; (5) recreation, relaxation, and even meditation should be encouraged; and (6) changes in the work setting that would produce any pleasant changes in stimulation,
visual or tactile, should be examined.

Programmatic approaches to stress management as a means of burnout intervention, prevention, and management are viable and necessary in health-care settings.

Patterson, C. H. Power, prestige and the rehabilitation counselor. Rehabilitation Research Practice Review, 1970, 1(3), 1-7.

The rehabilitation counselor has a job that is separate and distinct from that of the coordinator. To differentiate the two, the author proposes that the rehabilitation counselor's title be changed to "psychological counselor." Unlike the psycholoigcal counselor, the counselor-coordinator works with the clients and in general, integrates the rehabilitation process, etc. The psychological counselor "counsels." Though regarded as a lower-level professional the counselor-coordinator position is not any less important than the psychological counselor position, and perhaps is more important in the overall rehabilitation process.

Much of the confusion between these two roles has developed because of the rehabilitation counselor's desire for power and prestige. The individual who coordinates the rehabilitation process is seen as being in the public eye. In controlling the total rehabilitation process, the rehabilitation counselor gains public recognition and client applause. The author contends that power and prestige are not

the name of the game. Counselors should be more
concerned with the client's welfare. If power and
prestige are what is desired then perhaps the
counselor should be working as the coordinator
instead. "Power and prestige do not arise from the
counseling function, or the helping relationship."
It is time that the rehabilitation counselor act
in his capacity. The demand for counsel-
or-coordinators has been so great that they cannot
be supplied by programs preparing professional
counselors. The positions are often being filled
by those without any graduate preparation in
rehabilitation counseling.

Phillips, D. K., Ministerial burnout. Your Church,
    Nov./Dec., 1980, 26(6), 58-59.
    Ministerial burnout is similar to burnout in all
the helping professions because the helper is
involved in others' problems, often taking on those
symptoms himself, which renders him ineffective in
helping the client or parishioner to a hopeful
resolution. The resultant sense of futility is a
factor in burnout. Pastors also have to live with
unrealistic expectations held by both themselves,
colleagues, and others in the congregation and
community. They are supposed to be good in everything from preaching and counseling to administration and janitoring. A clinician in Texas
describes burnout as what happens when feelings are
no longer processed so that personal needs are not
met.
    Burnout often appears as fear, apathy, fatigue,
headaches, backaches, tension, and nervousness.
These can be overcome by a program of reestab-
lishing control over your own life. First, limitations must be accepted and dealt with. Routines
can and should be modified to provide a fresh
variety. The emotional climate including exercise,
vacation, and relaxing is another source of change.
Finally, everyone needs a support system for
sharing, for objectivity, and for growth.

Pines, A. M., Aronson, E., & Kafry, D. Burnout:

From tedium to personal growth. New York:
Macmillan, 1981.

Tedium and burnout are states of physical,
emotional, and mental exhaustion. They are characterized by physical depletion, by feelings of
helplessness, by emotional drain, and by the
development of negative self-concept and negative
attitudes towards work, life, and other people.
While tedium and burnout are similar in
symptomatology, they are different in origin.
Tedium is the result of any prolonged chronic
pressures; it is the result of having too many
negative and too few positive features in one's
environment--too many pressures, conflicts, and
demands, combined with too few acknowledgements and
meaningful accomplishments. Burnout is the result
of constant or repeated emotional pressure associated with intense involvement with people over long
periods of time. Such involvement is particularly
prevalent in all human-service professions.

Although the intensity, duration, frequency, and
consequences may vary, both tedium and burnout have
three basic components: physical, emotional, and
mental exhaustion. Physical exhaustion is characterized by low energy, chronic fatigue, weakness,
and weariness. Emotional exhaustion involves
feelings of depression, helplessness, and entrap-
ment leading in extreme cases to mental illness or
thoughts about suicide. Mental exhaustion is
characterized by the development of negative
attitudes towards oneself, toward work, and toward
life. People deal with tedium and burnout in
different ways. Some burned-out workers leave
their professions, change jobs within the organization, climb up the administrative ladder, never
quit and become "dead wood."

There are three common antecedents of burnout in
the human services. They include: work that is
emotionally taxing, certain personality characteristics that made people choose human service as
a career, and a shared "client-centered" orientation.

Bureaucratic organizations in general share three

antecedents of tedium: overload, lack of autonomy, and lack of rewards. Quantitative overload implies more work than can be completed in a given period of time. Qualitative overload implies that the job requires skill and knowledge exceeding those of the workers. Lack of control over one's environment is a highly stressful experience which may result in "learned helplessness" and depression. A perceived lack of autonomy appears to be a powerful antecedent of tedium. Frustration resulting from the lack of autonomy is a common antecedent of tedium in bureaucratic organizations. Complex organizations are inefficient distributors of rewards, appreciation, and recognition. Tedium comes in part from the feeling that one is working hard, beyond the requirements of the job, and yet one's efforts are not appreciated.

Organizational remedies for tedium and burnout are listed below:

1.   Reduce the client-staff ratio.
2.   Improve the availability of time out.
3.   Limit the hours of stressful work.
4.   Provide organizational flexibility to accommodate the individual.
5.   Improved training.
6.   Create positive work conditions.
7.   Communicate the significance of work completed.

An important development for combating burnout and tedium includes the fostering of social support systems. Social support is defined as information leading subjects to believe that they are cared for and loved, esteemed, valued, and that they belong to network of communication and mutual obligation. There are six functions of social support systems. They include:

1.   Listening (active).
2.   Technical appreciation.
3.   Technical challenge.
4.   Emotional support.
5.   Emotional challenge.
6.   Sharing social reality.

Social support systems can be seen as mediating

variables that act as buffers and supports to individuals in their social environment; these mediating variables reduce the effects of stressful environmental conditions and thus slow the tedium cycle.

Recommendations for intrapersonal coping are:

1. Examining individual coping by keeping a log of daily stresses, coping strategies, and success or failure in coping.
2. Goal setting is important for individuals to clarify priorities.
3. Acknowledging time as a precious and limited resource.
4. Acknowledging vulnerabilities.
5. Separating clearly the work sphere from life outside of work.
6. Providing one's own reinforcement.
7. Changing dispositional self-attributes.
8. Maintain a positive attitude.

Table of contents includes:

What is burnout? an overview
Burnout and tedium: the experience
Burnout among people in the helping professions
Occupational tedium among people in bureaucracies
Special issues concerning women
Organizational coping strategies
Social support systems
Intrapersonal coping strategies
Postscript: Burnout and tedium outside of work

Pines, A., & Maslach, C. Characteristics of staff burnout in mental health settings. Hospitals & Community Psychiatry, April 1978, 29(4), 233-237.
This study was designed to determine the characteristics of staff burnout and ways of coping with it from data on institution-related and personal variables for 76 staff members in the San Francisco area.

In a series of perliminary studies a sample of 200 health and social service personnel used a comparable set of techniques to try to combat burnout, including the following:

1. Detached concern.
2. Intellectualizing.
3. Compartmentalization.
4. Withdrawal.
5. Reliance on staff.

These preliminary studies indicated a high incidence of burnout in health and social-service professions and it was a major factor in low worker morale, absenteeism, high job turnover, and other indices of job stress.

The more intensive study reported in this article shows results on institutional and personal variables. The institutional variables were:

Overall staff-patient ratio--the larger the ratio of patients to staff, the less staff members liked their jobs and the more they tried to separate them from their personal lives.

Schizophrenic population--the higher percentage in the overall populations, the less job satisfaction expressed.

Work relationships--these were affected by certain working conditions and were related to staff members' attitudes toward their work, the institution, and the patients.

Staff-patient relationships--the quality of interaction between staff and patients was related to staff members' perception of the institution, other staff members, the work, and the patients.

Frequency of staff meetings--high frequency of staff meetings was correlated with very negative and dehumanizing attitudes toward patients.

Time-outs--staff who could afford to withdraw temporarily to other work activities showed more favorable attitudes toward patients.

Work schedules--longer work hours were correlated
    with more staff stress and negative feelings.
Time spent in direct contact with patients, with
    other staff, and in administrative
    duties--these items correlated with higher
    rankings on negative adjectives in
    questionnaires and more of a sense of failure on
    the job, with patients and achieving goals.
Work-sharing--if the general workload was shared,
    less stress was perceived.
  The findings of this study showed that mental-health workers experience personal stress as a
result of working closely and intensively with
patients over an extended time. There are several
steps recommended to reduce or cope successfully
with stress. The following set of recommendations
primarily emphasizes institutional changes:
reducing patient-to-staff ratio, shortening the
work hours, allowing more opportunities for
time-outs, sharing the patient load, changing the
function of staff meetings, improving work relationships, holding retreats for staff members,
taking precautions as an individual, and training
students to deal with future stresses.

Prentki, R. L. Burn-out in TR: A direct service
  phenomenon. Illinois Parks and Recreation, 1980,
  11(4), 12-13.
  Burnout is a term that has been defined as a
debilitating condition involving the development of
negative emotional, psychological, and physical
reactions to occupational stress. It has often
been used to describe the lack of satisfaction and
feelings of inadequancy common among personnel in
direct human-service contact. As in other
health-service fields, practioners in therapeutic
recreation, particularly those in treatment
settings, are extremely susceptible to this condition due to the unique pressures of constant direct
service contact with handicapped individuals.

Individuals involved in the burnout process frequently exhibit a negative change in behavior over
a period of time. The prevalence of burnout among
staff has been identified as being related to high
rates of job turnover, reduced staff morale, poor
quality of client care, and lack of job satisfaction.

To deal with burnout effectively the administrator
must   recognize   the   innate   properties   of
health-service professions such as the long hours,
extensive direct service, and large client to staff
ratios that often lead to burnout. In addition
there must be a realization and acceptance by both
the agency and the practioner of the burnout
potential of each individual and identification of
the specific causes associated with each direct-service position. Client-staff ratios should
be established to limit client-staff contact.
Related approaches include the rotation of work
schedules, the proper utilization of physical
exercise as a relaxant, involvement in professional
organizations, and the constructive use of nonwork
time to develop other recreational and outside
interests. These approaches can aid the individual
in maintaining a good self-image and a positive
attitude toward life in general. Burnout is an
occupational hazard of therapeutic recreation
requiring a sensitive awareness of individual
vulnerability and positive established procedures
for alleviating vocational stress.

Price, J. Stress requires new directions. School
   Guidance Worker, May 1977, 32(5), 27-29.
   Stress is an intrinsic part of life. Professionals in all occupations at one time or another
encounter stress-provoking situations. There are
some researchers who contend that at least a small
amount of stress is necessary for growth and
change.

In one instance, a counselor operating a counseling department in a modern secondary school also
experiences a certain amount of stress. Stress
resulted from the counseling experience itself and

other situations. To cope with this stress, a
reevaluation of the counseling program was done to
determine what the recipients of the service
wanted. Phases were introduced to help meet the
needs of the students as well as the teachers. As
a result, programs not already in existence were
begun. Those programs that were standing were
modified. Changes were made overall to improve
services and professionalism.

In all of this, stress was not totally eliminated.
What did occur, however, was that more time and
concentration was devoted to necessary services.
An overall improvement in the counseling department
could be noted. Change from routine daily tasks
helped to reduce the stress being experienced. In
short, since stress cannot be totally avoided,
finding ways to deal with it seems to be the next
best thing.

Quick, J. C., & Quick, J. D. Reducing stress
    through preventive management. Human Resource
    Management, 1979, Fall, 18(3), 15-22.
Stressor effects that lead to distress for an
employee are undesirable because distress is
associated with identifiable individual and organizational costs. Key stressors for people at
work, costs associated with the mismanagement of
stress, and ways managers can take a healthy,
preventive approach to stress are examined.
 Role factors and job factors are primary
stressors, but physical factors and interpersonal
factors are also significant creators of stress.
An employee can be expected to behave in a certain
manner, therefore causing moderate stress; if the
demands are ambiguous or unclear, the stress level
noticably rises. Job factors creating stress
include multiple tasks being included in the job,
performance appraisal, lack of hygienic job factors, and lack of autonomy in accomplishing various
tasks. Physical factors include high noise levels,
excessive vibrations, air currents, extreme temper-
atures, and floods. Interpersonal factors involve
personality conflicts or unpleasant results if the

individual deviates from the norm.

It is the individual's management of the body's stress outcome (fight or flight response) that determines whether the final outcome of the stressful experience is health and adaptive (eutress).

Individual costs include discomfort, disease, disability, or perhaps even death. Job dissatisfaction is one of the first symptoms of stress. Organizational costs take the form of industrial accidents, tardiness and absenteeism, turnover, and medical claims.

Preventive management can take the strain out of stress. Organizational activities are implemented through strategies, which include techniques such as role analysis, job enrichment, work redesign, and performance planning. Individual activities are implemented, which involve three categories: stressor- directed, symptom-directed, or generalized. Systematic desensitization is useful as a stressor-directed technique. Autogenic training and biofeedback are useful as symptom-directed techniques. In addition, relaxation response and aerobic exercise are recommended as generalized approaches to stress management. Other techniques such as acupuncture, hypnosis, and dietary therapy are also used, but not on a wide scale. These preventive-management techniques can enable employees to channel their responses to stressors so as to achieve eutress.

Rabkin, J. G., & Struening, E. L.   Life events, stress and illness. Science, December 1976, 194, 1013-1020.

An abundant amount of literature relating to life events, stress and illness is available. Unfortunately, however, many of these studies repeat the results and the errors of previous ones. In effect, there has been a delay in the growth and development of knowledge in this field.

Recently a study was conducted to review the literature on life-events stress and the onset of illness; to delineate trends in its development; to evaluate conceptual and methodological approaches

implemented; to identify primary variables mediating the impact of stressful situations on individuals and groups; and to recommend more comprehensive
approaches to substantive concerns.
  Life-events research is designed to demonstrate
the relationship between onset of illness and an
increase in the number of events that call for
socially adaptive responses by the individual. It
is believed that the greater the number of events,
the greater the effect. These events act as
participating factors that affect the timing but
have no affect on the type of illness episodes.
Other studies show similar relationship between the
number and the intensity of life events and the
forecast for the probability of specific illnesses.
  The literature presently available on the relationship of life events, stress, and illness does
not provide conceptual and theoretical orientation
in the design and execution of empirical studies.
To better understand illness onset, these studies
must include the complexity of the phenomena being
researched. More emphasis should be placed on a
detailed concept and sampling of the universe of
life events. Some improvement in data analytic
procedures is still a major challenge for researchers interested in life events, stress, and illness.

Raphael, A. J., Karpf, D. A., & Sills, F. W. Human
    relations training program: Prescription for
    rehab staff satisfaction. Rehabilitation
    Literature, Jan.-Feb. 1980, 41(1-2), 16-28; 23.
    Employees of rehabilitation facilities that offer
long-term care face the challenge of helping
patients through their emotional crises without
becoming depressed or emotionally drained. Facilities that are multiethnic (staff and patients) and
serve patients from a variety of social, psychological, intellectual circumstances/backgrounds
have a compounding of the difficulties encountered.
In an effort to help facility personnel provide
better services, a training program was developed
to develop interpersonal skills to increase sensitivity to the needs of patients; develop an

understanding of group dynamics to increase staff communications, support, and cohesion; and develop an understanding of themselves (insight) that would be beneficial in their personal as well as their professional lives.

Participants in the study included eleven licensed practical nurses, eight registered nurses and six nursing assistants. Results of the questionnaires indicate that the nursing profession has experienced positive changes overall and that nurses in particular have made positive gains.

Nursing personnel are now better trained and perform work of higher quality. As a group nursing personnel are more self-sufficient; they demonstrate more self-control, foresight, cooperation, and interpersonal sensitivity, than previously. Nursing assistants, as a subgroup, are gaining more acceptance, while becoming more responsive in general. Conversely, licensed practical nurses are becoming more cautious, although they recognize their value to the nursing profession and have, as a group, become more skilled. As a result of the training program, registered nurses became more responsible for patient care, more self-sufficient, and more plan-oriented. A majority of the nursing personnel felt that their patients benefited from the human-relations training because of the improved care received from the nurses.

The long-term effects of such training indicate that participants incorporate aspects of this into their personality as part of self-improvement. When rehabilitation personnel are able to use this training effectively to minimize the impact of psychological crises, they are more effective employees. The training allows an employee to maintain a higher morale and thereby reduce the rate of turnover caused by low morale or frustration.

Rediger, G. L. Clergy burnout. Church Management--the Clergy Journal. July, 1980, 56(8), 10-11, 27.

This article describes burnout as "the jargon

name for a syndrome identified with the helping professions." People have been involved in intense effort to help people for many years, which results in almost unbearable pressure, but it hasn't always been called burnout. The initial symptoms for clergy are exhaustion, apathy, despair, discouragement, and anxiety. These are often accompanied by irritation, cynicism and a "one-track mind." There are often sleep problems, lack of exercise and eating, with an inability to draw enjoyment from anything, including sex. At this point burnout becomes "the almost complete exhaustion of the physical, emotional and spiritual resources necessary for normal human functioning." There are specific reasons for clergy burnout:

> The pastor is the identified leader of society's chief valuing institution; the pastor must deal with polarities and conflict continually and is expected to resolve these; the pastor's clients are his employers; the pastor believes he is dealing with the key issues of life while society rewards and acknowledges the achiever, the manipulator and the accumulator, all of which violate the beliefs clergy are trying to teach. (p.10)

Faith, professional identity, and personal identity are all wrapped up together in a manner that is different from other jobs.

The author offers some specific advice to avoid burnout. The first suggestion is to increase awareness of the given realities of a situation in an objective manner, so as not to waste energy expecting unlikely behavior. Another idea is self-nuture, which includes exercise, leisure, hobbies and interests. Making decisions without expecting perfection helps to avoid or alleviate burnout. The last factor is an attitude of wholeness as a creation of God.

Reed, S. Teacher burnout: A growing hazard. The New York Times, January 1, 1979.

Thousands of teachers across the country will be struck by the debilitating disease of teacher

burnout. Not entirely a new phenomenon, nevertheless it is still harmful both to the individual and
psychologically to all those around the teacher.

Characteristics such as mental fatigue, anxiety,
depression, anger, insomnia, high blood pressure,
and psychotic collapse, are all symptoms of burnout
experienced by teachers. However, part of their
problems of stress goes beyond the individual and
lies in inadequate professional preparation, poor
organizational structures, and supervisors who are
themselves burned out. This leaves teachers with
the feeling of having less control over their
environment then they expected. Increased paperwork and lack of support from homes add to the
problem.

What is needed is a reorganization of the profession, as well as a change in the public attitude
towards teachers. Parents, teachers and the like
must all work together to help raise the status of
teachers in the professional field. The health of
our educational system depends on the effectiveness
and mental attitudes of its teachers. It is only
when teachers begin to feel they have an important
role in the future of our nation that we will have
fewer burned-out teachers.

Robinson, J. P. How americans use time: A
   social-psychological analysis of everyday
   behavior. New York: Praeger Publishers, 1977.

The results of the first national time-use study
in the United States, conducted by the Survey
Research Center in 1965-66, provide accurate data
on the public allocation of time. The ways in
which people allocate their time have been considered a social indicator (indexes of social or
economic status or process that indirectly affect
social welfare). The survey was designed to
represent a census of typical everyday behavior
across the country using a respondent time diary of
daily activites. Time use as inputs and outputs is
discussed in relation to the indexes.

Four major types of social-psychological comparisons of time-use data are distinguished:

cross-time, cross-sectional, cross-national, and
cross-activity. The internal structure of the
factors that determine the allocation of time are
personal, role, resource, and environmental. All
four sets of factors are treated as mutually
interacting. While these factors all directly
affect the way time is spent, so does time itself.
Individual decisions about time allocation ultimately determine how much time is available for
other activities.

One major impression about the impact of the sets
of factors is that personal factors explained
little variance in how time was spent. Presumed
differences by age, racial background, religious
area of upbringing, and attitudinal factors did not
materialize. The major exceptions are the factors
of education and sex. The better educated put
their leisure time to more active use and the many
differences associated with sex were induced by the
different role demands that women undertake. Role
factors exercised more control over time use than
any other set of factors. Of the three major
factors in this group, employment predominated over
marriage and parenthood; becoming a parent had
slightly more effect on time use than becoming a
spouse; and both parental and marital roles demand-
ed proportionately more from women than from men.
Minimal differences are associated with type of
occupation or employment of the spouse.

In terms of satisfaction associated with daily
activities, work rated higher than expected, only
slightly below the average for all free-time
activities; yet work was cited most often by
respondents as the least enjoyable aspect of their
day in the 1965-66 study.

No activity has as clearly demarcated the sexual
division of labor in our society as household care.
Women performed over 80% of both the housework and
child care in this country. While the employed
woman was able to complete her housework in about
half the time required by the housewife, this still
represented a considerable amount of time compared
to the time-use of other individuals.

The chapters of this book include the following:
Part I   Background and Analysis Model
   Ch. 1   Background and Methodology
   Ch. 2   Social-Psychological considerations in
       the Analysis of Time Data
Part II   Analysis of Daily Activities
   Ch. 3   Obligatory Activities
   Ch. 4   Free Time
Part III   Interpretations and Meanings of Time-Use
      Data
   Ch. 5   Meanings Attached to Everyday
       Activities
   Ch. 6   Free Time and Life Style
   Ch. 7   Summary and Conclusions

Rosenbaum, L. L., & Rosenbaum, W. B.   Morale and
   productivity consequences of group leadership
   style, stress and type of task.   Journal of
   Applied Psychology, 1971, 55(4), 343-348.
   This article concerns a study of 60 undergradu-
ates in an introductory psychology course to
examine a hypothesis that under stress and performing structured tasks, groups under authoritarian
leadership would perform better and be more satisfied, whereas, democratic-leadership groups would
perform better and be more satisfied under non-
stressful conditions and performing unstructured
tasks.
   Under stress, the present authors found greater
productivity for autocratically led groups, whereas, in the absence of stress, democratic leadership
was more productive.   The authors' hypothesis that
satisfaction ratings should parallel the productivity ratings was not confirmed.   However, the
subjects under authoritarian leadership conditions
took significantly longer to complete their tasks.
In addition, subjects performed better, worked
faster, and most enjoyed the structured task.

Sammons, D. L.   Burnout!   Working too hard for too
   long may be hazardous to your health.   INC.,
   December 1980, 2(12), 57-62.
   People, like machines, can burnout with overuse.

Burnout is a condition produced by working too hard
for too long in a high pressure environment.
Though the symptoms and intensity of the syndrome
vary, there are certain physical and psychological
warning signs. Executives under stress may have a
nagging sense of fatigue, feel physically run down,
be unable to shake a cold, or suffer from frequent
headaches or gastrointestinal disturbances. In
addition one may also experience sleeplessness, a
loss of weight, depression, or shortness of breath.
Feelings of boredom, disenchantment, and resentment
are not uncommon. A number of behavioral changes
including reduced sociability, increased anger, and
loss of flexibility are typical. Occasionally, many
people act as if they were burned-out; however, a
genuine burnout victim experiences these symptoms
as pervasive. They usually affect every aspect of
his or her life. A candidate for burnout refuses
to delegate authority and rarely, if ever, admits
the need for help in the job. The person's ability
to alienate people only further reinforces the
belief that only he or she can do the job right.
It is estimated that 10% of all Americans succumb
to burnout each year. Burnout does not strike
suddenly, leaving its victims sick where they were
well the day before. Instead, it develops gradually. So insidiously does burnout develop that its
victim does not realize the extent of his condition. A major obstacle to curing the burnout
victim is the denial and resistance that often
accompany the other symptoms. Before treatment can
progress, the victim has to recognize his own
psychological condition. Treatment consists of
learning or relearning how to relax, improving
one's self-image, spending more time with one's
family, and delegating more responsibility.
Prevention measures that can help reduce the
possibility of succombing to the condition include:
1. Avoid being the person who always handles
the tough jobs.
2. Limit the number of hours you work.
3. Take vacations, and make sure your staff
does, too.

4.   Promote a team approach.

Savidki, V., & Cooley, E. J.   Implications of
  burnout research and theory for counselor
  educators. Personnel and Guidance Journal, March
  1982, 60(7), 415-419.
  Savidki and Cooley relate that while burnout must
surely have existed before 1974, there is no record
to indicate that this term was actually used and
recognized before Freudenberger coined the term in
his 1974 paper on the affects of burnout. His
major focus was to place the malady in the proper
perspective. That was to indicate that the problem
was due to a phenomenon of the profession rather
than a defect or fault in the individual.
  While constant dealing with others in problem
situations seems to be the most likely catalyst for
this occurence, there are no set criteria for
determining a potential victim. Rather, recognizing, alleviating, and treating burnout seems to be
the future trend of the professional who encounters
such a disease. Symptoms of physical, cognitive,
emotional, and behavioral areas come into play when
defining the afflicted areas from over-stressful
situations leading to the formation of burnout. As
there are several areas into which burnout may
manifest, the forms in which it occurs are also
numerous. Maslach, offering the most researched
definition, concludes that the areas of emotional
exhaustion, depersonalization of clients, and lack
of feelings concerning personal accomplishment
assume the major share towards defining and compre-
hending burnout. As job intensity, the work
environment, and social supports can be leading
causes of this ailment, these categories can be
alleviated through the use of work sharing, feedback from other employees, and more control over
the use of adjustments to the work environment.
  Identification with clients to an unhealthy degree
supplies the ingredients necessary for the burnout
syndrome to manifest itself. While total unconcern
is impractical, there must remain a margin of
aloofness for the counselor to remain at his

professional best and supply the client with
support. While this research is merely in its
infant stages, awareness must be of a primary
concern in order to alter the organizational
structure because counselor-training programs are
often amiss in examining the organizational functioning. This in turn will allow the counselor
trainees to become aware of their own professionalism and be afforded the opportunity to incorporate some measures towards stress alleviation and
social support needed to eliminate the occurrence
of career burnout.

Sawyer, H., & Schumacher, B. Stress and the
    rehabilitation administrator. Journal of
    Rehabilitation Administration. May 1980, 4(2),
    49-55.
Functional stress is common among those individuals who must make difficult decisions about matters
that have important consequences once implemented.
The potential for stress exists when an environmental situation or interpersonal interaction is
perceived as presenting a demand that threatens to
exceed the administrator's capabilities and resources for adequate response. Acquisition of a
managerial role is the source of stress for the
newly assigned administrator. Administrators
usually experience high levels of stress because
they enter the position without adequate preparation, training, and experience. The demands of the
job and the dynamics of a rehabilitation facility
create a unique set of stresses, which make an
administrator highly susceptible to burnout. If
the stress is too great it may create problems
(physical, psychological, and emotional) for the
individual. Problems that may occur, such as
psychosomatic reactions, frequently reduce the
individual's quality of performance.
When the administrator acquires his position he
frequently encounters conflict with his role in
relation to workload and function. The individual
who is under great conflict experiences less job
satisfaction and more tension. An overload of work

or an uncomfortable feeling about the quality of work creates high stress in administrators. Positive correlations have been shown for high stress relative to poor health habits. The poor habits, such as smoking, increase the likelihood of physiological problems, heart disease, hypertension, or exhaustion. Role ambiguity results when knowledge possessed and information needed do not complement each other. When this is combined with other factors previously cited the likelihood of physiological or emotional problems is increased.

Adminstrators encounter stress when they are unable to easily accomplish certain tasks which are a part of their administrative function. Inadequacy in the performance of these tasks to the satisfaction of the administrator or his colleagues creates a unique type of stress. As a result the administrator is unable to develop long-term management strategies or establish programs that would increase the overall effectiveness of the organization because he is busy "fighting fires" which appear to have the same urgency.

Several methods for coping with stress and its physical symptoms have been suggested. Suggested methods include transcendental meditation, progressive relaxation, and emotional desensitization.

Schuh, A. J. The predictability of employee tenure: A review of the literature. Personnel Psychology, 1967, 20, 133-152.

The review found that there is no systematic relationship between intelligence test scores and length of service (clerical workers were the group most commonly studied). Aptitude tests, in addition, showed no systematic relationship to length of employment.

In three out of four studies, the persuasive scale on the Kuder Preference Record was found to relate to length of employment. On the Strong Vocational Interest Blank, the scale occupational level relates to length of service.

While personality tests were found to predict as well as the intelligence and aptitude scales, some items included in biographical data on the application blank in 21 studies were found to relate to tenure in jobs in all but 2 studies. But regardless of how long a study is carried out, the evidence indicates a steady decrease in the effectiveness of the application blank instrument.

Job-satisfaction questionnaires administered prior to employment may be useful as predictors of job tenure. No studies cited show negative or zero findings; therefore, it is concluded that tenure is positively related to worker's satisfaction. One indication was that job satisfaction may be a function of a relatively stable personality characteristic, thus relating to job tenure.

Recommendations include: 1) using several instruments validated against several tenure criteria to predict turnover, 2) look for curvilinear relationships between predictors and tenure criteria, 3) compare variances of the long and short tenure groups statistically, 4) reweigh the entire application blank every three years, assuming that trends will appear in the data, 5) cross-validate the predictor-criterion relationships, 6) conduct separate validity studies for males and females since they have been found to differ in the predictability of their tenure, 7) pay attention to the influence of other workers in the immediate work group; it is unclear whether long service is more attributable to individual characteristics or the influence of significant others, or the interaction of these two influences, and 8) emphasize subscores and individual item validities rather than total scores or profiles.

Schuler, R. S. Managing stress means managing time. Personnel Journal, Dec. 1979, 58(12), 851-854.

This article is concerned with the strategy of time management, which is defined as the process by which tasks and goals can be accomplished and in turn make jobs and careers more effective.

The author discusses some major stumbling blocks that are encountered when people strive to manage

their time.   These stumbling blocks are:
1.   Lack of awareness of job duties, authority, and responsibility levels.
2.   Lack of ability to prioritize tasks.
3.   The Pareto Principle, which indicates
that people spend 80% of their time doing
duties which are related to only 20% of
the total job results.
4.   Time robbers--incidents or situations
which, if repeated often or with some
frequency, tend to eat into time unduly.
Strategies that deal directly with these stumbling
blocks depend on awareness of:
1.   Your job duties, authority, and responsibility and their importance.
2.   Your own skills, needs, and abilities.
3.   How you currently allocate your time on
the job.
This is explained in more detail in the article
along with the next three steps of time management,
which are:
1.   Conserving time.
2.   Controlling time.
3.   Making time.
The author further explains how time management
practices can lower the overall stress level by
eliminating specific stresses such as those related
to achievement, growth, and certainty.

Schuler, R. S.   Effective use of communicating to
minimize employee stress.   The Personnel
Administrator, June 1979, 24, 40-44.
Stress results from many causes in our daily
lives as well as places of employment.   Stress
generally arises from not knowing what or how to do
a job, a new job, or a change in work schedule.
Stress often results from a lack of proper communication.   Therefore, if communication is initiated
at the right time, stress can be reduced.
A supervisor who has good communication skills can
reduce the stress in the people he supervises.
There are many categories of leadership behaviors
that effect employees.   The following are seven

behaviors that can be used by a supervisor or manager.

1. Achievement communication behavior conveys statements of goals and expectations by the supervisor that the employee can do the job. The specific effect is that the supervisor is conveying to the employee his or her confidence that the employee can do the job well. This increases the employee's feelings of self-worth, self-confidence, and satisfaction.

2. Ego deflation communication behavior reduces the employee's feelings of self-worth, self-confidence, and self-image. A supervisor who closely monitors the employee, indicates to the employee that he or she feels the individual cannot do the job well.

3. Contingent approval communication behavior aids employees in knowing what is expected of them. By praising the performance the supervisor is letting the employee know he or she is doing a good job.

4. Contingent disapproval communication behavior lets the employee know what is not rewarded, or more specifically, what results in disapproval. In order for this to be effective, the performance standards must be clear and the supervisor should indicate to the employee where the performance or work was not right; it should be clear that it is directed at the employee's performance and not directed at the employee as a person.

5. Participative communication behavior of the supervisor can help in establishing future goals for the employee and deciding how to best do the job. In a new work situation or job this can help clarify performance for the job, how it should be done, and reduce some

conflicts.
6. Directive communication behavior is especially appropriate when the employee wants directions and guidance when the circumstances call for it. It is also appropriate when the employee is not performing well and can help the employee produce the performance desired.
7. Supportive communication behavior indicates concern for the employee as a person. This helps increase the trust level between the employee and supervisor. Its impact on employee stress is indirect through increasing trust.

Each supervisor, to successfully utilize any of the leader communication behaviors, should have the basic skills of good listening, of good communicating, of receiving and giving specific task-related feedback, of nonverbal communicating and of diagnosing a situation.

Selye, H., & Cherry, L. On the real benefits of eutress. Psychology Today, March, 1978, pp. 60-63; 69-70.

Stress has been commonly known to have negative effects on the physiological mechanisms of the body. Selye believes, however, that a certain amount of stress is essential, even beneficial, to well being. He terms this type of stress eutress.

Stress is the body's nonspecific response to any demand placed on it, whether that demand is pleasant or not. Rather than trying to completely avoid stress, it is important to learn one's typical response to stress and modulate behavior accordingly. Two types of human beings are characterized: race horses who thrive on a stressful fast-paced lifestyle; and turtles who require a peaceful and tranquil environment. Although danger does exist if people mistake their type and push themselves beyond their limits, the concern about overwork seems to be exaggerated. In this light, all the stress inventories seem to be flawed because they do not account for individual differences.

Alcohol and drugs are common ways of trying to reduce stress, but the effects are usually temporary. Transcendental meditation is also useful in reducing stress in some people, but for others who suffer from hypostress (too little stress) there is actually a need for more activity. An alternate way of dealing with stress is recommended; that involves taking on a different attitude. A negative stress can be converted into a eutress by adopting the right attitude.

The amount of stress in society has not increased, rather the old stresses are replaced by new stresses. However, lack of motivation is one stress that has increased in recent years due to a loss of the stabilizing support of constructive goals. Science has destroyed the credibility of old beliefs. An altuistic egoism approach is suggested as a way of dealing with stress; one needs to find a place between being completely self-centered and being completely self-sacrificing. Three recommendation are made as an antidote to stress: 1) seek one's own stress level; 2) choose goals that are one's own; and 3) look outside of oneself by being necessary to others. The worst of all modern social stress is purposelessness.

Selzer, M. L., & Vinokur, A. Life events, subjective stress, and traffic accidents. American Journal of Psychiatry, 1974, 131(8), 903-906.

Many investigators have attempted to identify accident-prone drivers. The psychosocial variables such as aggressiveness, depression, and social maladjustment have been significantly related to traffic accidents. However, the correlations were too low to be used to create accident-prevention programs.

This study focused on three factors: (1) life changes and the response to these changes; (2) major distress experienced in such various contexts as marriage, job, and school; and (3) physical manifestations of stress in behavior.

If clinical depression is triggered by life

changes, then depression itself, which many studies
have correlated with traffic accidents, may be
regarded as an intermediary factor between life
changes and the accident. This change may modify
critical mental and emotional functions. One study
assessed the interpersonal and vocational-financial
stresses impinging upon 96 drivers involved in
fatal accidents and a matched control group. It
was found that 52% of the fatal-accident group
experienced such stresses as compared with 18% of
the control group.

The excessive use of alcohol as a response to
stress has been largely ignored. Such dependence
on alcohol usually aggravates the stress.

Shannon, C., & Saleebey, D. Training child welfare
   workers to cope with burnout. Child Welfare,
   September-October, 1980, 59(8), 463-468.

Child Protective Service workers of the Texas
Department of Human Resources conducted workshops
for their employees. The programs were designed to
give individual workers and groups of workers ways
to understand stress, their reactions to it, and
techniques for fighting the cumulative effects of
stress as well as ways of improving coping and
stress-management capacities.

Organizational structure and process are responsible for many of the conditions that promote stress
and increase the likelihood of burnout. Annoying
responses to the conditions include little control
over the environment, lack of organizational
support, excessive caseloads, insufficient time
away from stressful jobs, and inflexibility of
workloads, eventually leading to alienation from
the role of worker.

Forty-one child-care workers and supervisors who
particpate in the program were divided into sub-
groups in insure individual attention as well as to
aid in supportive group atmospheres. Each session
of the program introduced new material concerning
ways to cope with stress, each time building on
previously developed ideas. At the end of the
training period the workers evaluated the

effectivenes of the program.

The results indicated that one-half of the workers felt that the program was most helpful in all areas, while 70% thought the training would be most useful on the job. The positive attitudes felt by the workers in itself was helpful enough to handle stress and avoid burnout. The first step in coping with a stressful situation is the development of an adequate understanding of it.

Shea, G. F.   Cost-effective stress management training. Training and Development Journal, July 1980, 34(7), 25-26; 28-30; 32-33.

Learning to deal with stress is a most important aspect in big business. For this reason, stress-management techniques have been developed to assist individuals in coping with the difficulties they experience. In addition, it has been reported that stress management can save the company both time and money. Other studies confirm reported gains in productivity. The ability to manage stress effectively can make the difference between profit and loss.

In designing an effective stress-management program, such an agenda could have significant health advantages. All of the major techniques involve some form of exercise and result in a notable state of relaxation. Some of the major techniques include transcendental meditation, biofeedback, physical exercise, yoga/zen, self-hypnosis, and progressive relaxation. It is important that these techniques are explored at length as one may respond better to one technique than another. Of equal importance is the necessity that an individual is trained in the specific techniques utilized, as it may otherwise result in negative health effects.

When employing stress-management techniques, mediators in two Northeastern industrial firms reported that they were better able to: concentrate for a longer period of time on their work; conserve energy; avoid procrastination; use their energies more productively, etc. Stress management likewise is cost effective. However, in order to gain the most savings, some cost factors should be considered. First, it is important that one realize that all techniques do not require the same amount of training time. Some take more time than others to produce deep relaxation if needed. Secondly, some techniques will require more prac- tice following training in order for one to become skillful. Next, one should be aware that some methods more than others result in a faster, more efficient state of relaxation. Lastly, one must not overlook the fact that the beneficial effects of employing these techniques need to be added into the organizational cost analysis.

Sheafor, B. W. The effect of board members on staff of community mental health centers: A study of the relationship of their values to job satisfaction. Journal of Social Welfare, Spring 1976, 3, 75-82.
This study attempted to answer the question of mental health centers being dependent on the effectiveness of the working relationship of the board of directors, which establishes the policy, and the staff, which implements the policy. This was done by examining the influence of congruence in social values between board and staff members in 14 mental health centers and clinics in Colorado. The social values of all the respondents were measured through the use of the Meyer Social Value Test and the Brayfield and Roth Index of Job Satisfaction was used to measure the level of job satisfaction with staff members only.
The research identified that when the board members and the persons who constituted the clin- ical staff held similar social values, the staff members were likely to feel more satisfaction with their jobs. The data suggest the importance of mental health centers, and perhaps other social agencies, making a serious effort to achieve a good match between board and staff members on their social values; that the clinical staff be repre- sented on the agency boards; and that

administrators and other participants in establishing policy might effectively facilitate both the
decision making and the decision implementation by
raising the consciousness of all parties to the
value issues.

Sheridan, J. E., & Vredenburgh, D. J. Usefulness
   of leadership behavior and social power variables
   in predicting job tension, performance and
   turnover of nursing employees. Journal of
   Applied Psychology, 1978, 63(1), 89-95.
Two studies indicated that behavior and power
variables each explained unique and significiant
portions of variance in different criterion variables. This included measure of the subordinates'
satisfaction and their perceptions of the leader's
effectiveness. Subsequently, a study was conducted
extending this research. This study examined the
validity of leadership behavior and social power
variables to predict the behavioral criteria of
subordinates' job performance and decisions to
terminate employment as well as perceived job
stress.
   Questionnaires were distributed among nurses in
the Detroit area. Subjects were asked to describe
the leadership behavior of their head nurse. In
addition, three criteria variables were used,
namely, the subject's job tension, job performance,
and decisions to terminate employment.
   About three months following the completion of the
questionnaire, head nurses were asked to evaluate
the performance of her immediate staff members.
Subordinates were evaluated in the areas of knowledge and judgment, conscientiousness, skill in
human relations, organizational ability, and
observational ability.
   In the year following completion of the questionnaire, 54 of the subjects studied terminated their
employment at their hospital. Terminations were
not forced. None were a result of retirement,
leave of absence or the like. All were voluntary.
   Results of the study indicate significant demographic effect only between the subject's age and

her perceived tension on the job. Further, with regard to the head nurse, results show that consideration had an inverse relationship with nursing performance. In addition, consideration was related to job tension and turnover. With regard to structure, the head nurse's initiating it had a significant direct relationship with terminations. The head nurse's reward and expert power had significant inverse relationship with job tension.
  Generally speaking, the usefulness of the leaderhip behavior and social power variables to foretell job tension, performance and turnover can only be evaluated in comparison with other approaches. However, the number of studies available relative to nursing performance and job stress are few. Still, fewer can be compared in terms of predictor usefulness.

Shubin, S. Burnout: The professional hazard you face in nursing. Nursing 78, July 1978, 8(7), 22-27.
  Some signs of burnout in nursing personnel are distancing (by spending as little time as possible with patients), referring to patients by their symptoms, working overly long hours (saying they can't go home because there is too much to do), joking about a patient's illness, and becoming technical about machines or treatment in describing a patient's condition instead of referring directly to their patients.
  The initial step in preventing or salvaging oneself from burnout is to be aware one is in potential danger and to listen to oneself without dismissing feelings. Other methods are maintaining a high ratio of nurses to patients.
  Some methods the individual can use are taking care of yourself, pay attention to yourself, using a decompression routine, doing meditative kinds of things, sharing feelings and problems with other nurses. Analyzing and taking advantage of whatever choices and options are open to you including leaving your job, lateral job transfers, or sanctioned time-outs may be a way to deal with burnout.

Finally, if a nurse is in tune with feelings, trusts them, shares them, uses them constructively, and has social outlets and support, one will know when the edge of total detachment or overinvolvement is advancing and can do something in time to help oneself.

Smith, P. Coming to terms with job crisis. Personnel Management, January 1978, 10, 32-35.
Crisis is described as a critical disequilibrium in a relationship, a period of formulating or reformulating a balance in the demands of the job and the needs and capabilities of the individual. These crises represent significant decision points about the organization/individual relationship. The recognition of these stages is important to the management of personnel in general and especially to the appraisal, career planning, and management development. There may not be recognizable signs, but these crises may be indicated by signs of stress and ineffectiveness. There are five different identifiable stages when crisis may occur.
    1. The Induction Crisis occurs relatively early in the individual's relationship to his job. It is that event of establishing some relatively settled connection with an enterprise during which the expectations of the job held by the joiner and those held out during recruitment receive some mutual examination.
Induction crises do not only occur with new recruits. They are usually caused by disappointed expectations and a critical event that precipitates some action. Social acceptance (becoming part of a team) and good pay are influential factors in solving induction crisis.
    2. Crisis of Mastery is characterized by exposure to a special test and some examination standard in order to prove a satisfactory performance. Constant failure or difficulty in meeting the requirements of a job results in loss in self-esteem and feelings of isolation.
Mastery crisis can reappear as the job demands change. Positive feedback and supervisory support

are part of a positive organizational context that
will help to deal with mastery crisis.

3. Crisis of Development involves risk taking
in changing and evolving one's job. It means
stepping beyond the conventional boundries, expand-
ing the job, creating new relationships, and
setting new standards of performance. A positive
organizational context will provide encouragement,
opportunities, and expansive conditions during a
crisis development.

4. Crisis of Plateau is the flattening out of
the learning and developmental opportunities in a
job. Jobs that are quickly learned and whose
boundaries are fixed will produce plateau conditions early on in the job experience. Plateau is
reached when after some personal development of the
job, its activities no longer provide stimulus,
challenge, and interest.

5. Crisis of Transition may be passive
adaptation, living with the plateau and transferring energies and orientations elsewhere, or it may
be active; the individual may seek alternative
opportunities outside or inside the organization.
All of these crises involve stress of some kind.
They involve a process of individual reorientation,
a period of uncertainty, learning acknowledgement,
commitment, and risk taking.

Smits, S. J. Counselor job satisfaction and
    employment turnover in state rehabilitation
    agencies: A follow-up study. Journal of
    Counseling Psychology, 1972, 19(6), 512-517.
    Job satisfaction has become an important entity
in itself. A discussion of the humanitarian and
mental health as well as production-oriented points
view on job satisfaction are offered and what
research has shown job satisfaction to be. It is
felt that the positive relationship between job
satisfaction and productivity has been assumed
rather than demonstrated. The relationship between
job dissatisfaction and employment turnover has
been demonstrated rather consistently. The purpose
of this study was to assess the predictive validity

of the data bank of Job Satisfaction Inventory
scores obtained from counselors employed in 31
state rehabilitation agencies by conducting a
follow-up study of counselor employment status 1
year later. This study was conducted in 1970 with
263 counselors, 12-16 months after completing the
Job Satisfaction Inventory.

The rate of termination by size of the agency was
calculated by operationally defining small, medium-sized, and large agencies. It was found that
differences in scores between persons terminated
from and those retained in counseling positions in
small agencies are not statistically significant;
however in medium-sized agencies, significantly
lower scores were for terminators on four of the
eight variables. Terminators from large agencies
were significantly less satisfied in the areas of
relationships with associates, and interest in,
liking for, and emotional involvement in the job.

There were no significant differences in job
satisfaction among the three groups of terminators
in agency size and no significant differences for
those who were retained. The Inventory differenti-
ated between the terminators and the persisters,
but it did not differentiate within the two groups.
It is felt that while neither group was dissatisfied, the terminated counselors were consistently
less satisfied than those who retained their
positions.

Spicuzza, F. J., & DeVoe, M. W. Burnout in the
  helping professions: Mutual aid groups as
  self-help. Personnel and Guidance Journal,
  October 1982, 61(2), 95-98.

Burnout causes workers to be ineffective through
physical and emotional exhaustion resulting from
excessive demands on energy, strength, and resources of helping professionals. The constant
contact with clients causes those in the helping
professions to lose some of their idealism and
sense of purpose. The physical symptoms of burnout
are manifested as: increased anxiety, nervousness,
exhaustion, insomnia, headaches, and backaches.

Employees in the helping fields tend to be very dedicated, committed individuals. Some put themselves under pressure internally, to experience self-growth and excellence, and externally to meet client and program goals. The components of helping others often causes the worker to become emotionally involved to the point of losing objectivity. Workers also have difficulty balancing bureaucratic demands with their concept of ideal service. To add to their frustration many workers feel they do not receive sufficient support and recognition from their peers, administrators, and clients.

To help workers deal with the phenomenon of burnout, mutual aid groups have been formed. These groups help the worker to acquire the same level of efficiency achieved prior to burnout. In addition, mutual aid groups help workers avoid burnout through use of self-help strategies. Some strategies employed are: shorter work week, reduced case load, leaves of absence, varied responsibility, increased regular exercise, hobbies, development of relaxation skills, etc. Mutual aid group meetings are seen as ways individuals can discover or reassess their sense of self, can search for their own personal meaning in society, and can diminish their feeling of solitude within a group structure. A mutual aid group can offer individuals an influence to help them cope effectively with problems and provide a feeling of security and concern.

Meetings of mutual aid groups are for self-development and information dispersal. Information topics of concern are: the nature of stress, holostic health, alienation, organizational principles, and the art of effective management. Topics for self-development include: personal problems related to stress, loss of empathy, guilt, etc. Participants in the group are given opportunities to vent frustration and share concerns with other workers in similar circumstances. Through participation in mutual aid groups the individual is able to overcome negative feelings and perceptions to become more effective employees and happier individuals.

The most frequent help-giving activities within the mutual aid group setting are empathy, mutual affirmation, explanations of behavior that contribute to better understanding of self, reassurance that problems can be solved, sharing, and positive reinforcement. The benefit of a mutual aid group is that it helps professionals recognize their limits, align their expectations to reality, and take time for self-renewal.

Stelmach, M., Postma, J., Goldstein, S., & Shepard, K. F. Selected factors influencing job satisfaction of attendants of physically disabled adults. Rehabilitation Literature, May-June, 1981, 42(5-6), 130-137.

The use of attendants allows the physically disabled adult to live independently. These individuals are from a variety of backgrounds and have a wide range of skill levels. A good attendant is described as one who has willingness to learn, ability to follow directions, reliability, flexibility, an easy-going personality, and a willingness to work hard for minimal compensation. A study was conducted to determine the factors that influence job satisfaction of attendants.

Job satisfaction was difficult to determine accurately because the attendents willing to be interviewed are usually more interested in their jobs. They have a sense of value as to the worthiness of their work, they have a friendship with their employer, and they have a satisfactory schedule. The negative aspects listed that detracted from satisfaction were salary benefits and work schedule. Attendants working fewer than 25 hours a week had higher satisfaction rates, which may be attributed to other factors. The factors take into consideration that the more severely disabled usually have more complex physical and psychological needs, which require attendants to work more hours and which may not acknowledge the value of an individual attendant's work.

Interviews reveal that the most frequently mentioned positive component of attendant work was the opportunity to do work considered socially useful and personally rewarding.

Stocker, P. K. Burnout: Yes, It also happens to
Veterinarians. Modern Veterinary Practice,
October 1981, 751-755.

Veterinarians suffer from symptoms of burnout because of unrealistic demands from clients. They suffer from burnout which is manifested in the following characteristics: chronic fatigue, self-criticism for putting up with demands, cynicism, irritability, a sense of being besieged, anger at those making demands, and rapid display of emotions.

Burnout appears to be most prevalent among individuals who are not able to achieve their goals, especially if the person works in a people-oriented occupation. The impact on veterinarians is greater than in some other occupations because the veterinarian often is not equiped to handle the daily office routine. Often he does not have the experience or training to handle conflicts and other managerial tasks.

Suggestions made to reduce or eliminate burnout can be implemented by the individual:

1.   Recognize the existence of burnout.
2.   Be exposed to continuous challenge. Variety in one's daily routine allows for restoration of energy.
3.   Make use of mandatory vacations. Employ use of retreats, afternoons off, and trips to different geographic regions.
4.   Be actively involved in your professional field. The recognition is needed to maintain psychological needs.
5.   Keep abreast of current advances in your profession.
6.   Organize priorities in your work to maintain physical stamina.
7.   Appropriate expression of feelings helps maintain a mental and physical balance.

An expert in personnel management offers the solution to burnout in three stages: clarify values, list things that make life worth living, and identify things you want from your practice.

Swogger, G. Toward understanding stress: A map of the territory. Journal of School Health, January, 1981, 51(1), 29-33.

Burnout is a special form of stress that is a result of the reaction of a person to organization-al or work pressures. Burnout in this country used to be considered a small price to pay for success. However, with the advent of concern for ecology and conservation, the misuses of human potential is taken more seriously.

There are many symptoms of burnout: decreased performance and commitment to work, decline in self-esteem, depression, anger, guilt, marital conflict, divorce, and alcoholism.

Various causes have been identified: lack of a support group, increased knowledge which augments frustration, insufficient finances and authority to carry out personal or job goals, work overload, bureaucratic rigidity, avoidance of responsibility, and desire for status. Inadequate leadership and administrative support can increase burnout. Some companies also lack adequate performance review and reward. Work problems and family problems at the same time can compound the burnout. One of the major effects of burnout on the individual is an unpleasant change in self-concept. Through all the developmental stages people begin developing a sense of who they are; major upheavals in their lives or jobs can make major inroads into that concept.

Swogger suggests that we need to learn to ask the right questions in order to prevent or alieviate burnout. We must remember that stress for one person is distinct from stress for another. We could ask questions such as Who am I? What do I want to do with myself and for others? Am I happy with my work? What don't I like? We could ask the same questions or make the same assessment about the context in which we work, the support system we have developed, and our personal coping methods. Other factors that can be considered for burnout reduction are: physical needs for tension re- duction, exercise, nutrition, meditation, biofeedback, hobbies, and modification of Type A personalities. A planned balance is the key in burnout/stress reduction.

Tamerin, J. More about burnout. CAFC News, Sept.-Oct. 1982, 10(1), 1982, 10-13; 15.

The problem of burnout in counselors and thera- pists should be examined to reduce the occurance of countertransference. Counselors exhibit the signs of burnout such as loss of empathy, loss of sense of self, pessimism, sarcasm, depression, and even paranoid projection.

A mental health worker, such as an alcoholism counselor, should have a reliable support system in the advent of a relapse in either the client or the counselor. Reliable intervention systems allow the counselor to identify signs of burnout before a relapse can occur. The perspective of a counselor affects his or her ability to grow, change, and learn about himself and his clients. A counselor's ability to remain separate from a client's progress determines whether he or she is able to maintain self-esteem and adequately assist the client. A pitfall many alcoholism counselors experience is that of countertransference. The counselor who begins to experience negative feelings and projects feelings of rejection toward a client should examine personal feelings. If the counselor fails to examine and change perspectives, it could result in nonproductive therapy for clients.

It is suggested that the counselor can be most effective if he is alert to the feelings of his client and himself. It is important for the counselor to have realistic goals for his client. One's worth as a professional is not dependent upon whether or not each and every patient is saved from a life of alcoholism.

Tardy, W. Ten ways to cope with stress in your
  working environment. Black Enterprise, November
  1977, 8, 39-44.

Psychological stress seriously affects millions
of black workers, especially those advancing in
administrative positions. Due to increased opportunities and recruiting efforts, more blacks are
finding themselves in competitive work environments. Racism, real or imaginative, may be present. At higher levels, the racism often becomes
subtle. Tokenism in hiring practices is prevalent.
Responses by the black worker include fear of
repetition, shame over feeling helplessness, rage
at the source, and guilt or shame for aggressive
impulses.

Job stress is likely to result when workers' needs
are frustrated or their abilities are mismatched
with their responsibilities. Optional adaptation
to stress occurs when workers can anticipate
stressful events and predict their response to it.

Ten suggestions are made for black workers to deal
with stress:
1. Know your style of coping with stress.
    Avoid stress situations.
2. Be aware of company politics. Get real
    facts and do not blur reality.
3. Confront racism; talk it over with a
    coworker.
4. Maintain interpersonal relations; do not
    become withdrawn.
5. Avoid alcohol or drug use.
6. Watch physical health and nutrition.
    Medical   problems   complicate
    stress-provoking conditions.
7. Keep job separate from social and home
    life.
8. Make good use of leisure time and va-
    cations.
9. Get adequate rest; know your capacity.
10. Seek professional help early.

Tucker, L. Stress: Its consequences for drug
  therapy. American Pharmacy, August 1979, 19(9),

13-16.

Although the use of psychotherapeutic drugs for treatment of anxiety has declined in the last few years, these drugs are still the most prescribed medications in the world.

According to a recent survey there is a new awareness regarding the dangers of overmedication. This survey indicated that doctors are too quick to prescribe medication and that there is too much emphasis on taking pills to feel better, on taking miracle drugs, and on taking tranquilizers and sleeping pills. It also indicated a pressing need, on the part of the surveyed families, to reduce the amount of stress in their lives and a lack of appropriate information on how to go about dealing with stress.

Concerning the types of persons who need tranquil- izers, it has been shown that not only high-powered executives but also blue-collar workers are prone to disease associated with stress. Common to almost all of the high-stress occupations were long working hours and repetitive and/or boring job tasks.

New investigations are searching to determine the reasons why the use of antianxiety sedative drugs appears to be twice as high among women as men in almost all countries studied. Different expla- nations have been suggested, but they are all simply speculations.

Maladaptive responses to stress result from falsely triggered emergency reactions and a failure to turn off the process. Some of the consequences of nonadaptive stress responses are: functional disorders such as gastrointestinal upsets, irri- tability, lowered threshold for anger or frus- tration, and the aggravation of existing diseases such as asthma, diabetes or coronary heart disease.

There is a tendency for the public to view stress-related problems as personal emotional weakness, which leads the victim of stress to endure mild symptoms and delay in seeking help. As a result, those who are uninformed about health matters may be drawn to alcohol, tobacco, and various chemical preparations.

The preferred medications for anxiety are the benzodiazepines. Among drugs of this class are valium, librium, the world's most widely prescribed drugs, and dalmane, the most widely used prescription sleeping capsule.

There are different opinions among physicians on the prescriptions of psychotheropeutic drugs. Physicians who pride themselves on their skills in counseling may refuse to prescribe tranquilizers for a patient who desires more. On the other hand, physicians also may prescribe tranquilizers too easily to avoid taking the time for personal communication with patients. There is a need that patients should be clearly advised that tranquilizers do not cure anxiety, but merely relieve symptoms. The goal is to substitute a nondrug approach as soon as possible. Recent investigations are searching for a safer class of tranquilizers: the brain's chemicals.

Vachon, M. L. S., Lyall, W. A. L., & Freenam, S. J. J. Measurement and management of stress in health professionals: Working with advanced cancer patients. Death Education, 1978, 1, 365-375.

Staff working with advanced cancer patients may experience considerable stress but there have been few attempts to measure such. This paper presents preliminary studies of staff stress in two cancer centers. Nurses in a cancer hospital were found to focus on problems with dying patients as a displacement of their feeling. Major problems with the work situation, and with staff communications were cited just as often as in watching patients suffer and die as causes of stress. A series of group discussions lasting eight sessions was held with the nurses to facilitate communication with other staff and to promote understanding of life-threatening illnesses and death.

Staff on a newly opened palliative care unit were found to experience only slightly less stress than a group of newly widowed. While the stress decreased over time, indications are that some staff working in newly developed Hospice centers may be at considerable risk.

With regard to physicians, seminars and meetings have been developed as part of the oncologist's teaching program. In these sessions, the groups focus on the problems faced by patients and families coping with cancer. Physicians are provided with answers to common problems. From the authors' perspective, the most effective solution is a good referral system with psychologists to meet the needs of their patients. Other training is available to make one nurse in a unit a resource person for the other nurses. Consultation was also made available to the nurses for personal needs.

Van Auken, S. Youth counselor burnout. Personnel and Guidance Journal, 1979, 59(10), 143-144.
The phenomenon of burnout is found in every field in which people are called upon to help others cope with their problems. The symptoms include glassy eyes, listlessness, anxiety, psychosomatic illness, and unusual speech patterns. Burnout occurs from prolonged involvement either with a few extremely troubling cases, or with too many cases.

The author presents a short case study of a counselor trying to work with a 16-year-old runaway and her family. The counselor becomes overinvolved in the case and develops both emotional and physical problems.

There are several suggestions for minimizing exposure to stressful situations and for managing stress.

1. Avoid being taken in by parents seeking to abdicate their responsibilities.
2. Keep meetings brief. Several short ones are less tiring than one long one.
3. Exercise selectivity in responding to emergency calls. Most problems will keep until morning.
4. Remind yourself you cannot control other people's behavior.
5. Stick to your professional objectives.

You can't change a person overnight and progress includes setbacks.

6. Develop a circle of associates with whom you can discuss cases.
7. Take the least dramatic steps first.
8. Maintain your sense of humor.
9. Take time off for vacation when you feel the onset of burnout.
10. Expect a process of trial and error and you won't be dissappointed.
11. Avoid panic.
12. Sometimes the best thing to do is withdrawal your attention from an uncooperative client.

The author's final recommendations is to model one's behavior after more experienced caseworkers who are maintaining their effectiveness.

Vander Kolk, C. W. Counselor stress in relation to disabled and minority clients. Rehabilitation Counseling Bulletin, 1977, 20(4), 256-274.

Counselor physiological and self-reported reactions to various disabled and minority clients were explored to help further understand counseling relationships. Relatively little research has been done on counselor attitudes towards disabled clients, although the observation of a disabiltiy seems to arouse a strong physiological reaction in some people. Several studies have shown a marked discrepancy between self-reported discomfort and measured physiological stress.

This study found support for the notion that counselors' physiology does change as various clients are encountered. Significant stress above the baseline was found with all six categories (five disabilities and one minority). Minority clients elicited the greatest stress for both minority and majority counselors. The blind client elicited the greatest stress in the disabiltiy category (other categories included mental retardation, amputee, paraplegia, and cerebral palsied). Rehabilitation and nonrehabilitation counseling students, minority and majority students, and males and females did not differ significantly form one another in the stress they experienced towards the six categories.

Although both minority and majority subjects were found to be physiologically most uncomfortable with minority clients, the self-reported data showed minority clients as being ranked the most comfortable to work with. For majority students, the largest discrepancy between self-report and measured physiological response was with paraplegia; for minority students, the greatest discrepancy was with mental retardation.

It is suggested that the lack of significant differences in stress levels between rehabilitiation and nonrehabilitation counseling students may be attributable to the limited exposure of beginning students to disabled persons. High stress on the part of minority students may be attributable to their feeling the need to perform effectively with minority clients, to the fact that several minority students felt it devaluing to include a minority client picture, and to the students' tendency to identify themselves with the majority or to feel the client identifies them with the majority.

Vattano, A. J. Self-management procedures for coping with stress. Social Work, March 1978, 23(2), 113-119.

Recently there has been an increased emphasis on teaching people to cope directly with the symptoms of stress through self-management procedures. Relaxation training, systematic desensitization, and meditation, are three important coping techniques.

Relaxation in its usual version consists of relaxing 20 major muscle groups. Each muscle group is tensed and relaxed in several different ways during a 60-minute period every day.

Various versions of muscle relaxation are effective for dealing with stress and the transitory state of anxiety. Relaxation training can be taught to individuals or to groups.

Systematic desensitization refers to a set of procedures for treating problems associated with inappropriate conditioned anxiety. These procedures consist of: 1) relaxation training, 2) creating a scale to measure anxiety responses, 3) constructing a hierarchy of anxiety-provoking stimuli, and 4) maintaining the relaxed state while imagining progressively more stressful stimuli.

Through this process, individuals learn a new response to the stimuli, which was previously associated with stress and fear. They are then able to transfer their new, relaxed response from mere visualization to the real life experiences. Research indicates that this procedure is far superior to more traditional approaches to anxiety-related behavior problems.

Meditation techniques in recent investigations indicate that for some people the regular practice of meditation can serve to counteract stress and anxiety. Meditation can produce an alteration in consciousness that involves a shift in mental process, alertness, and visual imagery. This is accompanied by hypometabolic changes that can produce deep rest and restoration of physiological and psychological functioning, which help reverse the effects of stress.

Relaxation training appears most appropriate for situation-specific problems. Systematic desensitization is most effective for conditioned anxiety. Meditation is a general preventive measure for counteracting the stress of modern living.

Veninga, R. Administrator burnout--Causes and cures. Hospital Progress, February, 1979, 45-52.

A study of over 100 occupations indicates that administrators/managers are one of the most stressed. With the multitude of pressures, challenges, and criticisms, practicing health administrators in growing numbers are succumbing to a condition called burnout. This term originated in the streets and referred to the irreversible drug addict. The term has been successfully applied to a condition among employees who, because of

contradictory pressure and unrealistic precon-
ceptions of the job, become depressed and unable to
work effectively. The symptoms are paranoia,
depression, poor health, and absenteeism. The net
result contributes to poor delivery of health and
welfare services.

The most susceptible administrator is the idealistic administrator. The idealistic administrator
works very hard to achieve unrealistic goals.
After years of overtime, taking work home, and
neglecting family for the sake of work, he or she
eventually perceives that the battle is endless,
and that objectives will not be met.

The burnout victim copes in different ways. For
example, some find new jobs. Others remain in
their positions, but withdraw from conflict.
However, others fight the source of frustration.
Whenever possible the administrator should engage
in preventative measures. The most important thing
for any administrator is to find satisfaction in
social obligations apart from work.

Feedback is of great importance between the
administrator and the employees. Only through
feedback can an accurate assessment of realistic
goals be achieved.

The entire human being must be considered by
himself before becoming too involved in obsessive
work habits. Only through personal and professional growth can the administrator ensure his continued effectiveness both privately and professionally. The balanced, realistic life should be the
objective toward which the administrator must
strive. Though this sounds simplistic, it is hard
for the workaholic administrator to see. Not until
some means of educating administrators is created
will burnout cease to be a problem in health care
administration.

Veninga, R., & Spradley, J. P. How to cope with
   job burnout. Reader's Digest, December, 1981,
   109-112.
The psychological response to unalleviated work
stress is called job burnout. It is manifested in

ailments such as headaches, excessive drinking, backaches, insomnia, depression, ulcers, and high blood pressure. Difficulty in decision making and inability to gain perspective on job realities are also symptoms of burnout.

Various pressures contribute to the development of burnout: pressures from superiors, work deadlines, inadequate compensation, ambiguity, and performance expectations that are unreasonable. As these stressors increase, the response of the person may go to the point of being life threatening. Coping can be the focus of flight, chemical additions, mental illness, and suicide.

More effective coping mechanisms include getting away physically from the job, hobby interests, avocations that are radically different from job processes, exercise, and mini-vacations. One factory offered a running program for employees and absenteeism due to sickness dropped 90%. The apparent solution to burnout is to make a radical and frequent change in the routine, especially if the worker can control the change in the routine and make his own choices. The article reports burnout occurs from too much pressure as well as too little. Setting realistic goals is another method of avoiding burnout; redesigning the job is another solution. The important thing to consider is that burnout will affect us if we don't learn how to deal with it.

Vessel, R. The devastating costs of professional burnout. Therapeutic Recreational Journal, 1980, 14(3), 11-14.

Burnout is commonly observed, yet little under-stood, as a problem that seems to unfairly afflict those professionals who were the most enthusiastic and motivated members of their field. Terms such as occupational stress and professional stagnation are often linked with burnout. Burnout is often defined as exhaustion, lack of energy, or loss of commitment.

The psychology of stress, stress in the work environment, and coping behavior of individuals are current areas of investigation that have identified internal (personal) and external (work environment or organizational) characteristics of burnout. The personal features of burnout are loss of a positive attitude substituted by apathy, fatigue, aches and pains, even ulcers. The organizational features include costly increases in absenteeism, increased tardiness, increased turnover, and the subsequent negative influence on the work environment.

More specifically, the activity of therapeutic recreators is further challenged by three performance characteristics that are likely to prove stressful: frequent contact beyond the boundaries of one's department, frequent contact beyond one's agency, demand for innovative and creative problem solving. Suggested remedies include:

1. Critical self-assessment. Identification of stress symptoms and burnout victims potential. Prevention is still the best cure.
2. Setting realistic personal goals. Emphasizing self-care and caring for others should be encouraged.
3. Develop a positive support system among the staff.
4. Reduce high patient-staff ratios, nonproductive meetings, job ambiguity, and job conflict.
5. Maximize potential. Provide a sense of growth for the employee.
6. Time-out. Periodic staff retreats or hide-away seminars for discussion of issues apart from work.

Walsh, D. Classroom stress and teacher burnout. Phi Delta Kappan, December 1979, 253.

In Chicago a teachers union survey found 56.6% of 5,500 respondents claiming physical and/or mental illness as a direct result of their jobs. Last year 70,000 teachers in the nation's public schools reported being physically assaulted. In 1962 more than one-fourth of all teachers had 20 years of experience; by 1976 this proportion had been cut in

half.   There have been a number of conditions
characteristic of burnout or its effects:
1.   A reaction of the nervous system to
     stress, leading to a variety of physical
     diseases.
2.   A disruption of personal or professional
     life as a result of occupational stress.
3.   Destructive feelings of emotional stress
     as a result of ineffective coping.
4.   Loss of concern and detachment from those
     with whom you work.
5.   A cynical and dehumanized perception of
     students accompanied by a deterioration
     of the quality of teaching.
The current causes of teacher burnout include such
varied stresses as harassment by the administration, assaults by students, paper work pressure,
and isolation.   Anger, fear, and frustration are
frequent responses, leading to such behavior
reactions as absenteeism, alcoholism, and abandon-
ment of the profession.   The list of physical
ailments ascribed to school stress by Chicago
teachers ranges from colitis or ulcers to high
blood pressure, depression, eye problems, headaches, ear disease, kidney problems, and stomach
problems.   Burnout seems to be lower for those
helping professionals who have access to some sort
of social-professional support systems.

Warheit, G. J.   Life events, coping, stress and
    depressive symptomatology. American Journal of
    Psychiatry, 1979, 136 (4B), 502-507.
Researchers have attempted to identify the
processes by which social, psychological, and
environmental stressors act as precursors to
physical and/or mental disorders.   Stress is
generally conceptualized as the altered state of an
organism produced by agents in the psychological,
social, cultural, and physical environments.
Efforts have been made to establish a qualitative
and quantitative relationship between particular
classes of life events and illness behavior.   Two
purposes exist for this paper.   One is to report

empirical data on life events, coping, resources, stress, and depressive symptomatology. The second is to analyze these variables within the context of longitudinal data that permit comparisons of depressive symptomatology before and after the occurrence of loss-related life events.

Theoretical models relating life events to psychosocial stress and illness have become more complex to include coping and adaptation variables. One criticism of many of these models, however, is that stressor events, coping, and illness continue to be viewed as static and occurring within a closed system. In addition, statistical models often assume unidirectional causality and do not provide for reciprocal interactions. A model is provided by the author detailing the life events arising from three sources: the individual's constitution, the culture, and the social environment.

The major findings of this study are:

1. Persons having high loss scores had higher depression scores than those with low/moderate loss scores.

2. Spouse presence was significantly correlated with lower depression scores for both the low/moderate and high-loss groups (other relatives were not significant).

3. Friend availability was significantly correlated with lower depression scores for the high-loss group; the low-loss group had no significant differences.

4. Significantly more of the high-loss group were using the services of physicians and clinics than were those with low losses.

5. Those utilizing mental-health services in both groups had higher depression scores.

6. Low socioeconomic status was significantly interrelated with higher depression scores in high-loss groups.

7. Losses and absence of resources were significant variables when used to predict high depression scores.

Warnath, C. F., & Shelton, J. L.   The ultimate
    disappointment: The burned out counselor.
    Personnel and Guidance Journal, December 1976, 55
    (4), 172-175.
Graduate students in counseling assume that the
act of helping people will furnish all the satisfaction they will require of life.   Nevertheless,
the movement of counselors out of full-time positions and the loss of counselors to other occupations raises questions about the ability of the
counseling role to meet the expectations that
graduate students have of their future position.
This article looks at some of the issues related to
why initially enthusiastic people lose their
commitment to direct-service work.
 Counselors in training are encouraged by their
instructors to adopt an orientation toward personal
responsibility, which assumes that individuals
possess adequate resources to control the circumstances of their lives if they will only assume
responsibility for their own decisions.   On the
job, the realization that people do not and cannot
control all the variables that affect them in every
situation becomes clear.   They also find out that
there are no clear-cut solutions as they had come
to expect from discussing counseling cases in the
abstract; there are only temporary solutions that
require a trade off of positive and negative
effects.   Some of the problems discussed are that
the freedom of choice may be limited by the needs
of their colleagues or the agency; client turnover
is high and allows little opportunity for the
personal relationship between counselor and client
implied in the literature; they may find themselves
isolated from others in their institutions and
agencies, distanced from the population they serve
because of their role as professional helpers; and
they are often distanced from each other because of
their own uncertainties about the effectiveness of
their work.
 No solution is offered, but a list of eight
suggestions might stimulate some open discussion
among counselor-education staff and between staff

and students. Such discussion may assist in bringing the reality of the job together with the counselor-education program.

Warshaw, L. J. <u>Managing stress</u>. Reading, Mass.: Addison-Wesley, 1979.
The stressors that arise within the work setting may be divided into the following categories:
    1.   Job content and environment.
    2.   Job structure.
    3.   Role in the organization.
    4.   Interpersonal relations.
    5.   Change.
Stress-management programs may be divided into two prototypes: a clinical or medical model and an organizational model or approach. The former deals on a one-to-one basis with individuals and the latter deals with units or segments of the work force or the employee population as a whole. The clinical approach components are: first aid; case finding; evaluation; treatment; referral; rehabilitation; screening; and prevention. The organizational programs are sometimes extensions of the clinical program and are run as a staff function; however, they more often function independently under the direction of the person responsible for operations. Fundamentally, these programs address the policies and practices of the organization as they relate to job stress and the emotional climate of the workplace.
Important stress reactions include alcohol and drug abuse, backache, mass psychogenic illness, and absenteeism. The above list represents types of behavior or patterns of reaction that are encountered frequently in the work setting.
Mechanisms for coping with stress include a variety of approaches and techniques including: medical therapy, group approaches (AA, meditation, Yoga, assertiveness training, physical exercise, etc.), exercise (sports and recreational activities, aerobic or cardiovascular fitness, muscular fitness strength, and tension-relieving exercises), diet, meditation and relaxation, biofeedback,

career counseling, and biorhythms. Table of contents includes:
Stress in the work setting
1. Introduction
2. What is stress?
3. Stress in the work setting
Stress-management programs
4. Stress management in the work setting
5. Kinds of helpers
6. Prototype clinical programs
7. Organizational programs
8. Psychological testing
Reactions and stressors
9. Important stress reactions
10. Change as a stressor
Coping and preventing
11. Mechanisms for coping with stress
12. Mechanisms for preventing stress reactions
Organizational considerations
13. Accidents and worker compensation awards
14. Evaluation and research

Watkins, B. T. A new academic disease: Faculty "burnout." Chronicle of Higher Education, March 24, 1982, pp. 1; 8.
Burnout is a condition characterized by physical and emotional exhaustion. Twenty percent of the population suffer from it. This disease has spread among faculty and college administrators. They suffer from a feeling of being professionally stuck, with declining economic and social status. Many experience fatigue and a lack of challenge. The reasons one experiences burnout are varied.
Some people suffer from burnout because they are high achievers. These individuals do more than their share of work and do not know when to quit. Burnout can also occur when one fails, gets worn down, or becomes exhausted from demands resources that one cannot meet. Faculty members and college administrators may experience this. As a result, they become torn different ways.
Some faculty members and administrators may

experience burnout because they feel they have no
significance in their work and an absence of
control over their environment. Some begin to feel
that what they do does not matter. Teaching
subjects that they really do not want to teach can
also cause faculty and college administrators to
burnout quickly. Some believe that the student
body contributes to faculty burnout.

After the cause has been determined, the next
thing to do is to learn to cope with burnout.
Long-range career planning can assist in the fight
against burnout. Being able to express one's
feelings on the issue can also release some tension. Developing workshops to learn more about
cause, effect, and treatment can additionally help
ease the condition.

Watkins, C. E., Jr.   Burnout in counseling
   practice: Some potential professional and
   personal hazards of becoming a counselor.
   Personnel and Guidance Journal, Jan. 1983,
   61(5), 304-308.

Burnout is a syndrome that afflicts many individuals employed in professional fields in which
they exhibit dedication and commitment to their
work. It is a pervasive phenomenon that results in
a change in attitude and behavior. There is a loss
of motivation, enthusiasm, and energy and a marked
departure from the individual's behavioral norm.
Burnout affects every aspect of the individual's
life, including social and professional behavior.

There are four categories of burnout: cognitive,
affective, behavioral, and physical. Symptoms of
burnout, cognitively expressed, usually result in a
personality change. There is a conflict of
emotions, with guilt or depression being the most
prominent. The emotions experienced cause a sense
of helplessness or loss in the individual. Behavioral symptoms vary from repetitive actions, to
reduction in work, to an increase in detrimental or
very negative actions. The physical symptoms of
burnout usually manifest themselves in illness or
reduction of stamina.

The counselor experiences certain hazards, which have an impact both interpersonally and intrapersonally. Interpersonal difficulties manifest themselves in a sense of despair, emptiness, and a sense of role meaninglessness. When this is experienced the counselor may resort to self-destructive behaviors in an effort to free himself of the pain he feels. Interpersonal difficulties are most apparent in intimate relationships with friends and relatives.

Three methods were suggested for dealing with burnout. The first method is personal therapy. The counselor who seeks therapy often experiences increased understanding and insight into self, clients, and the counseling enterprise. The second method is free private time. This is a period of time filled with an activity that the individual enjoys. This offers him or her: an opportunity to add variety to the day; a time of contemplation, or a time of relaxation. Free, private time can result in physical and mental rejuvenation. The third method is association with healthy souls. By spending time with family and friends, personal enrichment is achieved. Contact with other professionals leads to enhancement of professional capabilities. Overall, association with well-adjusted individuals improves the perspective of the counselor in all areas of life.

Weitzel, W., Pinto, P., Dawis, R. V., & Jury, F. A. The impact of the organization on the structure of job satisfaction: Some factor analytical findings. Personnel Psychology, 1973, 26, 545-557.

This paper presented a study directed toward ascertaining the impact an organization has on the structure of job satisfaction for its members. The article presupposed that there would be variances from company to company because there are distinctions in size, structure, means of reporting, and types of activities.

The responses that received the highest reaction to the general factor of satisfaction were:

recognition by supervisors, individual identity, overall satisfaction, credibility and confidence in management, and regularity of communication with supervisors.

There were two subgeneral factors analyzed. The first was satisfaction with job, under which the highest responses were: opportunity for advancement, promotion practices, satisfaction with progress of career and choice of career, amount of compensation, and comparison and practices of compensation. The other subfactor was satisfaction with the organization. The highest reported factors here were: openness of communication, cooperation, confidence in management, company aims and plans, and regular communication with management.

There were also four first-order-level factors. These were: satisfaction with personal progress and development, satisfaction with compensation, satisfaction with organizational context, and satisfaction with superior-subordinate relationships. They found that all of these factors were important in job satisfaction.

Whitehead, R. Bio-feedback: Plug into a piece of infinity. Industry Week, 1977, 193, 64-66.

Biofeedback is beginning to be an important aid to personal development in management-training programs. Biofeedback offers three electrical devices that measure the physical responses of the psyche: brain wave production, muscle tension, and skin resistence. An individual is taught to relax by combining hypnosis-like suggestion and training with one of these instruments. As a result, the individual can be taught to relax, thus increasing the efficiency of his energy use. In addition, biofeedback response and learning training time are much shorter than yoga or transcendental meditation.

Biofeedback has been found to allow an individual to see this emotion from the inside and identify the inner feelings that go with tenseness. Western culture tends to make us objective, ignoring what goes on inside of us. Businessmen and executives are problem-oriented, objective, and outward looking; emotion is equated with weakness.

Medical and scientific people should be in charge of biofeedback for several reasons. It is possible to have a psychotic episode, and lay operators may not be equipped to handle the situation. In addition, an individual is protected from faulty equipment and possibly misleading information. Furthermore, professionals can teach the individual to relax in private without the use of a machine.

Coping with stress can involve drugs, alcohol, or other ineffective mechanisms resulting in body breakdown. Biofeedback provides an acceptable replacement and ways of identifying oncoming stress through physical cues. In addition, it takes only hours to gain control, vs. years needed to master meditational techniques.

Witty, M. Keeping your cool. Quest, July/August, 1980, pp. 97-98.

Some people in stress-prone jobs do manage to stay healthy and keep their cool. People can learn to minimize stress by turning a demand into a learning challenge, or converting a feeling of helplessness into one of mastery. This article looks at seven people who have been able to do this and assesses their strategies for reducing stress.

The types of stressful jobs looked at are a police bomb squad commander, an air traffic controller, a renowned brain surgeon, a risk arbitrator at a Wall Street brokerage house, the medical director of the Lockheed Missile and Space Co., a concert pianist, and the department head at the Center for Stress-Related Disorders. Some of the strategies used by these people are ample sleep and occasional nights on the town with spouses, being involved in rough or active sports, being active in a diversity of interests, being highly organized, taking weekend vacations as often as possible, pacing oneself, and being able to minimize the stress.

Wubbolding, R. E., & Kessler-Bolton, E. Reality

therapy as an antidote to burn-out. <u>American</u>
<u>Mental Health Counselors Association Journal</u>,
1979, <u>1</u>, 39-43.
Counselor burnout is characterized by feelings of
frustration, rigidity, omnipotence, and fatigue.
Burned out staff members appear overly suspicious
and easily irritated. Burned-out counselors work
harder and harder, yet due to their growing ineffectiveness they accomplish less and less. A study
of 200 professionals in the helping profession
found that they tend to cope with stress by distancing themselves (both physically and psychologically) from their clients. Further damage is
caused by increased cynicism and negativism about
clients. Perhaps the most serious result of
burnout is the poor, even inhumane quality of
treatment allotted to the client.
 Antidotes to burnout have included sanctioned
time-outs, formal and informal support systems, and
physical exercise. Yet the problem of burnout
apparently cannot be solved exclusively by
on-the-job counter-measures. Reality therapy
offers an organized and systematic method of
self-help that can be identified and implemented by
workers suffering from varying degrees of burnout.
Reality therapy is based on the belief that individuals have the power to control their lives, to
change, to attain feelings of success or a successful identity. In reality therapy there are four
pathways to success: love, worth, fun, and
self-discipline. Burnout may be effectively
combated through the combination of a specific plan
of action and opposite behaviors (goals) the person
wishes to adopt. By examining interpersonal
relations in terms of the four pathways, specific
deficits should be noted, then matched with a goal
and specific steps to restore balance.

Yankelovich, D. New rules in American life:
  Searching for self-fulfillment in a world turned
  upside down. <u>Psychology Today</u>, April 1981, pp.
  35-91.
  Tomorrow is being shaped by a cultural revolution

that is transforming the rules of American life and moving us into wholly uncharted territory, not back to lifestyles of the past. Shared meanings are the essence of culture--the common understanding we hold about the varied particulars of social life and individual behavior. The cultural revolution now taking place has four outstanding characteristics; they are:

1. Breadth. The changes encompass the full sweep of American life--the private space of our inner lives; the semipublic space of our lives within the family, at work, in school, at church, and in our neighborhoods; and the public space of our lives as citizens.

2. The self-fulfillment contradiction. This is a mismatch between the goals of Americans seeking self-fulfillment and the means they deploy to achieve those goals.

3. Conflict and confusion. The search for self-fulfillment and the contradiction within it creates intense social conflict and confusion.

4. The stakes are high. Given the great reversal of culture and economy, and the intensity of the search of self-fulfillment, we have been plunged into a struggle that is both historic and mundane. In a matter of a few years, we have moved from an uptight culture set in a dynamic economy to a dynamic culture in an uptight economy.

The outcome of this cultural revolution depends on how we define, approach, and resolve the contradictions associated with the search for self-fulfillment and how we nurture the still-embryonic new rules of conduct.

There are two categories that depict the magnitude of the quest for self-fulfillment. The strong-formers are the people most thoroughly trapped in the self-fulfillment contradiction: they are the most ardent seekers of new meanings, but they pursue self-defeating strategies to define them. A confusing triple bind ensnares the strong form. First, they are faced with an abundance of choices without the knowledge to make the right ones; secondly, they desire forms of self-fulfillment and success that presuppose a cooperative economic and social environment. Thirdly, they are preoccupied with their inner psychological needs, and they think of the self as assemblage of needs.

The weak-form majority retain many traditional values, including a moderate commitment to the old self-denial rules, even as they struggle to achieve greater freedom, choice, and flexibility in their lives. The weak-form majority find family obligations, inflation worries, health cares, kids with school problems, and neighborhood crime important concerns not to be forgotten or overlooked.

In the coming two decades Americans will be called upon to make many changes to accommodate new economic realities. We need a new social ethic. There are now scraps and shreds of evidence that American culture is evolving toward a new ethic of commitment. The word commitment shifts the axis away from the self towad connectedness with the world. Two kinds of commitments are emerging. The first involves the forming of closer and deeper personal relationships, and the second involves trading some instrumental values (people and objects are viewed in terms of their immediate use or how they might satisfy limited or narrowly defined objectives) for sacred/expressive ones (people and objects are valued for themselves, apart from their instrumental use). A successful social ethic demands that people form commitments that advance the well-being of the society as well as their own. The process of developing new social signals, transmitting them, and assimilating them will take several decades, so the new giving/getting compact is unlikely to reveal all of its ramifications much before the end of the century.

Young, F. Stress it's good for you. Data
    Management, October 1980, pp. 22-25.
Stress can be a positive factor in some people's
lives as it can force them into using untapped
resources within themselves in order to resolve or
face a new situation. A direct link has been
established, however, between the mental and
physical functions of an individual. Consequently,
stress can lead to diseases in the human body if a
person fails to adapt to the stressors, or agents,
that are causing the initial stress. Hypertension,
migraine headaches, and duodenal ulcers can be
considered diseases that are caused by a person's
inability to adapt to stress. It is important,
therefore, to be aware of the optimal stress level
that is right for a person in order to maintain a
healthy existence. Three elements can be controlled in a person's life. The physical condition
of a person based on the way that person chooses to
live his or her life, the emotional pattern which
is developed from a person's early stages, and
finally the immediate environment
Several techniques can be utilized effectively to
cope with stress. It is important to analyze
strengths and weaknesses, clarify goals, recognize
symptoms of stress and what causes stress, understand various techniques of coping with stress, and
seek professional help if it is required.

Zaharia, E. S., & Baumeister, A. A. Technician
    turnover and absenteeism in public residential
    facilities. American Journal of Mental
    Deficiency, 1978, 82(6), 580-593.
Staffing is a recurrent problem in mental institutions to the degree that even court-ordered
requirements are impossible to maintain. This
study deals specifically with turnover and absenteeism, as an end result to a process of withdrawal
that begins with tardiness and poor job performance.
Besides the cost factor of training a series of
new people, there is an emotional cost to the
patients when the average resident would have to

adjust to 20 new caretakers over a six month period. The instability of the environment on the continuity of care is a factor to which no dollar sign can be attached.

Causes for turnover can be attributed to three areas: extrainstitutional factors, intrainstitutional factors, and the personal characteristics of the workers. Extrainstitutional factors include wages and the fact that the kind of wage structure often attracts people who are not highly motivated to work and may not even report initially after being hired. Low status and local economic conditions also may play a part in extrainstitutional factors. Intra-institutional management problems result often from outdated forms of management, although now there have been some new programs written for this kind of management.

The personal characteristics of the technicians themselves have the most variety in terms of turnover. Salary and benefits seem to affect some people more than others. Job content and autonomy have a great impact on most people. Sometimes vocational factors and personality types might affect turnover but not absenteeism. The types of patients in a ward may affect the turnover, as some types are more frustrating to work with. The nature of the institution in regard to size is not as important as the structure within the institution's divisions. Smaller groups may be more cohesive and allow closer relationships and more ownership.

Some specific findings in regard to absenteeism are: older workers have fewer but longer absences; the greater the travel distance, time and effort, the poorer the attendance record; the fewer family responsibilities, the poorer the record; and weather affects absenteeism.

There are some suggestions for controlling such withdrawal: inservice training, clear job descriptions before starting, four day work weeks, close watch on the initial four-month period to be supportive of the adjustments of the technician, and raising the status of the job.

Compendium

Signs and Symptoms

Physical
  substance abuse
    susceptibility to
      illness
    fatigue
    cardiopulmonary
    sleep problems
    psychosomatic complaints
    pain/tension
    physiological changes
  Emotional/mental
    mental illness
    depression
    isolation
    marital/family conflict
    self-esteem
    loss of coping mechanism
    cynicism
    rigidity/passivity
    aggression

Organizational
  job dissatisfaction
  attitudes twd.
  clients/patients
  unprofessionalism
  decreased productivity
  absenteeism/tardiness
involvement
  administration
  personnel activity
  accident proneness
  turnover

Causes and Sources

Personal
  loss/separation
  type A behavior
  pollyanna principle
  personal standards
  conflicts/crisis
  disequilibrium
  communication
  relationships
  fear
Environmental

Organizational
  clients/patients
  tedium/tension
  communications
  feedback
  involvement
  rewards
  role
  politics
  management
  supervision

tedium	changes/decisions
rewards	time
physical factors	status
society/economy	
conflicts	
living	

Coping Strategies

Personal	Organizational
biofeedback	performance standards
planning	involvement
support systems	tasks
relaxation/meditation	expectations
exercise/nutrition	job definition/role
leisure time	conflict resolution
personal	management
psychological	sharing/communications
	rest

Signs and Symptoms

Physical

Substance Abuse

Bies & Molle, 1980
Bricklin, 1981
Briley, 1980
Caplan, Cobb & French,
  1975
Cherniss, 1980
Cooper, 1979
Cooper & Marshal, 1976
DuBrin, et al, 1979
Fooner, 1981
Freudenberger, 1974
Freudenberger, 1975

Knutsen, 1977
Maslach, 1976
Maslach, 1978
McConnell, 1981
Mirkin, 1979
Selzer & Vinokur,
  1974
Swogger, 1981
Tucker, 1979
Veninga, 1979
Veninga & Spradley,
  1981
Warshaw, 1979

Susceptibility to Illness

Adler & Gosnell, 1980
Beech, Burns, &
  Sheffield, 1982
Bies & Molle, 1980
Blake & Mouton, 1980
Briley, 1980
Cherniss, 1980
Cohen, 1978
Collins, 1979
Cooper & Edson, 1979
Emener, 1979
Freudenberger, 1974
Freudenberger, 1975
Gardner, 1981
Hyson, 1982

Johnson, 1981
Kehl, 1981
Kobasa, 1979
Lunn, 1975
Margolis, Kroes & Quinn 1974
Matteson & Ivancevich, 1979
Mechanic, 1975
Patrick, 1979
Quick & Quick, 1979
Rabkin & Struening, 1976
Sammons, 1980
Watkins, 1983
Young, 1980

Fatigue
Bach, 1979
Beehr, 1981
Berstein, 1982
Bies & Molle, 1980
Briley, 1980
Chance, 1981
Cherniss, 1980
Christensen, 1981
Clark, 1980
Collins, 1979
Cooper, 1979
Daley, 1979
DuBrin, et al, 1979
Dunham, 1978
Edelwich & Brodsky,
  1980
Emener, 1979
Forney, et al, 1982
Freudenberger, 1974
Freudenberger, 1975
Freudenberger, 1977
Kahn, 1978

Kehl, 1981
Kyriacou & Sutcliffe,
  1978
Leffingwell, 1979
Maslach, 1978
Maslach & Jackson,
  1978
Maslach & Pines, 1977
McConnell, 1981
McMinn, 1979
Moracco, 1981
Patrick, 1979
Pines, Aronson & Kafry
  1981
Raphael, Karpf &
  Sills, 1980
Rediger, 1980
Reed, 1979
Sammons, 1980
Spicuzza & DeVoe, 1982
Stocker, 1981
Vessel, 1980
Watkins, 1982
Watkins, 1983
Wubbolding & Kessler-
  Bolton, 1979

Sleep Problems
Briley, 1980
Cherniss, 1980
Christensen, 1981
Cooper, 1979
Emener, 1979
Freudenberger, 1974
Freudenberger, 1975
Johnson, 1981

Kahn, 1978
McMinn, 1979
Mirkin, 1979
Patrick, 1979
Rediger, 1980
Reed, 1979
Sammons, 1980
Spicuzza & DeVoe, 1982
U.S. News and World
  Report, 1978
Veninga & Spradley,
  1981

Psychosomatic Complaints

Alexander, 1980
Bloch, 1978
Brocher, 1979
Clark, 1980
Colligan & Murphy, 1979
Cooper & Edson, 1979
Freudenberger, 1975

Knutsen, 1977
McLean, 1979
Sawyer & Schumacher, 1980
Van Auken, 1979
Vessel, 1980
Warshaw, 1979

Pain/Tension

Adler & Gosnell, 1980
Antonovsky, 1972
Cooper, 1979
DuBrin, et al, 1979
Gardner, 1981
Greenberg, 1977
Johnson, 1981

Kahn, 1973
Lustman & O'Hara, 1981
Miller, 1981
Miller & Roberts, 1979
U.S. News and World Report, 1978
Vessel, 1980
Warshaw, 1979
Young, 1980

Psychological Changes

Barrows & Prosen, 1981
Beech, Burns & Sheffield, 1982
Blake & Mouton, 1980
Bloch, 1978
Brocher, 1979
Cohen, 1978
Duemer, 1978ld, 1982
Emener, Luck & Gohs, 1982
Fooner, 1981
Greenberg, 1977
Holland, 1982

Kahn, 1978
Levi, 1981
Lipton, 1981
Lutz & Ramsey, 1976
Mason, 1975
McLean, 1979
Mirkin, 1979
Newman & Beehr, 1979
Notarius & Levenson, 1979
Parrina, 1979
Walsh, 1979

Emotional/Mental

Mental Illness

Beech, Burns & Sheffield, 1982
Bloch, 1978
Boronson, 1976

Knutsen, 1977
Lipton, 1981
Maslach, 1976
McLean, 1979

Bricklin, 1981
Colligan & Murphy,
 1979
Colligan, Smith &
 Hurrell, 1977
Cooper, 1979
Cooper & Marshal, 1976
Emener, 1979
Freudenberger, 1975
Kanner, Kafry & Pines,
 1978
Kasl, 1973

Mirkin, 1979
Pines, Aronson & Kafry,
 1981
Reed, 1979
Tamerin, 1982
Walsh, 1979
Watkins, 1983
Young, 1980

Depression
Beehr, 1976
Beehr, 1981
Bies & Moole, 1980
Chance, 1981
Christensen, 1981
Clark, 1980
Collins, 1979
Cooper, 1979
DuBrin, et al, 1979
Freudenberger, 1974
Freudenberger, 1975
Freudenberger, 1977
Hyson, 1982
Johnson, 1981
Kehl, 1981
Klerman, 1979
Knutsen, 1977
Lunn, 1975

McCarley, 1975
McConnell, 1981
McMinn, 1979
Mechanic, 1975
Mirkin, 1979
Moracco, 1981
Patrick, 1979
Pines, Aronson & Karfy,
 1981
Raphael, Karpf & Sills,
 1980
Rediger, 1980
Reed, 1979
Sammons, 1980
Selzer & Vinokur, 1974
Swogger, 1981
Tamerin, 1982
Veninga, 1979
Vessel, 1980
Warheit, 1979
Watkins, 1983

Isolation
Bach, 1979
Beehr & Gupta, 1978
Bermak, 1977
Colligan & Murphy,
 1979

Kehl, 1981
Laron, Gilbertson &
 Power, 1978
Lattanzi, 1981
Lubin, 1982

Cooper, 1979
Emener, 1979
Fooner, 1981
Freudenberger, 1975
Grater, Kell & Morse,
  1961
Gruneberg, Startup
  & Tapsfield, 1974
Jones & Emanuel, 1981
Kanner, Kafry & Pines,
  1978

Lunn, 1975
Maslach & Jackson,
  1979
Maslach & Pines, 1978
McConnell, 1981
Moracco, 1981
Newman & Beehr, 1979
Pines & Maslach, 1978
Spicuzza & DeVoe, 1982
Veninga, 1979

Marital/Family Conflict
  Cherniss, 1980
  Cooper & Edson, 1979
  Hauenstein, Kals &
   Harburg, 1977
  Maslach, 1976
  Maslach, 1978

Maslach & Jackson, 1978
Maslach & Jackson, 1979
Reed, 1979
Swogger, 1981

Self-Esteem
  Allen, 1979
  Bach, 1979
  Barrow & Prosen, 1981
  Beehr, 1981
  Cherniss, 1980
  Cole & LeJeune, 1972
  Cooper & Marshal, 1976
  Dunham, 1978
  Forney, et al, 1982
  Holland, 1982
  Jones & Emmanuel, 1981
  Kahn, 1973

Kahn, 1978
Kalleberg, 1977
Margolis, Kroes &
  Quin, 1974
Meadow, 1981
Moracco, 1981
Patrick, 1979
Pines, Aronson &
  Kafry, 1981
Prentki, 1980
Stocker, 1981
Tamerin, 1982
Tardy, 1977

Loss of Coping Mechanism
  Antonovsky, 1972
  Bermak, 1977
  Coburn, 1975
  Colligan, Smith &
   Hurrell, 1977
  Edelwich & Brodsky,
   1980

Lunn, 1975
Lustman & O'Hara, 1981
Mason, 1975
Morocco, 1981
Newman & Beehr, 1979
Parkington & Schneider
  1979

Forney, et al, 1982
Freudenberger, 1974
Gardner, 1981
Holland, 1982
Hyson, 1982
Jones & Emanuel, 1981
Knutsen, 1977
Lattanzi, 1981

Parrina, 1979
Phillips, 1980
Pines, Aronson &
  Kafry, 1981
Shea, 1980
Warheit, 1979
Watkins, 1982
Young, 1980

Cynicism
Bach, 1979
Berstein, 1982
Briley, 1980
Chance, 1981
Collins, 1979
Edelwich & Brodsky,
  1980
Emener, Luck & Gohs,
  1982
Fooner, 1981
Freudenberger, 1974
Freudenberger, 1977

Holland, 1982
Maslach, 1976
Maslach, 1978
McMinn, 1979
Patrick, 1979
Rediger, 1980
Stocker, 1981
Tamerin, 1982
Vessel, 1980
Wubbolding &
  Kessler-Bolton, 1979

Rigidity/Passivity
Berstein, 1982
Blake & Mouton, 1980
Bloch, 1978
Christensen, 1981
Dunham, 1978
Freudenberger, 1974
Freudenberger, 1975
Freudenberger, 1977
Kahn, 1978

Kyriacou & Sutcliffe,
  1978
Leffingwell, 1979
Lenhart, 1980
McMinn, 1979
Moracco, 1981
Patrick, 1979
Sammons, 1980
Wubbolding &
  Kessler-Bolton, 1979

Aggression
Bach, 1979
Chance, 1981
Christensen, 1981
Cooper & Edson, 1979
Emener, 1979
Emener, Luck & Gohs,
  1982

Mirkin, 1979
Moracco, 1981
Organ, 1979
Patrick, 1979
Reed, 1979
Sammons, 1980
Selzer & Vinokur, 1974

Freudenberger, 1975
Greenberg, 1977
Hyson, 1982
Johnson, 1981

Stocker, 1981
Tardy, 1977
Wubbolding &
   Kessler-Bolton, 1979

Organizational

Job Dissatisfaction

Armstrong, 1971
Atkins, Meyer & Smith,
   1982
Bach, 1979
Beehr, 1981
Berlin, 1969
Bies & Molle, 1980
Carpenter, 1971
Cherniss & Egnatios,
   1978
Cooper & Marshal, 1976
Daley, 1979
Freudenberger, 1977
Frew, 1974
Geist & Backes, 1978
Grossnickle, 1980
Gruneberg, 1979
Gruneberg, Startup &
   Tapsfield, 1974
Hamner & Oldham, 1974
Hanson, 1968
Hauenstein, Kals &burgStelmach, et al, 1981
   Harburg, 1977

Ivancevich, 1976
Jones & Emanuel, 1981
Kahn, 1973
Kalleberg, 1977
Kasl, 1973
Keller, 1975
Labovitz & Orth, 1972
Lunn, 1975
Nicholson & Miljus,
   1972
Osborn & Vicars, 1976
Pacinelli & Britton,
   1969
Parkington & Schneider
   1979
Prentki, 1980
Quick & Quick, 1979
Raphael, Karpf &
   Sills, 1980
Sheafor, 1976
Smits, 1972
Weitzel, et al, 1973

Attitudes Toward Clients/Patients

Atkins, Meyer & Smith,
   1982
Bach, 1979
Bermak, 1977
Bies & Molle, 1980
Bricklin, 1981
Cherniss, 1981
Colligan, Smith &
   Hurrell, 1977
Cooper, Mallinger &

Kahn, 1978
Lamb, 1971
Maslach, 1976
Maslach, 1978
Patrick, 1979
Shubin, 1978
Tamerin, 1982
Vander Kolk, 1977
Walsh, 1979
Wubbolding &

Kahn, 1978
Dunham, 1978
Holland, 1982
Justice, Gold & Klein, 1981

Kessler-Bolton, 1979

Unprofessionalism
Bach, 1979
Bardo, 1979
Bricklin, 1981
Chance, 1981
Frew, 1974
Geist & Backes, 1978
Holland, 1982
Humphrey, 1978

Jones & Emanuel, 1981
Justice, Gold & Klein, 1981
Knutsen, 1977
Maslach, 1976
Prentki, 1980
Veninga, 1979
Walsh, 1979

Decreased Productivity
Briley, 1980
Bryan, 1981
Cooper, Mallinger &
  Kahn, 1978
Cooper & Marshal, 1976
Daley, 1979
Freudenberger, 1974
Freudenberger, 1975
Freudenberger, 1977
Gruenberg, 1979
Hanson, 1968
Kahn, 1973
Kahn, 1978

Laron, Gilbertson
  & Power, 1978
Macy & Mirvis, 1976
Maslach & Jackson, 1978
Maslach & Pines, 1978
Matteson & Ivancevich,
  1979
Moracco, 1981
Shea, 1980
Swogger, 1981
Wubbolding & Kessler-
  Bolton, 1979
Zaharia & Baumeister,
  1978

Absenteeism/Tardiness
Bardo, 1979
Beehr, 1981
Beehr & Gupta, 1978
Briley, 1980
Bryan, 1981
Cherniss, 1980
Cooper & Marshal, 1976
Daley, 1979
Fooner, 1981
Gardner, 1981

Lyons, 1972
Macy & Mirvis, 1976
Maslach, 1978
Maslach & Pines, 1978
Moracco, 1981
Pines & Maslach, 1978
Quick & Quick, 1979
U.S. News and World
  Report, 1978
Veninga, 1979

Kasl, 1973
Lunn, 1975

Vessel, 1980
Zaharia & Baumeister,
  1978

Involvement
  Ball, 1977
  Bardo, 1979
  Batlis, 1980
  Boy & Pine, 1980
  Briley, 1980
  Chance, 1981
  Collins, 1979
  Edelwich & Brodsky,
    1980
  Freudenberger, 1977
  Grater, Kell & Morse,
    1961
  Hamner & Tosi, 1974

Lammert, 1981
Lantos, 1952
Malone & Falkenberg,
  1980
Maslach, 1976
Maslach, 1978
Maslach & Jackson, 1978
McKenna, 1980
Parkington & Schneider,
  1979
Phillips, 1980
Veninga & Spradley,
  1981

Administration
  Austin & Jackson, 1977
  Boy & Pine, 1980
  Cooper, Mallinger &
    Kahn, 1978
  Fooner, 1981
  Gardner, 1981
  Holland, 1982

Kahn, 1978
Karasek, 1979
Lutz & Ramsey, 1976
Macy & Mirvis, 1976
Osborn & Vicars, 1976
Tardy, 1977

Personnel Activity
  Lutz & Ramsey, 1976
  Daley, 1979
  Gardner, 1981
  Geist & Backes, 1978
  Holland, 1982
  Kasl, 1973

Lutz & Ramsey, 1976
McKenna, 1980
Nicholson & Miljus,
  1972
Osborn & Vicars, 1976
Tardy, 1977
Zaharia & Baumeister,
  1978

Accident Proneness
  Bricklin, 1981
  Macy & Mirvis, 1976
  Mirkin, 1979

Selzer & Vinokur, 1974
U.S. News and World
  Report, 1978

Warshaw, 1979

Turnover

Atkins, Meyer & Smith, 1982
Beehr, 1981
Beehr & Gupta, 1978
Bryan, 1981
Campbell, 1977
Campbell & Frail, 1975
Cherniss, 1980
Cleland & Peck, 1959
Daley, 1979
DuBrin, et al, 1979
Francis, 1980
Frew, 1974
Gardner, 1981
Hamner & Oldham, 1974
Holland, 1982
Jones & Emanuel, 1981
Labovitz & Orth, 1972
Lyons, 1972

Macy & Mirvis, 1976
Maslach, 1978
Maslach & Jackson, 1978
McMinn, 1979
Nicholson & Miljus, 1972
Parkington & Schneider, 1979
Pines, Aronson & Kafry, 1981
Pines & Maslach, 1978
Prentki, 1980
Quick & Quick, 1979
Raphael, Karpf & Sills, 1980
Schuh, 1967
Sheridan & Vredenburgh, 1978
Smits, 1972
U.S. News and World Report, 1978
Veninga, 1979
Vessel, 1980
Warnath & Shelton, 1976
Zaharia & Baumeister, 1978

Causes and Sources

Personal

Loss/Separation
  Johnson, 1981
  Klerman, 1979
  Kobasa, 1979
  Kobasa, Hilker &
    Maddi, 1979
  Lattanzi, 1981

  McLean, 1979
  Mechanic, 1975
  Rabkin & Struening,
    1976
  Warheir, 1979
  Watkins, 1983

Type A Behavior
  Beech, Burns &
    Sheffield, 1982
  Bricklin, 1981
  Caplan, Cobb & French,
    1975
  Caplan & Jones, 1975
  Cooper & Edson, 1979
  Cooper & Payne, 1980
  Edelwich & Brodsky,
    1980
  Freudenberger, 1975
  Frew, 1974
  Greenberg, 1977
  Hauenstein, Kals &
    Harburg, 1977

  Ivancevich, 1976
  Kasl, 1973
  Matteson & Ivancevich,
    1979
  McConnell, 1981
  Selye & Cherry, 1978
  Spicuzza & DeVoe, 1982
  Veninga, 1979
  Vessel, 1980
  Watkins, 1982
  Yankelovich, 1981

Polyanna Principle
  Boronson, 1976
  Boy & Pine, 1980
  Edelwich & Brodsky,
    1980

  Grater, Kell & Morse,
    1961
  Kanner, Kafry & Pines,
    1978

Matlin & Stang, 1978

Personal Standards
Barrow & Prosen, 1981   Gatre & Rosenblum,
Boronson, 1976   1978
Briley, 1980   Ivancevich, 1976
Chance, 1981   Kehl, 1981
Cherniss, 1980   Keller, 1975
Clark, 1980   Lattanzi, 1981
Freudenberger, 1975   Maslach & Jackson, 1978
Gardell, 1976   Moracco, et al, 1982
                               Selye & Cherry, 1978

Conflict/Crisis
Adams, 1978   Klerman, 1979
Blake & Mouton, 1980   Laron, Gilbertson,
Brief & Aldag, 1976   & Power, 1978
Gardell, 1976   Miller & Roberts, 1979
Hyson, 1982   Mirkin, 1979
Johnson, 1981   Mitchell, 1979
Kahn, 1973   Organ, 1979
Kahn, 1978   Parkington & Schneider,
Kehl, 1981   1979
                               Rediger, 1980
                               Smith, 1978

Communication
Baron & Cohen, 1982   Patrick, 1979
Mitchell, 1979   Tucker, 1979
Moracco, 1981

Relationships
Ball, 1977   Mitchell, 1979
Bermak, 1977   Moracco, 1981
Berstein, 1982   Moracco, et al, 1982
Freudenberger, 1977   Newman & Beehr, 1979
Frew, 1974   Osborn & Vicars, 1976
Grater, Kell & Morse,   Pines & Maslach, 1978
 1961   Quick & Quick, 1979
Kalleberg, 1977   Smith, 1978

Kasl, 1973
Klerman, 1979
Lazarus, 1979
Maslach, 1978
McConnell, 1981
Mirkin, 1979

Smits, 1972
Warshaw, 1979
Watkins, 1983
Yankelovich, 1981

Fear
Berlin, 1969
Bloch, 1978
Brocher, 1979
Gardner, 1981

Grater, Kell & Morse,
  1961
Grossnickle, 1980
Phillips, 1980

ENVIRONMENTAL

Tedium
Bach, 1979
Bies & Molle, 1980
Chance, 1981
Colligan & Murphy,
  1979
Cooper, Mallinger &
  Kahn, 1978

Freudenberger, 1977
Kanner, Kafry & Pines,
  1978
Pines, Aronson & Kafry,
  1981
Sammons, 1980

Rewards
Atkins, Meyer & Smith,
  1982
Edelwich & Brodsky,
  1980
Gardell, 1976
Gardner, 1981
Geist & Backes, 1978

Gruneberg, 1979
Kalleberg, 1977
Rediger, 1980
Stelmach, et al, 1981

Physical Factors
Bailey & Walker, 1982
Beech, Burns &
  Sheffield, 1982
Blake & Mouton, 1980
Daley, 1979
Dunham, 1978
Francis, 1980
Gardner, 1981

Hayson, 1982
Kasl, 1973
Labovitz & Orth, 1972
Levi, 1981
McLean, 1979
Patrick, 1979
Quick & Quick, 1979

Grossnickle, 1980
Gruneberg, Startup &
  Tapsfield, 1974

Society/Economy
Barch, 1979
Bennett, 1979
Chance, 1979
Cherniss & Egnatios,
  1978
Cole & Lejeune, 1972
Emener, 1979
Emener, Luck & Gohs,
  1982
Gardell, 1976
Grossnickle, 1980
Hauenstein, Kals &
Harburg, 1977
Jenkins, 1976

Johnson, 1981
Kahn, 1978
Lenhart, 1980
Lutz & Ramsey, 1976
Macy & Mirvis, 1976
McLean, 1979
Mechanic, 1979
Mitchell, 1979
Organ, 1979
Rediger, 1980
Watkins, 1982
Yankelovich, 1981

Conflicts
Atkins, Meyer & Smith,
  1982
Blake & Mouton, 1980
Brief & Aldag, 1976
Edelwich & Brodsky,
  1980
Gardell, 1976
Hyson, 1982
Kahn, 1973
Kahn, 1978
Kehl, 1981

Kierman, 1979
Levi, 1981
Miller & Roberts, 1979
Mitchell, 1979
Organ, 1979
Parkington & Schneider,
  1979
Rediger, 1980
Warshaw, 1979
Yankelovich, 1981

Living
Boronson, 1976
Brown, 1977
Cole & LeJeune, 1972
Cooper, 1979
Cooper & Payne, 1980
Cummings & Cooper, 1979
Emener, Luck & Gohs,
  1979

Kahn, 1973
Kanner, Kafry & Pines,
  1978
Kasl, 1973
Kobasa, Hilker & Maddi,
  1979
Lecker, 1978
Macy & Mirvis, 1976

Forney, et al, 1982
Freudenberger, 1975
Glaser, 1976
Hulin & Smith, 1964
Johnson, 1981
Justice, Gold & Klein,
  1981

Organ, 1979
Price, 1977
Rabkin & Struening,
  1976
Selzer & Vinokur, 1974
Selye & Cherry, 1978
Warheit, 1979

Organizational

Clients/Patients
  Bailey & Austin, 1982
  Bermak, 1977
  Cherniss, 1981
  Colligan, Smith &
    Hurrwll, 1977
  Collins, 1979
  Dunham, 1979
  Edelwich & Brodsky,
    1980
  Francis, 1980
  Gardner, 1981
  Grossnickle, 1980
  Holland, 1982
  Kyriacou & Sutcliffe,
    1978
  Lamb, 1971
  Lenhart, 1980
  Maslach, 1978

  McCarley, 1975
  Moracco, 1981
  Patrick, 1979
  Pines, Aronson & Kafry,
    1981
  Pines & Maslach, 1978
  Raphael, Karpf & Sills,
    1980
  Savidki & Cooley, 1982
  Spicuzza & DeVoe, 1982
  Stocker, 1981
  Tamerin, 1982
  Vachon, Lyall & Freenam,
    1978
  Van Auken, 1979
  Vander Kock, 1977
  Watkins, 1982

Tedium/Tension
  Cherniss, 1980
  Colligan & Murphy,
    1979hn, 1978
  Cooper, Mallinger &
    Kahn, 1978
  Cooper & Marshall,
    1976
  Daley, 1979
  Freudenberger, 1977
  Gardner, 1981

  Hauenstein, Kals &
    Harburg, 1977
  Kanner, Kafry & Pines,
    1978
  Pines, Aronson &
    Kafry, 1981
  Sammons, 1980
  Sheridan & Vredenburgh
    1978

Communications

Austin & Jackson, 1977
Baron & Cohen, 1982
Beech, Burns &
  Sheffield, 1982
Carpenter, 1971illo, 1980
Casas, Furlong &
  Castrillo, 1980
Colligan & Murphy,
  1979
Dunham, 1978
Flood, Kashka & Tweed,
  1981
Glaser, 1976

Kahn, 1973
Lipton, 1981
Miller, 1981
Pacinelli & Britton,
  1969
Pines, Aronson &
  Kafry, 1981
Pines & Maslach, 1978
Schuler, 1979
U.S. News and World
  Report, 1978
Vachon, Lyall &
  Freenam, 1978
Vessel, 1980
Weitzel, et al, 1973

Feedback

Bloch, 1978
Bryan, 1981
Cherniss & Egnatios,
  1978
Cooper & Payne, 1980
Cummings & Cooper, 1974
Daley, 1979
Glaser, 1979
Grossnickle, 1980

Lammert, 1981
Moracco, 1981
Pacinelli & Britton,
  1969
Quick & Quick, 1979
Schuler, 1979
Swogger, 1981
Veninga, 1979

Involvement

Austin & Jackson, 1977
Bermak, 1977
Boy & Pine, 1980
Brocher, 1979
Collins, 1979
Cooper, Mallinger &
  Kahn, 1978
Daley, 1979
Hamner & Tosi, 1974
Lammert, 1981
Maslach, 1978
McConnell, 1981

Patrick, 1979
Phillips, 1980
Price, 1977
Rediger, 1980
Savidki & Cooley, 1982
Smits, 1972
Spicuzza & DeVoe, 1982
Swogger, 1981
U.S. News and World
  Report, 1978
Veninga, 1979
Warnath & Shelton,
  1976
Watkins, 1982

Rewards
  Bailey & Walker, 1982
  Bryan, 1981
  Chance, 1981
  Edelwich & Brodsky,
    1980
  Emener, 1979
  Flood, Kashka & Tweed,
    1981
  Gardell, 1976
  Gardner, 1981
  Geist & Backes, 1978
  Grossnickle, 1980
  Gruneberg, 1979
  Hulin & Smith, 1964
  Kalleberg, 1977
  Kasl, 1973

  Macy & Mirvis, 1976
  Maslach & Jackson,
    1978
  Moracco, 1981
  Moracco, et al, 1982
  Nicholson & Miljus,
    1972
  Osborn & Vicars, 1976
  Pines, Aronson &
    Kafry, 1981
  Sheridan & Vredenburgh
    1978
  Spicuzza & DeVoe, 1982
  Stelmach, et al, 1981
  Veninga & Spradley,
    1981
  Weitzel, et al, 1973
  Zaharia & Baumeister,
    1978

Roles
  Armstrong, 1971
  Batlis, 1980
  Beech, Burns &
    Sheffield, 1982
  Beehr, 1976
  Beehr, 1981
  Berlin, 1969
  Boy & Pine, 1980
  Cherniss, 1980
  Cherniss, Egnatios &
    Wacker, 1976
  Coburn, 1975
  Colligan, Smith &
    Hurrell, 1977
  Cooper & Marshal, 1976
  Cooper & Payne, 1980
  Daley, 1979
  Dunham, 1978
  Francis, 1980
  Gardell, 1976
  Gardner, 1981

  Holland, 1982
  House, 1981
  Hyson, 1982
  Kahn, 1973
  Kahn, 1978
  Keller, 1975
  Lecker, 1978
  Levi, 1981
  McLean, 1979
  Meadow, 1981
  Pacinelli & Britton,
    1969
  Parkington & Schneider,
    1979
  Patterson, 1970
  Quick & Quick, 1979
  Sawyer & Schumacher,
    1980
  Warnath & Shelton, 1976
  Warshaw, 1979
  Watkins, 1982

Hamner & Tosi, 1974
Hauenstein, Kals &

Politics
Austin & Jackson, 1977
Beech, Burns, &
  Sheffield, 1982
Bloch, 1978
Campbell & Frail, 1975
Cherniss & Egnatios,
  1978
Cherniss, Egnatios &
  Wacker, 1976
Edelwich & Brodsky,
  1980
Fooner, 1981

Holland, 1982
House, 1982
Lenhart, 1980
Parkington & Schneider,
  1979
Patterson, 1970
Sheafor, 1976
Sheridan & Vredenburgh,
  1978
Tardy, 1977

Management
Adams, 1978
Bailey & Walker, 1982
Barnes & Crutchfield,
  1977
Bloch, 1978
Brocher, 1979
Campbell & Frail, 1975
Carpenter, 1971
Casas, Furlong &
  Castrillo, 1980
Cherniss, 1980
Cherniss & Egnatios,
  1978
Colligan & Murphy,
  1979
Cooper & Maslach, 1976
Cummings & Cooper, 1979
Daley, 1979
Emener, 1979
Flood, Kashka & Tweed,
  1981
Fooner, 1981
Gardell, 1976
Geist & Backes, 1978
Grossnickle, 1980

Kahn, 1973
Karasek, 1979
Lamb, 1971
Levi, 1981
Lipton, 1981
Maslach & Jackson,
  1978
McLean, 1979
Miller & Roberts, 1979
Moracco, 1981
Moracco, et al, 1982
Nicholson & Miljus,
  1972
Patrick, 1979
Pines & Maslach, 1978
Rosenbaum & Rosenbaum,
  1971
Reed, 1979
Sawyer & Schumacher,
  1980
Sheafor, 1976
Shannon & Saleebey,
  1980
Spicuzza & DeVoe, 1982
Veninga & Spradley,

Gruneberg, Startup &
  Tapsfiled, 1974
Holland, 1982
House, 1981

Supervision
  Aiken, Smits & Lollar,
    1972
  Austin & Jackson, 1977
  Campbell & Frail, 1975
  Carpenter, 1971
  Casas, Furlong &
    Castrillo, 1980
  Chance, 1981
  Cherniss & Egnatios,
    1978
  Colligan & Murphy, 1979
  Cooper & Marshal, 1976
  Flood, Kashka & Tweed,
    1981
  Gardell, 1976
  House, 1981

Changes/Decisions
  Adams, 198
  Beech, Burns &
    Sheffield, 1982
  Berlin, 1969
  Cherniss, 1980
  Cooper & Edons, 1979
  Cooper & Payne, 1980
  Dunham, 1978
  Edelwich & Brodsky,
    1980
  Emener, 1979
  Gardell, 1976
  Hackman & Oldham, 1975

1981
Watkins, 1982
Weitzel, et al, 1973
Zaharia & Baumeister,
  1978

Hulin & Smith, 1964
Kasl, 1973
Lipton, 1981
Lutz & Ramsey, 1976
Osborn & Vicars, 1976
Pacinelli & Britton,
  1969
Pines, Aronson & Kafry,
  1981
Reed, 1979
Rosenbaum & Rosenbaum,
  1971
Schuler, 1979
Sheridan & Vredenburgh,
  1978
Veninga & Spradley,
  1981

Humphrey, 1978
Johnson, 1981
Lamb, 1971
Lipton, 1981
McLean, 1979
Miller, 1981
Patrick, 1979
Smith, 1978
Warshaw, 1979
Yankelovich, 1981

Time

Bermak, 1977
Boy & Pine, 1980
Bricklin, 1981
Colligan & Murphy, 1979
Collins, 1979
Cummings & Cooper, 1979
Daley, 1979
Greenberg, 1977
Johnson, 1980
Kahn, 1973
Kahn, 1978
Kyriacou & Sutcliffe, 1978

Lamb, 1971
Leffingwell, 1979
Meadow, 1981
Patrick, 1979
Pines, Aronson & Kafry, 1981
Pines & Maslach, 1978
Robinson, 1977
Sammons, 1980
Schuler, 1979
Shannon & Saleebey, 1980
Stelmach, et al, 1981
Veninga & Spradley, 1981

Status

Austin & Jackson, 1977
Berlin, 1969
Brief & Aldag, 1976
Caplan & Jones, 1975
Carpenter, 1971
Chance, 1981
Edelwich & Brodsky, 1980
Emener, 1979
Garnder, 1981
Glaser, 1976
Havenstein, Kals & Harburg, 1977

Hulin & Smith, 1964
Jenkins, 1976
Lamb, 1971
McConnell, 1982
Patterson, 1970
Rediger, 1980
Reed, 1979
Swogger, 1981
Tardy, 1977
Zaharia & Baumeister, 1978

Coping Strategies

Physical

Biofeedback

Bailey & Walker, 1982
Barrow & Prosen, 1981
Beech, Burns &
 Sheffield, 1982
Blake & Mouton, 1980
Cooper & Edson, 1979
Gardner, 1981
Greenberg, 1977
Hassett, 1978

Lustman & O'Hara, 1981
Parrina, 1979
Quick & Quick, 1979
Sawyer & Schumacher,
 1980
Shea, 1980
Vattano, 1978
Warshaw, 1979
Whitehead, 1977

Planning

Adams, 1978
Adams, 1979
Bies & Molle, 1980
Briley, 1980
Bryan, 1981
Duemer, 1978
Fooner, 1981
Gatre & Rosenblum, 1978
Genevay & Simon-Backes,
 1979
Girodo & Stein, 1978
Holland, 1982
Hyson, 1982
Johnson, 1980

Johnson, 1981
Jones & Emanuel, 1981
Leffingwell, 1979
Malone & Falkenberg,
 1980
McKenna, 1980
Newman & Beehr, 1979
Quick & Quick, 1979
Smith, 1978
Swogger, 1981
Watkins, 1982
Wubbolding &
 Kessler-Bolton, 1979
Young, 1980

Support Systems

Adams, 1979
Antonovsky, 1972
Atkins, Meyer & Smith,

Lammert, 1981
Laron, Gilbertson &
 Power, 1978

1982
Beehr, 1976
Bennett, 1979
Berstein, 1982
Briley, 1980
Bryan, 1981
Caplan, Cobb & French, 1975
Casas, Furlong & Castrillo, 1980
Clark, 1980
Cohen, 1978
Collins, 1979
Cooper, 1979
Cooper & Payne, 1980
Daley, 1979
DuBrin, et al, 1979
Dunham, 1978
Emener, 1979
Flood, Kashka & Tweed, 1981
Fooner, 1981
Francis, 1980
Freudenberger, 1974
Grossnickle, 1980
Hendrickson, 1979
Holland, 1982
House, 1981
Kahn, 1978
Klerman, 1979

Leffingwell, 1979
Levi, 1981
Lunn, 1975
Malone & Falkenberg, 1980
Maslach & Jackson, 1978
McCarley, 1975
McLean, 1979
McMinn, 1979
Meadow, 1981
Mechanic, 1975
Morallo, 1981
Morallo & McFadden, 1982
Phillips, 1980
Pines, Aronson & Kafry, 1981
Savidki & Cooley, 1982
Spicuzza & DeVoe, 1982
Tamerin, 1982
Vachon, Lyall & Freenam, 1978
Van Auken, 1979
Vessel, 1980
Warshaw, 1979
Watkins, 1983
Wubbolding & Kessler-Bolton, 1979

Relaxation/Meditation
Ball, 1977
Barrow & Prosen, 1981
Beech, Burns & Sheffield, 1982
Blake & Mouton, 1980
Briley, 1980
Brown, 1977
Clark, 1980
Cooper, 1979
Cooper & Edson, 1979

Kovecses, 1980
Kuna, 1975
Lunn, 1975
Lustman & O'Hara, 1981
Mitchell, 1979
Morallo, 1981
Newman & Beehr, 1979
Parrina, 1979
Patrick, 1979
Phillips, 1980

DuBrin, et al, 1979
Dunham, 1978
Emener, 1979
Frew, 1974
Gardner, 1981
Genevay & Simon-Backes,
  1979
Greenberg, 1977
Hassett, 1978

Quick & Quick, 1979
Sammons, 1980
Sawyer & Schumacher, 1980
Shea, 1980
Spicuzza & DeVoe, 1982
Vattano, 1978
Warshaw, 1979

Exercise/Nutrition
  Adams, 1978
  Adams, 1979
  Bailey & Walker, 1982
  Blake & Mouton, 1980
  Briley, 1980
  Chance, 1981
  Clark, 1980
  Cooper, 1979
  Cooper & Edson, 1979
  DuBrin, et al, 1979
  Emener, 1979
  Freudenberger, 1974
  Freudenberger, 1975
  Gardner, 1981
  Gatre & Rosenblum, 1978
  Holland, 1982
  Johnson, 1980
  Johnson, 1981
  McKenna, 1980

  Mechanic, 1975
  Mirkin, 1979
  Mitchell, 1979
  Morallo, 1981
  Phillips, 1980
  Prentki, 1980
  Quick & Quick, 1979
  Rediger, 1980
  Shea, 1980
  Spicuzza & DeVoe, 1982
  U.S. News and World
    Report, 1978
  Veninga & Spradley,
    1981
  Warshaw, 1979
  Witty, 1980
  Wubbolding &
    Kessler-Bolton, 1979

Leisure Time
  Bailey & Walker, 1982
  Ball, 1977
  Borowson, 1976
  Bricklin, 1981
  Briley, 1980
  Chance, 1981
  Collins, 1979
  Daley, 1979
  DuBrin, et al, 1979

  McConnell, 1981
  McKenna, 1980
  Miller, 1981
  Mirkin, 1979
  Patrick, 1979
  Phillips, 1980
  Prentki, 1980
  Rediger, 1980
  Sammons, 1980

Dunham, 1978
Freudenberger, 1974
Freudenberger, 1977
Gatre & Rosenblum,
  1978
Hendrickson, 1979
Kovecses, 1980
Lunn, 1975
Maslach, 1978

Tardy, 1977
U.S. News and World
  Report, 1978
Van Auken, 1979
Veninga & Spradley,
  1981
Watkins, 1983
Witty, 1980

Personal
  Adams, 1978
  Adams, 1979
  Barrow & Prosen, 1981
  Beech, Burns &
    Sheffield, 1982
  Brief & Aldag, 1976
  Dunham, 1978
  Emener, 1979
  Genevay & Simon-Gruen,
    1979
  Hanson, 1968
  Hassett, 1978
  Hendrickson, 1979
  Johnson, 1980
  Jones & Emanuel, 1981
  Kehl, 1981,
  Kobasa, 1979
  Kobasa, Hilker & Maddi,
    1979
  Laron, Gilbertson & Power,
    1978

  Levi, 1981
  Malone & Falkenberg,
    1980
  Maslach & Jackson,
    1978
  McConnell, 1981
  Mirkin, 1979
  Phillips, 1980
  Pines & Maslach, 1978
  Rediger, 1980
  Sammons, 1980
  Selye & Cherry, 1978
  Shubin, 1978
  Vachon, Lyall
    & Freenam, 1978
  Vessel, 1980
  Watkins, 1983
  Young, 1980

Psychological
  Adams, 1978
  Adams, 1979
  Allen, 1979
  Beech, Burns &
    Sheffield, 1982
  Bermak, 1977
  Bloch, 1978
  Brief & Aldag, 1976
  Daley, 1979

  Johnson, 1978
  Knutsen, 1977
  Kobasa, Hilker & Maddi,
    1979
  Kovecses, 1980
  Lantos, 1952
  Lazarus, 1979
  Maslach & Jackson,
    1978

Forney, at al, 1982
Genevay & Simon-Gruen,
 1979
Grater, Kell & Morse,
 1961
Hassett, 1978

McConnell, 1981
Morallo, 1981
Rediger, 1980
Sammons, 1980
Selye & Cherry, 1978
Wubbolding &
 Kessler-Bolton, 1979

Organizational

Performance Standards
 Bailey & Walker, 1972
 Boy & Pine, 1980
 Bricklin, 1981
 Briley, 1980
 Bryan, 1981
 Collins, 1979
 DuBrin, et al, 1979
 Duemer, 1978
 Emener, 1979
 Fruedenberger, 1975
 Hackman & Oldham, 1975
 House, 1981
 Laron, Gilbertson &
  Power, 1978

Lenhart, 1980
Lubin, 1982
Lutz & Ramsey, 1976
Nicholson & Miljus,
 1972
Pines & Maslach, 1978
Sammons, 1980
Spicuzza & DeVoe, 1982
Stocker, 1981
Van Auken, 1979
Veninga, 1979
Vessel, 1980

Involvement
 Adams, 1979
 Atkins, Meyer & Smith,
  1982
 Boy & Pine, 1980
 Duemer, 1978
 Dunham, 1978
 Grater, Kell & Morse,
  1961
 Jones & Emanuel, 1981
 Kahn, 1978
 Labovitz & Orth, 1972
 Lunn, 1975

McConnell, 1981
Meadow, 1981
Pines, Aronson
 & Kafry, 1981
Prentki, 1980
Rediger, 1980
Stocker, 1981
Tardy, 1977
Van Auken, 1979
Veninga, 1979
Witty, 1980

Tasks
  Armstrong, 1971
  Beehr, 1981
  Berlin, 1969
  Clark, 1980
  Daley, 1979
  Duemer, 1978
  Freudenberger, 1974
  Freudenberger, 1975
  Hackman & Oldham, 1975
  Ivancevich, 1976

  Kahn, 1978
  Maslach & Pines, 1978
  McConnell, 1981
  Miller & Roberts, 1979
  Pines, Aronson & Kafry, 1981
  Pines & Maslach, 1978
  Price, 1977
  Schuler, 1979
  Van Auken, 1979

Training
  Alken, Smits & Lollar, 1972
  Austin & Jackson, 1977
  Bailey & Walker, 1982
  Barrow & Prosen, 1981
  Bermak, 1977
  Brocher, 1979
  Chance, 1981
  Christensen, 1981
  Daley, 1979
  DuBrin, et al, 1979
  Dunham, 1978
  Forney, et al, 1982
  Freudenberger, 1974
  Freudenberger, 1975
  Genevay & Simon-Gruen, 1979
  Hendrickson, 1979
  Holland 1982
  House, 1981
  Hyson, 1982
  Jones & Emanuel, 1981
  Knutsen, 1977
  Kovecses, 1980
  Laron, Gilbertson & Power, 1978

  Lubin, 1982
  Lutz & Ramsey, 1976
  Margolis, Kroes & Quinn, 1974
  Maslach & Jackson, 1978
  Miller & Roberts, 1979
  Morallo & McFadden, 1982
  Pacinelli & Britton, 1969
  Pines, Aronson & Kafry, 1981
  Pines & Maslach, 1978
  Raphael, Karpf & Sills, 1980
  Shannon & Saleebey, 1980
  Shea, 1980
  Vachon, Lyall & Freeman, 1978
  Veninga, 1979
  Zaharia & Baumeister, 1978

Expectations
  Barow & Cohen, 1982
  Beehr, 1976

  Laron, Gilbertson, & Power, 1978

Bies & Molle, 1980
Boy & Pine, 1980
Bryan, 1981
Chance, 1981
Cherniss, EgnatiosalkeMaslach & Jackson,
 & Walker, 1976
Daley, 1979
Duemer, 1978
Forney, et al, 1982
Genevay & Simon-Gruen,
 1979
Kehl, 1981
Keller, 1975

Levi, 1981
Margolis, Kroes
 & Quinn, 1974
Maslach, 1978
Maslach & Jackson,
 1978
McConnell, 1981
Nicholson & Miljus,
 1972
Parkington & Schneider,
 1979
Reed, 1979
Warnath & Shelton, 1976
Zaharia & Baumeister,
 1978

Job Definition/Role

Batlis, 1980
Beehr, 1976
Beehr, 1981
Bies & Molle, 1980
Boy & Pine, 1980
Chance, 1981
Freudenberger, 1977
Gruneberg, 1979
Hackman & Oldham, 1975
House, 1981
Kahn, 1978

Karasek, 1979
Lunn, 1975
Margolis, Kroes, &
 Quinn, 1974
Miller & Roberts, 1979
Morallo, 1981
Pines, Aronson
 & Kafry, 1981
Quick & Quick, 1979
Reed, 1979
Van Auken, 1979
Vessel, 1980

Conflict Resolution

Austin & Jackson, 1977
Bailey & Walker, 1982
Berlin, 1969
Duemer, 1978
Edelwich & Brodsky,
 1980
Gardner, 1981
Humphrey, 1978
Karasek, 1979

Lazarus, 1979
Leffingwell, 1979
Maslach & Pines, 1978
Patrick, 1979
Sheafor, 1976
Tardy, 1977
U.S. News and World
 Report, 1978
Vessel, 1980

Management

Adams, 1979

Laron, Gilbertson

Barrow & Prosen, 1981
Bloch, 1978
Carpenter, 1971
Cooper & Payne, 1980
Daley, 1979
Duemer, 1978
Emener, 1979
Flood, Kashka & Tweed,
  1981
Forney, et al, 1982
Glaser, 1976
Holland, 1982
Hyson, 1982
Johnson, 1980
Johnson, 1981
Kovecses, 1980

& Power, 1978
Lubin, 1982
Maslach, 1978
Maslach & Pines, 1978
McConnell, 1981
Meadow, 1982
Miller & Roberts, 1979
Mitchell, 1979
Patrick, 1979
Prentki, 1980
Quick & Quick, 1979
Schuler, 1979
Warshaw, 1979
Zaharia & Baumeister,
  1978

Sharing/Communications
Austin & Jackson, 1977
Bailey & Walker, 1982
Bennett, 1979
Berstein, 1982
Clark, 1980
Daley, 1979
Dunham, 1978
Emener, 1979
Flood, Kashka & Tweed,
  1981
Freudenberger, 1975
Freudenberger, 1977
Glaser, 1976

Grater, Kell & Morse,
  1961
Hackman & Oldham, 1975
House, 1981
Hyson, 1982
Lammert, 1981
Lubin, 1982
Malone & Falkenberg,
  1980
Miller, 1981
Pines, Aronson
  & Kafry, 1981
Schuler, 1979
Watkins, 1982

Rest
Alexander, 1980
Bies & Molle, 1980
Boronson, 1976
Bricklin, 1981
Briley, 1980
Daley, 1979
Freudenberger, 1974
Freudenberger, 1975
Kovecses, 1980

Maslach, 1978
Maslach & Pines, 1978
McConnell, 1981
Meadow, 1981
Morallo, 1981
Patrick, 1979
Pines & Malsach, 1978
Sammons, 1980
Shubin, 1978

Laron, Gilbertson
  & Power, 1978
Levi, 1981

Tardy, 1977
Vessel, 1980